Created and Directed by Hans Höfer

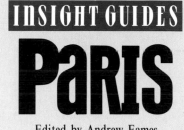

INSIGHT GUIDES
PARIS

Edited by Andrew Eames

Main photography: Ping Amranand and Bill Wassman

Editorial Director: Brian Bell

HOUGHTON MIFFLIN COMPANY

APA PUBLICATIONS

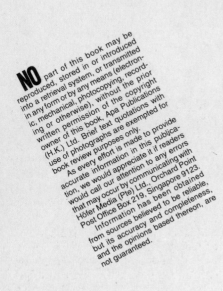
PaRIS

Fourth Edition
© **1994 APA PUBLICATIONS (HK) LTD**
All Rights Reserved
Printed in Singapore by Höfer Press Pte Ltd

Distributed in the United States by:	Distributed in Canada by:	Distributed in the UK & Ireland by:	Worldwide distribution enquiries:
Houghton Mifflin Company	**Thomas Allen & Son**	**GeoCenter International UK Ltd**	**Höfer Communications Pte Ltd**
222 Berkeley Street	390 Steelcase Road East	The Viables Center, Harrow Way	38 Joo Koon Road
Boston, Massachusetts 02116-3764	Markham, Ontario L3R 1G2	Basingstoke, Hampshire RG22 4BJ	Singapore 2262
ISBN: 0-395-71077-4	ISBN: 0-395-71077-4	ISBN: 9-6242-063-2	ISBN: 9-6242-063-2

ABOUT THIS BOOK

How many guide-books will tell you that Alexandre Gustave Eiffel, as well as designing a tower, also created the garter belt? How many will note that Métro trains run every 80 seconds in the rush hour, that one in three Parisians lives alone, or that every Paris street is swept by hand at least once a day? This one does, and in addition explains why Parisians will suffer a torrent of verbal abuse without batting an eyelid but will never forgive someone who neglects to say *bonjour* or *merci*. It also tells you how to spot a local, what it gives the Métro its distinctive smell.

Paris is a world unto itself, standing apart from the rest of the great nation that it heads. Victor Hugo, who lived in Paris, appreciated the mingled pride and frustration with which the rest of the country viewed their capital: "Paris goes her own way," he said, "and France, irritated, is forced to follow".

In some fields, it has not just been France, but the rest of the world, which has been forced to follow. Today, Paris is still a major hub of intellectual, cultural and artistic pursuits. It is universally known for its cuisine, wine, *haute couture*, painting, theatre and museums. It is also known for its revolutions, and for embracing innovation – witness the Pompidou Centre, the new pyramids in front of the Louvre, and the ambitious development at La Défense. This may be one of the best preserved cities in Europe, but it has not been content to let time stand still.

The *Insight Guides* approach fits Paris perfectly, combining as it does fine writing, objective journalism and outstanding photography to produce a unique form of travel literature which gives serious travellers an insight into a destination's history and culture. The purpose, says the company's founder **Hans Höfer**, is not to promote tourism but "to contribute to positive communication between the local people and visitors." The success of the series, which has grown to nearly 200 titles, in addition to 80 *Insight Pocket Guides*, is proof that such an idea can find an enthusiastic market.

The whole experience of Paris – historical, contemporary, artistic and intellectual – is thus packed into this book, with in-depth street by street explorations of all the key downtown areas from Montmartre to Montparnasse, as well as trips to the inspiring new development at La Défense to Versailles, Euro Disney and Chartres.

Old and New

Just as Paris has changed, so this book has altered radically from its first edition in the 1980s. This edition, thoroughly overhauled by Insight Guides' executive editor **Andrew Eames**, builds on the work done for the first edition by editor **Grace Coston**, the core of whose *City on the Seine* and *Day Trips* chapters still remain, and by principal photographer **Ping Amranand,** whose classic work has been supplemented by recent images from other regular Insight photographers **Bill Wassman** and **Catherine Karnow**.

In preparing an edition which would look forward to the Millennium as well as backwards to the Revolution, Eames decided to keep much of the history section by **Marton Radkai**, an American-educated travel writer and photographer who spent part of his youth in Paris, but is now based in Munich. Radkai charts the city from its very beginnings – including the various origins of its name – up

Eames

Coston

Amranand

Radkai

to the latest upheavals in its long love affair with revolution.

Also making the leap between old and new editions is French contributor **Philippe Artru**, who writes about the city's architecture.

In order to strengthen the essays section at the front of the book, Eames enlisted the wit and knowledge of **Jonathon Brown**, a Scottish-born artist and writer who is now living in the south of France. Brown suggests, in his chapter on *Paris without Tears*, that the best way to appreciate Paris is not to bother with the city sights, but to sit down and observe. In his chapter on *Paris through Paintings*, Brown selects some of the most famous images of the city and reveals something of the lifestyles of the artists who created them.

Also in the first section is a new and invaluable chapter by **Philip** and **Mary Hyman** on the Parisian eating experience. The Hymans, Americans living in Paris, are acknowledged as real experts by the French government, for whom they are completing a survey of local specialities. Supplementing the chapter is the Hymans' list of recommended restaurants which appears in the *Travel Tips* section at the back of the book.

Susan Bell, who works in Paris for the London *Times*, reworked the original chapter on the Parisians and introduced new boxes on the Métro, on street-cleaning, on the demise of the local café, and on the Académie Française. She also put together a detailed survey of the city's best shopping.

The word-processor and shoe-leather behind the largest single contribution to this book belong to **Jim Keeble**, a bilingual graduate of Oxford University who divides his time between Cambridge and the Côte d'Azur. It was Keeble who walked the length and breadth of Paris for the Places section of this book, unearthing many gems as he did so. The origins of the name "bistro", why the Latin Quarter is so named, the wine bar that discourages the drinking of water "because fish make love in it" and the description of the Mona Lisa's smile as that of a "woman who has just dined off her husband", all lie within his text. Keeble's contribution, as well as covering all the downtown areas, also extended to the outlying parks, to the markets, to La Défense and to Euro Disney, which he found surprisingly stimulating.

Winding up the book with a comprehensive new *Travel Tips* section is **Hilary Macpherson**, originally from Glasgow, Scotland, but now a long-term resident of Paris, where she writes, brings up a family, and shows guests the city she loves. Proofreading and indexing were completed through Insight Guides' London editorial office by **Mary Morton**.

Scents and Sensibility

Every writer worth his or her salt has found something superlative to say about Paris. Ernest Hemingway, who described the city as "a moveable feast", has long been associated with Paris, and his contemporary John Steinbeck was even more enthusiastic: "No other city in the world has been better loved or more celebrated." Even the great foreteller Nostradamus had his own prediction for the city: "As long as Paris does not fall, gaiety will exist in the world". The English writer G. K. Chesterton stated: "If a man fell out of the moon into the town of Paris, he would know that it was the capital of a great nation". This book sets out to capture something of everything in this most loved of world cities.

Brown *Bell* *Keeble* *Macpherson*

History & Features

Places

Maps

TRAVEL TIPS

Compiled by
Hilary Macpherson

For detailed information
see page 241

THE CITY ON THE SEINE

All channels of communication lead to Paris: highways, railways, airways and even Hertzian waves. Situated on longitude 2° 20'14"W (Greenwich meridian) and latitude 48° 50'11"N, Paris is in the centre of a vast land depression known as the Parisian Basin. It is the political, economic, historical, artistic, cultural and tourist hub of France. According to writer Jean Giraudoux the Parisian is more than a little proud to be part of these 5,000 hectares where "the most thinking, talking and writing in the world have been accomplished."

Paris covers an area close to 10,000 hectares or 100 sq. km (40 sq. miles), running 12 km (7½ miles) east and west, and 9 km (5½ miles) north and south. On the map, 20 *arrondissements* (administrative districts) spiral out like a snail's shell, a pattern reflecting the city's historical development and successive enlargements. The site of medieval Paris corresponds roughly to the first six *arrondissements*. The Revolution of 1789 added the land that comprises the next five, while the territory covered by the last nine was acquired in the 19th century by the annexation of a dozen neighbouring villages, including La Villette, Belleville, Auteuil and Montmartre.

Today's inner city limits are marked by *le périphérique*, a circular highway stretching 35 km (22 miles) around Paris. Constructed in 1973 in an attempt to reduce traffic jams, *le périphérique* is invariably congested itself, particularly at rush hours (7–10am and 5–7.30pm), when an estimated 130,000 cars storm its 35 exits leading to the suburbs.

Paris is a city of reliefs. Starting from Grenelle, the lowest point at 26 metres (85 ft) above sea level, the banks of the Seine river swell gently north and south, forming two chains of hillocks. To the north, on the right

Preceding pages: Toulouse-Lautrec's *The Ballerina La Roue* (frontispiece); the Eiffel Tower; the Seine and Île de la Cité; the view from Alexandre III Bridge; the Eiffel Tower from Trocadéro; a celebrated café. **Left**, barging through the city.

bank (*rive droite*), the gentle group of hills includes Montmartre, the highest at 420 ft (128 metres), Ménilmontant, Belleville and the Buttes Chaumont. The left bank (*rive gauche*) has Montsouris, the Montagne Ste-Geneviève, the Buttes aux Cailles and Maison Blanche at 256 ft (78 metres). Mont Valérien stands at 528 ft (161 metres). This is the highest point on the city's outskirts and it provides an immense panoramic view of Paris from the west.

The suburbs (*banlieue*) form two concentric rings around Paris. Wrapped tightly about the city, the inner ring is made up of three counties or *départements* (Hauts-de-Seine, Val-de-Marne and Seine-St-Denis), and is itself enclosed by an outer ring of four *départements* (Seine-et-Marne, Essonne, Yvelines and Val-d'Oise). These counties, together with Paris, constitute the greater Paris area (Île-de-France), and extend over 770 sq. miles (2,000 sq. km). The counties are linked by eight major highways, four RER lines and an extensive railway network branching out in all directions from six train stations in Paris.

At the beginning of the 19th century, Napoleon Bonaparte imposed a special status on the city of Paris in order to maintain a firm hold on the capital's politics and populace. It wasn't until 25 March 1977 that Paris voted into office a city council which in turn elected the first mayor, Jacques Chirac. Today, each *arrondissement* also has its own council and mayor. Paris, with its double status as both city and county, is represented nationally by 21 delegates and 12 senators in the two houses of Parliament.

On the Seine: "She is buffeted by the waves but sinks not": so reads the inscription on the city's coat-of-arms, symbol of Paris born on the flanks of the Seine river. The Gaulish village of Lutetia was indeed founded on the largest island, as these lines suggest, but today it is the Seine that cuts a swathe through the middle of the city. The river is the capital's widest avenue; it is spanned by a total of 35 bridges which provide some of the loveliest views of Paris. The Seine is also the city's calmest artery, barely ruffled by

Right, the Paris the satellites see.

22

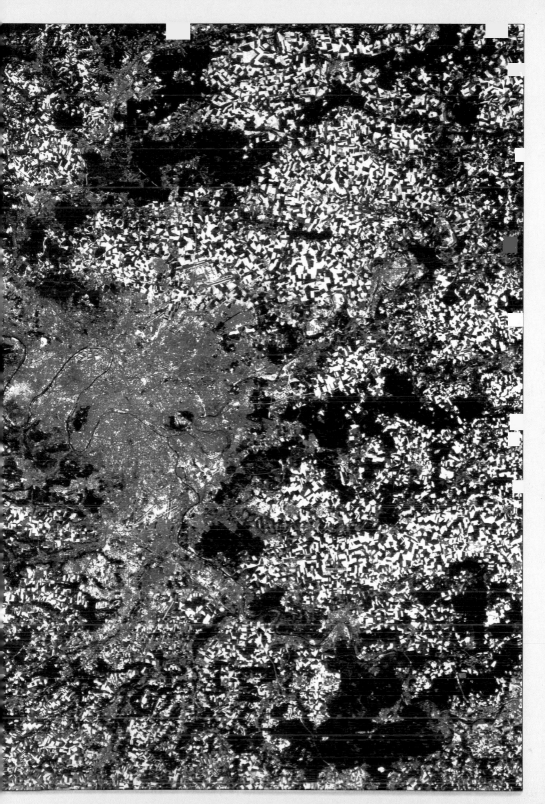

the daily flow of tourist and commercial boat traffic. In the 19th century, the banks were encumbered with wash-houses and water-mills and its waters heaved with ships hailing from every corner of France.

Even more difficult to imagine now are the 700 brightly painted Viking warships which used the river to invade Paris from the north in the 9th century, or the thousands of bodies that floated past in 1572, victims of the Saint Bartholomew Day Massacre. Today, barges and pleasure boats on their lazy way to Burgundy, source of the Seine 300 miles (500 km) away, use the St-Martin and St-Denis canals to shorten their trip, cutting across northeastern Paris. Downtown, the Seine flows for tourists, poets and lovers.

Both divided and united by the river, Paris is a mosaic of 80 villages or *quartiers*, each noted for its own distinctive character and activity: the Odéon quarter with its publishing houses, Faubourg St-Antoine with its cabinet-makers, the garment wholesalers at Sentier, universities and colleges in the Latin Quarter, department stores at the Chaussée d'Antin and the business district around the Bourse (the Stock Exchange), the Opéra or at La Défense.

One of the most persistent images of Paris is its long avenues and boulevards graciously lined with chestnut and plane trees. Flowers and plants abound in a patchwork of 338 squares, parks and gardens, tended in the formal French tradition.

Underground Paris is a labyrinth of Metro lines, 2,000 miles (3,200 km) of sewers, scores of garages and dozens of miles of ancient quarries. These Gallo-Roman stone quarries were converted into catacombs in the 18th century, when the remains of nearly six million bodies were rescued from various defunct graveyards elsewhere in the city, notably the Innocents Cemetery, a breeding ground of infection which was evacuated in 1785. Guided tours of the Catacombs are given at 2B Place Denfert Rochereau in the 14th *arrondissement*. Over the entrance a sobering inscription reads: "Stop. Here lies death's empire" – a warning largely unheeded by daring young explorers in search of nocturnal adventures.

Right, art fountain by the Pompidou Centre.

LVTETIA 1600

Jacques Desreveaulx 1609 sculp. inv.

CLOVIS I.

As with many of the world's great cities, the mysterious mists of antiquity veil the origins of Paris. In 500 BC when the Celts were chasing each other around Europe, one tribe, the Parisii, settled on the Seine river. They were good farmers and active traders, hence the name "Parisii", which is said to be derived from a Celt word for "boat". However, perhaps a more imaginative theory on the origins of the city's name claims that the tribe's founder was Paris, the émigré son of King Priam of Troy.

Lutetia: In 53 BC a number of Gallic tribes failed to appear at the annual council summoned by the Romans in Ambiani (Amiens). Roman Emperor Julius Caesar, sensing rebellion in the air, quickly transferred the council into the midst of the restless tribes, to the Parisii town of Lutetia – at that time nothing more than an agglomeration of huts on an island in the Seine.

Lutetia thrived under the sudden Roman presence. A wooden bridge connected the island (Île de la Cité) to the left or south bank where a residential neighbourhood sprawled, replete with temples, baths, a theatre and other hallmarks of Roman civilisation (relics visible at the Cluny Museum).

Dominating the right or north bank from its hilltop perch, stood a temple to Mercury where, in AD 287, St Denis, a Christian agitator and the first bishop of Paris, was beheaded. Thereafter, the hill was named *Mons Martyrium*, Montmartre. According to legend, St Denis picked up his severed head and walked 6,000 steps before being buried by one of his apostles.

Lying as it did exposed on a plain, Lutetia fell victim to frequent sackings by marauding barbarian tribes. In AD 358, Emperor Constantine sent his son-in-law, Julian, to Gaul to fight the barbarians. The young man promptly fell in love with Lutetia and its inhabitants. When not on the battlefields, he sat in the *palais* on the Cité, enjoying Lutetian

Preceding pages: Paris in 1600. Left, Clovis I gave the city its name. Right, Paris coat of arms.

wine and figs and putting the town's finances in order. The Lutetians returned the favour in AD 360, by proclaiming him emperor.

About a century later, Attila the Hun appeared with his hordes in the Île de France. The Lutetians prepared to flee but were stopped by the 19-year-old Geneviève who assured them that the Huns would not harm the city. Lo and behold, the Huns passed southwest of Lutetia and ran straight into the swords of a hastily raised army of legion-

naires. Thereafter Geneviève became the patron saint of Paris.

The Dark Ages: Sainte-Geneviève was still alive when Clovis I, king of the Salian Franks and founder of the Merovingian dynasty, invaded much of Gaul, converted to Christianity and swept into Lutetia which he promptly made his capital and (according to some accounts) renamed it Paris. Like Julian, he installed himself in the *palais* and later had a basilica built where he and Sainte-Geneviève were buried. The so-called church of the Apostles ultimately became the Panthéon, the last resting place for France's great men, including Rousseau, Mirabeau, Victor Hugo and Jean Jaurès.

Merovingian law of succession was simple: the empire was divided among the previous ruler's offspring. As a result, family members spent the better part of 250 years squeezing each other out. Paris, instead of being used as an administrative centre, served as a favourite battleground for the murderous bickering of Clovis's descendants. Nature also conspired, with floods, fires, epidemics and hurricanes. The brief rule of Dagobert (AD 629–639) brought a flicker of relief. He organised an annual trade fair at Lendit, and his minister Saint Eloi struck

tribute and let them sail up the Seine to pillage Burgundy. As a result, Paris and the French felt betrayed.

In defiance of the Emperor, Eudes was crowned King of France. Carolingian unity dissolved. The French crown shifted from one dynasty to the next. The Saracens appeared in the south, Hungarians in the east, and the Vikings ran amok. All in all, it was not a happy time for France.

By hook, crook, marriage and force, Duke Hugo the Great, a descendant of Eudes, forged a French federation. When the German Kaiser Otto II invaded France in AD 978, he met a resolute French army at the

Parisian coins and looked after the municipal finances. The Carolingians, who ruled from AD 751, felt more comfortable nearer to their homelands in the lower Rhine. Paris was put in the charge of a count who created a municipal guard.

The Norman invasions of the mid-9th century brought Paris back into the limelight. After several sackings, in AD 885, Count Eudes decided to resist. The first siege of Paris lasted an entire year and almost bore fruit: the Carolingian army came to the rescue. But Emperor Charles the Fat, instead of attacking the siege-weary Vikings, paid them

gates of Paris. The victory led to their general, Hugo Capet, son of Hugo the Great, becoming King of France, and starting a new, long-lasting dynasty.

The Middle Ages: Though the early members of the dynasty preferred crusading and hunting to governing, Paris prospered under the Capetians. New fountains brought fresh water to the citizens and the streets were paved. *Sergents de ville* armed with clubs walked a beat and public punishment were common.

With its new cloisters and churches and cosmopolitan population, Paris rapidly became an intellectual centre. Monks, scholars, philosophers, poets and musicians flocked to the city to learn, to argue and to teach. Abélard and Saint Bernard hurled logic at each other in the open air – although the former got into hot water after starting a relationship with his student Heloïse. He was castrated and sent to a monastery, but not before she'd borne him a child. The University of Paris was founded in 1231 and hardly a European scholar failed to visit its prestigious faculties.

Economic life in Paris was in the hands of merchants and craftsmen who wisely organised themselves into guilds. The most pow-

officers. The number increased later to 24 and they met in regular sessions to discuss municipal business. Louis IX (1226–70) created three governing chambers.

The concessions to the commoners had a long-lasting effect on Parisian and French political life. These *bourgeois* (city dwellers) became an independent political force, often corrupt, but equally often striving for democratic reforms.

The first revolution: By the mid-14th century the Capetians had given way to the Valois and the devastating Hundred Years' War began. The French knights seemed powerless before the English foot soldiers. The

erful one was the water merchants' guild, which included all river workers and gave its coat-of-arms to the city.

Philippe Auguste (1180–1223) built Les Halles for the guilds, and improved the Seine docks. The guilds took care of levying taxes, town-crying and other municipal duties. In 1190 six guild members, so-called *grands bourgeois,* were chosen to act as the king's

Far Left, Roman stonework in the Cluny Museum. Left, tragic lovers Heloïse and Abélard. Above, boatmen jousting in front of the former Notre Dame bridge, 1756.

plague made its first deadly appearance. In 1356, the English captured King John the Good at Poitiers. The citizens of Paris, tired of incompetent leadership, rebelled. Their leader, Etienne Marcel, a clothmaker and guild chairman, was the first in a long string of genial, corrupt demagogues to emerge on Paris's political horizon. A motley crew of poor townspeople and peasants under Jacques Bonhomme chose the moment to begin a revolt, later known as the Jacquerie.

For support, Marcel unwisely chose the King of Navarre (Charles the Bad), an English ally. When the Parisians found out about the alliance, they turned on Marcel. On 31 July 1358, he was assassinated by a loyalist; three days later John the Good's son, Charles, entered the capital.

The new regent, who later became Charles V, hammered out a truce with the English allowing France some time to put its house in order. Paris was well-treated considering its fickle loyalties: the Parliament still met but its powers were curtailed.

Behind a calm exterior, Paris seethed. In 1382, a group of citizens calling themselves the Maillotins rebelled against high taxes and were brutally repressed. Then, in 1407, the Maillotins became enmeshed in the vio-

Seeing France torn apart by civil war, the English resumed hostilities. Siding with the Burgundians, they defeated the Armagnacs at Agincourt in 1415.

In 1419, John the Fearless was murdered, whereupon Henry V of England married Catherine, daughter of mad King Charles, and occupied Paris in December 1420.

English law-and-order was initially welcomed after the anarchic years of John the Fearless and Caboche, but radical application of the gallows soon began to gall. Charles VII, the legitimate king, had some support in the capital, but the bulk of Parisians remained convinced that his vengeance would

lent struggle for power between the Burgundian John the Fearless and his cousin Louis d'Orléans, brother of the mentally deranged Charles VI. John had Louis murdered and in 1409 took control of Paris, which backed the Burgundians.

While Louis' son raised a new army, Paris celebrated. Into the fray stepped a butcher, Caboche, demanding fiscal and administrative reforms. All hell broke loose as John's authority slipped into the hands of Caboche and his butchers. The ensuing Reign of Terror gave Charles and his Armagnac army a chance to re-enter and "pacify" the city.

be merciless. And so when Joan of Arc besieged Paris in 1429, the population put up a stiff resistance.

Six years elapsed before Charles VII recaptured his capital and drove the English back to the Channel coast. His main task consisted of reconstructing the nation. Elected magistrates upheld public life in Paris and the kings, wary of the city, moved out to luxurious castles on the Loire river.

Renaissance and religious troubles: With peace came prosperity, but with prosperity came war. By the early 16th century, Louis XII (1498–1515) was rummaging around

Italy. François I (1515–47) began the struggle against the Habsburgs in Europe. In 1525, he was captured at Pavia. The Parisians paid his ransom and he promptly moved into the Louvre. In his wake came hordes of Italian architects, painters, sculptors, goldsmiths, cabinet-makers and masons who set about reshaping the city's lugubrious Gothic face.

With the rebirth of the capital under François I's graceful, iron hand, French culture also returned to life. Ronsard, Du Bellay and other members of the Pléiades carried French poetry to new heights while Clément Jannequin put the French *chanson* on the map. The printing press increased the range

try and to condemn – usually to burning – religious agitators.

Henri II's heirs, François II (1559–60), Charles IX (1560–74) and Henri III (1574–89) were not competent enough to control France's religious factions. Nor were they helped by the endless intrigues of their mother, Catherine de Médicis.

In August 1572 Paris gave the signal for the Saint Bartholomew massacre. Thousands of Protestants died, including most of their leaders. Among the few to escape was Henri of Bourbon, King of Navarre, cousin of the King of France.

War between the Henris: King Henri III's

of these creative activities, but it also helped spread the new gospel of Protestantism through Catholic France. François I was prepared to tolerate the new religion as long as its converts remained orderly.

Paris, dominated by the conservative Sorbonne theologists, was outraged by this attitude. Under the reign of Henri II (1547–59), the city pushed for measures against the Protestants, creating the *chambre ardente* to

<u>Left</u>, Joan of Arc beseiged Paris. <u>Above</u>, Henry III and <u>right</u>, Charles IX, sons of the scheming Catherine de Médicis.

concessions to the Protestants infuriated the Catholics led by the popular Henri de Guise and the Paris-based Holy League. In 1584, the Navarre Henri became heir to the throne but he had to fight for the right. In 1589, Henri III had Henri de Guise assassinated. Paris threw up its barricades and a Council of Sixteen took power and deposed Henri III who willy-nilly joined forces with the Protestant Navarre. His army, however, joined the Catholics. On the first day of August, a friar, Jacques Clément, murdered Henri III and Henri of Navarre became Henri IV.

Civil war dragged on for another five

years. Paris was the stage for the Council of Sixteen's gruesome repression of real and perceived plots. In 1593, Philip II of Spain, who had entered the war on the Catholic side, pressed to usurp the French throne. The Paris parliament, however, solemnly declared that no foreigner would rule. Henri IV opportunely chose that moment to convert back to Catholicism, whereupon Paris opened its doors to him and overnight the war-weary nation fell in line.

Henri IV patched up France spiritually and economically. In 1598, his Edict of Nantes set up guidelines for cohabitation between the two religious groups. His (Protestant)

adviser, Sully, reformed the tax system and balanced the budget.

The glorious epoch: Despite massive deficits incurred by their violent foreign policy, the Bourbons lavished huge sums on Paris, while keeping it on a short political leash. Two deserted islets behind the Cité became the residential Île Saint-Louis. New bridges crossed the Seine. Avenues cut through the dingy labyrinth. Architects built new houses, palaces, schools and restored the old ones. Parks appeared, where society could stroll in the shade and exchange ideas, gossip or tender glances. Cardinal Richelieu, who

looked after most governing tasks on the behalf of the young Louis XII, founded the Académie Française.

Under Louis XIV (1643–1715) the spending spree reached its peak. His minister, Colbert, sanitised entire sections of the city and set up manufacturing plants to provide the French with luxury items. Louis XIV also had hospices built for the poor and the Invalides was built to house war veterans.

The influx of money and the proximity of the court attracted a huge crowd to the capital. Rich wives and courtesans opened their living rooms to conversationalists. Theatres echoed with the verse of Racine and Corneille, the booing of the *cliques* and the applause of the *claques*. The first cafés appeared on the boulevards. Everyone laughed at the writings of Molière, Boileau, and de la Fontaine satirising the hustling and bustling society.

But storm clouds were gathering. In 1648, Paris revolted, demanding greater political representation. The 12 provincial parliaments joined, as did a conspiracy of nobles under Prince Condé. The Fronde, as it was called, eventually collapsed, but Louis XIV later had his lavish palace, Versailles, built outside the city limits to keep his distance from the unruly Parisian mob.

The beginning of the 18th century was a period of great inequality in Paris. French high society was having a fine time in the court of King Louis XIV, who set up manufacturing industry specifically for luxury items. Theatres were busy, the café scene was lively, and the city positively buzzed by night. But all this activity ignored the needs and wishes of the poor, who were swept aside in the modernisations of the city.

The road to Revolution: Louis XIV's immediate successor in 1715, the regent Duke of Orléans, moved back into the city but he left government to his ministers, while he engaged in amorous pursuits. King Louis XV continued likewise, giving his mistress, Madame de Pompadour, the power to select ministers, generals and other functionaries. Meanwhile, the nation's budget deficits grew and the financial situation seriously worsened. The city was ready for revolution.

<u>**Left**</u>, **Richelieu**. <u>**Right**</u>, **Louis XIV, the Sun King.**

LUDOVICO MAGNO

35

REVOLUTION!

The building of the fabulous palace at Versailles was one of the last grand gestures of a fated monarchy. By building it, Louis XIV hardly endeared himself to the population at large, already grumbling with discontent. Moving to Versailles also took the monarch and court away from the little contact with reality that they still had.

France lost a drawn-out war against England (1756–63) and satire turned to dissent. In the *salons* surly philosophers replaced the brisk talkers. French reputation no longer rested on royal glory but on the wisdom of its intellectuals – Voltaire, Rousseau, Diderot and Quesnay. It was as if Paris was nonchalantly sitting in the restaurant car while the train headed for the precipice. Entertainment grew more extravagant and cafés were full. When a bad harvest in 1788 increased the price of bread, Queen Marie-Antoinette is supposed to have made her famous pronouncement that the hungry should eat cake.

By 1789 France's debts had reached a critical stage. The King summoned the Estates General, a legislative body made up of the clergy, the aristocracy and the bourgeoisie. For the sake of fairer representation, the latter created the National Assembly. But by the time the King reacted, the absolute monarchy had ended. On 14 July, Paris's populace proclaimed a Commune, formed a National Guard and, uniting under the leadership of Lafayette, stormed the Bastille prison for its weapons.

The revolutionary century: The explosion of 1789 swept the past away. Radicals of one hour became the conservatives of the next. Streets changed names, newborn babies were baptised Égalité, Liberté, or République. A statue of a ballerina representing Liberty sat on the altar of Notre Dame. The First Republic was proclaimed and, in January 1793, King Louis XVI was decapitated in public on Place de la Concorde.

Paris was the burning centre of the Revo-

Preceding pages: Delacroix's depiction of the Revolution. **Left, detail from the Arc de Triomphe.**

lution. Its temperamental and bloodthirsty mob was the force behind increasingly radical leaders, from Mirabeau, to Brissot, to Danton, Robespierre and Marat, whose scrofulous constituents regularly filled the Assembly's gallery. Power in France was centralised in the capital and, by 1893, anyone proposing a federal system was dragged off to the guillotine.

It was Napoleon who brought order and respectability to the Revolution. He also reconfirmed Parisian centralism. No French leader until Adolf Thiers in 1871 dared to alter that status. "Paris goes her own way," wrote Victor Hugo in the mid-19th century.

"enemy's" own *salons*. The hirsute Berlioz deafened his audiences, Victor Hugo wrote epically about the poor, and Baudelaire, steeped in absinthe and hashish, glorified *ennui* disenchantment in the scintillating city.

The spirit of 1789 also survived in the Republican forces who reached for the Parisian mob whenever despotism reared its head. In 1830, Charles X (1824–30) revoked certain electoral laws. After three days of bloody rioting, he abdicated in favour of his cousin, Louis-Philippe, who 18 years later succumbed to another Parisian insurrection. When Louis Napoleon, Napoleon's nephew and president of the Second Republic,

"France, irritated, is forced to follow."

Romantic Paris: The glorious Napoleonic empire ended sadly with Paris occupied by three allied armies from 1815 to 1818. Louis XVIII, another Bourbon, headed a constitutional monarchy with emphasis on law-and-order and *laissez-faire* economics.

The Industrial Revolution might have turned Paris into an opulent and mediocre business centre were it not for the apostles of romanticism. Inspired by the anti-establishment spirit of 1789, they waged a struggle against creaky academics and bourgeois respectability in garrets, cafés, journals and the

crowned himself emperor in 1852, he preemptively arrested more than 20,000 suspected political opponents, just to make sure.

The Second Empire (1852–70) was a gaudy and grandiose period in Paris history. Thousands of kilometres of new railway track connected it with other European capitals. Twice, in 1855 and 1867, it hosted the World Fair. Basking in financial ease, the city abandoned itself to the pleasures of masked balls, Offenbach operettas and *salon* conversation.

<u>Above</u>, the revolutionaries stormed the Bastille prison on 14 July 1789 – Bastille Day.

Aided by eager speculators and fat taxes, the Prefect Haussmann gave Paris a brand-new face. He gutted and rebuilt the downtown area. New water mains and a sewage system were installed to service the by now two million Parisians. Elegant boulevards, avenues and *places* appeared: Champs-Elysées, St-Michel, St-Germain, Etoile, to name a few. These served an aesthetic purpose, but they also facilitated troop deployment in the event of trouble.

Families dispossessed by the construction were forced to move to eastern Paris. This influx only added to that area's already notoriously seditious spirit.

The Commune: In 1870, Napoleon III went to war with Prussia. Parisians lined the streets to cheer the ill-equipped, ill-led and ill-fated army as they marched east. Two months later, Napoleon was beaten, the Second Empire had become the Third Republic, and the Prussians were besieging Paris. In Bordeaux the government of Adolph Thiers waited for a *levée en masse* in heroic revolutionary style that never materialised.

In Paris, the National Guard and regulars, mostly from the poor classes, milled around preparing for an heroic *sortie* that failed. To kill time, wealthy Parisians carried on with their social life, though restaurant fare became more exotic as butchers bought their stock from the zoo at the Jardin des Plantes. The poor simply went hungry.

On 28 January 1871, Thiers, without consulting Paris, finally agreed to a ceasefire. A month later the National Assembly ratified a peace treaty. The Prussians triumphantly marched through Paris avoiding, however, the eastern districts, home of the belligerent and vengeful National Guard who felt betrayed by the French government. Sensing trouble, Thiers ordered the National Guard to disarm and moved the government to Versailles. He barely escaped the ensuing explosion of rancour.

On 28 March, a Commune was proclaimed at the Hôtel de Ville after a municipal election was boycotted by the bourgeoisie. Civil war erupted.

While the Communards hoisted red flags and argued over political and military strategies, Thiers was busy raising a new army.

The government forces succeeded where the Prussians had failed. Working from house to house, they pushed the Communards back into the eastern districts of Ménilmontant, Belleville and La Villette until reaching the graves of the Père-Lachaise cemetery. The Paris bourgeoisie came out to jeer at the columns of pathetic bedraggled-looking prisoners. *Le Figaro* windily raved against the "moral gangrene" and called for summary justice. Some 25,000 Communards died fighting or were executed in the last weeks of May. With them went the revolutionary spark that had defied tyrants and kindled republics since 1789.

La Belle Epoque: Life quickly returned to normal after the Commune but gunshots crackled even while Paris began clearing away the battle debris. By 1878, the city was ready for the World Fair and in 1879 the government moved back from Versailles.

Paris no longer played a guiding role in French politics. With the insurrectionist working class brutally tamed, it became merely the stage for the squabbles, plots, demonstrations, counter-demonstrations, and oral and written polemics of the Third Republic. The Republicans split into pro-clerical and anti-clerical factions. In the 1890s, after recovering from the Commune, the left gathered around the socialist, Jean Jaurès. On the right was an array of diehard monarchists and nationalists with a strong vein of anti-Semitism, as revealed by the Dreyfus Affair in the late 1890s. (That *cause célèbre* revolved around the Jewish army captain, Dreyfus, who was deported on trumped-up spying charges.)

Though crackling with tension, Paris seemed more than ever ready to accept the controversial and the provocative. The Metro was dug, the Eiffel Tower built and the first films were shown. Between 1880 and 1940, Paris housed more painters, sculptors, writers, poets, musicians and other creative artists per acre than any other metropolis in the world. They chattered with philosophers, theorists, critics, brawny syndicalists, gazetteers, anarchists and socialites in smoke-filled cafés.

Almost every literary movement flourished in Paris – Realism, Impressionism,

Cubism, Surrealism, Dadaism, and so on. In the pawnshops of Montmartre, paintings by Picasso, Utrillo and Modigliani were hung up by clothes pegs. Debussy, Zola, Cocteau and his apostles strolled through town. Diaghilev's *Ballets Russes* presented Nijinsky to full houses that broke into riots if Stravinsky was performed.

World War I dampened spirits as the city turned to the slaughter at hand. In September 1914, the German army came within earshot. The military governor Gallieni rushed reinforcements to the counter-offensive on the Marne using every means he could lay his hands on, including the Paris taxi service.

effects of the war. The far right, meanwhile, made important gains.

Fascist-type organisations developed in France in the late 19th century. Charles Barras and Léon Daudet, pornographic novelists, founded *Action Française* in the 1890s. In the 1920s and '30s such groups proliferated, fuelled by general discontent and the fear of Bolshevism and inspired by the successes of Mussolini and Hitler. They focused their efforts on Paris which at that time was enjoying the new "thing", swing music. The fascists paraded in paramilitary garb, campaigned against the internationalists, the socialists, and above all the Jews.

Normal life began to return after the armistice was declared in 1918. From the east came Russian émigrés, from the west came American writers and composers. In the 1930s Paris was a temporary haven to the refugees of fascism.

Between the wars: With 1½ million dead, millions of others crippled and the agricultural north destroyed by bombings, France's part in the victory over Germany in 1914 was Pyrrhic. Conservative Republicans and left-wing coalitions, including the Communist Party (founded in 1920), tried to come to grips with the economic and social after-

On 6 February 1934, a coalition of fascist factions attempted a *coup d'état* in Paris. It failed, but the left was finally goaded into concerted action. In 1936, a front of radicals, socialists and communists, headed by the socialist Léon Blum, won the election. The so-called *Front Populaire* promised to fight fascism and improve the French worker's lot. After major strikes, employers reluctantly agreed to wage increases, paid vacations and reduced hours.

Initial euphoria was short-lived. The struggle against fascism split the *Front* when Blum refused to send help to the Spanish

Republicans against Franco. He also interrupted the labour reforms because of their negative effect on the economy. In 1937, in a wave of wildcat strikes, the shattered *Front Populaire* sank into the past. "Rather Hitler than Blum," the Conservatives muttered.

World War II: When war broke out against Nazi Germany in September 1939, France shored up the utterly useless Maginot Line, mobilised an ill-equipped army and waited. In Paris, statues were sandbagged and the Louvre curators carefully prepared paintings in readiness for transport to safety.

On 14 June, the Nazis marched into the city having simply gone round the Maginot

Choltitz, the German commander, received orders to blow up the city but chose to surrender instead. On 26 August General de Gaulle paraded with his forces down the Champs-Elysées. Crowds rejoiced and collaborators scrambled into hiding or suffered the pains of summary justice. The war still had nine months to rage on but with Paris liberated light at last returned to the European continent.

Paris since World War II: With the bane of fascism at last gone, the poets and artists regained their chairs at their favoured watering-holes, the Flore, the Lipp and the Coupole. Political quarrelling resumed without the

Line. There was no siege, no National Guard, no *levée en masse*, no cabbies hauling howitzers. Instead Pétain, withered hero of Verdun, became the titular head of a puppet régime in Vichy.

Some Parisians welcomed the Nazis as racial cleansers, others because they expected the trains to run on time. But there were those who bravely resisted, sacrificing their lives.

On 6 June 1944, Allied forces landed in Normandy and advanced on Paris. Von

extreme right. The tourists returned in droves. Bebop, and rock 'n' roll arrived from across the Atlantic.

But the war and its horrors cast long shadows: the stench of the Holocaust and the indelible proof of man's capacity for evil. Postwar thought was dominated by the dark existentialism of Jean-Paul Sartre and Albert Camus. In addition, France lost two major colonial wars, the first in Indochina (1946–54) and the second in Algeria (1954–62).

May 1968: A bloody wave of bombings swept Paris in the early 1960s, when it became clear that General de Gaulle, who came

Left, the Opéra shortly after construction in 1888. **Above**, the liberation of Paris, 1944.

out of retirement to head the Fifth Republic, wanted to pull out of the Algerian quagmire. De Gaulle's manner in internal matters was patriarchal and authoritarian. His ideas, with few exceptions, were conservative. Time had eroded the legend. A generation had grown up that had not heard the comforting speeches beamed into occupied France by the BBC. It had other ideas and other idols.

The 1968 agitation began uneventfully enough in March with a sit-in by students to demand changes in the antiquated university system. But instead of initiating a civil discussion with the students, the *ancien régime* promptly called in the CRS, France's dreaded riot police, to restore what they saw as a breakdown of order.

Push led to shove. On the night of 10 May 1968, the police stormed 60 barricades in the Latin Quarter. Unrest spread to the factories and other cities. France was soon paralysed and Paris was left in a state of siege. Petrol was rationed and cautious housewives began to hoard sugar and other essential foodstuffs. The state-run media shuffled along with ersatz programming, while Parisians got the news from the privateers on France's periphery or, ironically, from the BBC in London.

On 30 May, de Gaulle announced new elections and warned against impending totalitarianism. The Parisian bourgeoisie awoke. An hour later over 500,000 de Gaulle supporters were flowing down the Champs-Elysées. May 1968 was the most important upheaval in the city since the war.

June came and the Gaullists won the election. Parisians headed toward the seashore for a well-deserved vacation, and the *événements* of 1968 became part of history.

The 1970s appeared tame, but, when the conservative President, Giscard d'Estaing, lost to socialist leader François Mitterrand, in 1981, a huge crowd emerged to march to the Bastille in celebration.

However, in 1986, the exigent Parisian character revealed itself again, during the legislative elections. Voters on the left were dismayed by what they viewed as Mitterrand's sell-out, and conservative forces, led by Paris mayor Jacques Chirac and his Gaullist Rally for the Republic party swept in with a rightist coalition. Chirac was well-suited to the population in his inconsistencies. In his student days, he had been a member of the communist youth movement, then a gung-ho lieutenant fighting with French anti-independence forces in Algeria, and later Prime Minister for two years under Giscard d'Estaing in the early 1970s.

May 1968 reaffirmed Paris's old rebellious spirit. Parisians still demonstrate at the drop of a hat – anti-racism, pro-gays, against altering university entrance requirements, whatever. The zeitgeist of the 1990s has found much to admire in the legacy of the *événements* as, once again, many Parisians have been trying to find alternative ways of living (*vivre autrement*). The 1993 elections confirmed the swing to the right and strengthened Chirac's credentials to succeed Mitterrand as France's president.

Mitterrand, an increasingly isolated figure warring with his own government ("Machiavelli versus the Medicis," as one commentator put it), seemed helpless as the socialist party experienced *effondrement* – a "melting away" of its support. But at least he could console himself that, however much his political dreams had been diluted, he would be remembered as a latter-day Sun King, the promoter of many of the *grands projets* that changed the face of Paris. Even this achievement began to turn sour, though, as critics piled scorn on the last of the *grands projets*, the Très Grande Bibliothèque, the world's biggest book depository, described by one commentator as "an upturned table with towers forming the legs; an insane way to house books or people wishing to study them."

The undeniable charm of Paris lies in these exquisite tensions and juxtapositions – political, artistic, social and architectural. The old lives together with the new. Beaubourg stands an equal to Notre Dame. Brash young businessmen, punks and Dior-dressed ladies share the streets used by beslippered *ménagères* clutching shopping nets bristling with baguettes and smelling faintly of aged camembert. Paris, modern and sophisticated, can claim to be the heart of western civilisation, but in its veins still flows the blood of the rustic, untamed, refractory Gaulois.

Right, La Défense, symbol of modern Paris.

Question: how can you spot a true Parisian in Paris? Answer: he's the only one who can get a cab at six o'clock on a Friday evening.

For many of the inner-city's 2.2 million residents and the 20 million tourists who visit each year, Paris is a grand seductress, a mistress or a lover. Hundreds of thousands of people are carrying on an illicit affair with her. Some manage a quick fling. For others, the love affair endures a lifetime.

"No other city in the world has been better loved or more celebrated," wrote American author John Steinbeck. "Scarcely has the traveller arrived than he feels himself in the grip of this city which is so much more than a city." A great part of the allure of Paris undoubtedly lies with the Parisians themselves, with their charm, their individualism, their diversity.

So who are the Parisians? They are the prostitutes in the leather mini-skirts on the Rue St Denis, the *clochard* sleeping off a bottle of red in the Metro, the society hostess in Chanel, the yuppie stockbroker weaving home from the Bourse on his scooter, the children of the Opéra ballet school affectionately known as "les petits rats", the au pairs, hiding from their mothers in the city's American bars, the Algerian greengrocer and the Portuguese concierge, the stately African chief from Sierre Leone, the law student from the Sorbonne and the old lady in the park in her bedroom slippers feeding the pigeons. People are what lend any city its vibrancy and Paris is no exception. Stripped of its human population, Paris would be no more than a collection of buildings and monuments, architecturally beautiful maybe, but a sad, cold place nonetheless.

Cold front: There is an old joke, not familiar to many Parisians but much told in bars where foreigners congregate. It goes like this. On the 8th day, God created a city in the

image of paradise and named it Paris. It was a city so beautiful, so perfect, he was afraid lest the rest of the world became jealous. And so, to redress the balance, on the 9th day he created the Parisians.

This joke may not go down too well in the capital, but you can bet that the rest of France is joining in the laughter. A recent national survey put Parisians at the top of the list of most hated people in France (31 percent), easily outclassing the traditional targets such as civil servants (21 percent), Corsicans (23

percent) and even policemen (18 percent).

Visitors and Parisians have their favourite stereotypical Parisian whom they love to hate, from the haughty, patronising shop assistant too busy adjusting her lipstick to give her customers the time of day, to the swearing, gesticulating taxi driver, who refuses to let you enter his cab because you are not heading in "his" direction, and to the indifferent bureaucrat who keeps you waiting for three hours only to inform you that you lack a vital document (usually your electricity bill) without which he is unable to help you. (Although the French invented the

Preceding pages: lady and friend in the Latin Quarter; art students in the Luxembourg Gardens. **Left,** Paris messenger. **Right,** traffic policeman.

concept of bureaucracy, it is unforgivable to call a person "bureaucrat" to his face. The polite reference is *fonctionnaire*).

Recent articles in the French press exhorting Parisians to good behaviour and deploring the unfriendly welcome they extend to tourists does mean that at least today's Parisians are no longer under any illusions. Only 38 percent consider themselves kind, while an almost unanimous 92 percent admit to being under stress. Eighty-two percent also own up, undoubtedly with more than a touch of Gallic pride, to being *individualistes*, a description which anyone who has had more than a passing acquaintance with the city

may be difficult to get to know, once he lets you into his life he'll be your friend forever."

Human underneath: Once one transcends the stereotype and becomes acquainted with the individual, the Parisian is no longer the intimidating, disdainful creature of legend, but actually quite human. Beneath that studied Parisian indifference beats a heart of intelligence, loyalty and warmth. Courtesy, charm and consideration are not, perhaps, qualities which spring to mind while trying to navigate the busy intersection at Charles de Gaulle Etoile, and yet they are abundantly evident in everyday life: in the friendly concern of Mme Defreitas, the concierge; the

may suspect of doubling as a convenient excuse for a multitude of sins of the "me first" variety.

And yet the American author Henry Miller, who spent many years in the capital and was better placed than most to make an objective judgement of the national character, stated that he has more respect for the French "than any other nationality on the face of the earth." While conceding that "the French may not be the jolliest, happiest or the easiest people to get along with," Miller could not praise them highly enough, saying that "a Frenchman makes the best kind of friend. Though he

cheerful greeting of Monsieur Durand, the baker and the welcoming smile of Henri behind the counter at the Café des Sports.

For despite the legendary rudeness, Paris is a city in which the majority of the population are chivalrous to a fault and in which good manners are considered an essential part of everyday life. While a volley of verbal abuse – including many expressions which cannot, for reasons of propriety, be reproduced here – will barely cause the average Parisian to bat an eyelid, forgetting to say *bonjour* or *merci* is considered unforgivable.

Living in Paris: "I have before me the most

thought about, the most spoken of, the most written about five thousand hectares in the world," author Jean Giraudoux wrote of Paris. In the 18th century Jean Baptiste Louis Cresset added that "It is only in Paris that one truly lives, elsewhere one just vegetates."

Given this universal acclaim for the city, it is hardly surprising that many millions want to live in Paris. The greater metropolitan area contains 10½ million people, one-fifth of France's total population. As a result, Paris is more densely populated than Tokyo, London or New York. The Parisians' high stress level – and thus their rudeness – can be partly put down to the fact that they live literally on

apartment at any one time. It is an oft-cited paradox that this battle for a place to live occurs in a city where 16 percent of apartments lie vacant.

Competition to live in the capital may be stiff but for the 2.2 million souls fortunate enough to have made it to Paris's inner sanctum, the privileged kernel of 20 affluent *arrondissements* or city districts within the *périphérique* – the ring road which separates the city proper from the often grim suburbs of decaying high rises and barrack-like apartment blocks – the rewards are undoubtedly very high. While many cities in other countries seem to be disintegrating from the ef-

top of one another, squeezed into, what are by most standards, extremely small apartments packed into the city's 105 sq. km (40½ sq. miles).

Virtually all Parisians live in apartments in a city where a house and garden is an almost unheard of luxury. Nor is accommodation easy to come by, with families holding on to their homes for generations. There is intense competition for desirable living space, with an average of 150,000 people looking for an

Far left, pretty *parisiennes* in pink. **Left**, a café intellectual. **Above**, dowager in fur.

fects of poverty and crumbling infrastructure, Paris is thriving, not only as one of the world's most beautiful cities, but also as one of the best run.

Good management: Generous financing and sound administration mean that Paris functions as a smooth-running modern metropolis. Mail is delivered three times a day, during rush hour the Metro trains arrive every 80 seconds, rubbish is collected seven days a week and every one of Paris's 1,300 km (800 miles) of streets is swept by hand at least once every day.

Middle-class flight, which has adversely

affected so many American cities, barely exists in Paris, where the affluent are queuing up to live in a city which offers excellent public school education, first-class amenities, and a culture budget to rival that of most Third World countries' overall spending for a year. As an urban planner explained it: "One reason Paris has so few problems is that the type of people who make problems can't afford to live in Paris."

A microcosm of privileged Parisian society is the idyllic Jardin du Luxembourg in the 5th *arrondissement*. This famous garden has 80 gardeners, or more than one per acre, and is an oasis from the traumas suffered by most

arrondissements means that the city falls into easily recognised "quartiers" or neighbourhoods, each with its own shops, markets, cafés and local eccentrics. Parisians develop lifetime attachments to their own neighbourhoods. While large supermarket chains exist, Parisians continue to support local merchants and to shop in small specialised shops and the local markets. By always frequenting the same fishmonger or baker and taking their morning *café crème* at the local corner café, loyalties are soon built up and each *quartier* takes on a village atmosphere in which everyone is known, at least by sight and frequently by name. Paris works

cities. Each year more than 350,000 flowers are planted or transplanted in the garden and each spring 150 orange and palm trees are brought out after spending the winter months lovingly sheltered from the cold. In the summer months, chattering students from the Sorbonne compare notes around the splashing fountain, while designer-dressed toddlers, their elegant mothers in tow, come for pony rides or to sail toy boats on the pond, old men play chess or draughts under the trees, and lovers hold hands over an apéritif in the *salon de thé*.

The organisation of the capital into 20

therefore as a series of small communities coexisting under the umbrella of a big city. As a result it is hard to imagine feeling lonely or intimidated here as one might in London or New York.

Lovers and lights: The city's image as the capital of romance has been built up by countless novels and films. It's an image that holds true for visitors, but for locals the reality fails to live up to the myth: one in three Parisians lives alone and half the city's marriages end in divorce. It is hard to be sad in Paris for long, though. The capital's reputation as a good-time girl stretches back before the bright lights came to Pigalle. In the Middle Ages, Nostradamus, prophet of gloom, offered the comforting thought that there was one spot on earth which could be relied on to lift the spirits: "As long as Paris does not fall, gaiety will exist in the world," he wrote in the 16th century.

Parisians as a whole form such a diverse collection of races and cultures that it is almost impossible to characterize them. On the radio there are local stations broadcasting 24 hours a day to African, Arab and Portuguese listeners. Tune in to Radio Nova (101.5 FM), the city's most popular music station (and started by an Irishman), to hear

These Marie-Chantals and Charles-Henris are easy to recognise. They are the ones sporting the Hermès scarves decorated with dead grouse, the velvet hairbands and the Chanel quilted handbags – real, not imitation. And that is just the women. For men, Lobb shoes, Dunhill pipes and even cravates are still in vogue.

This group is also known under the acronym CPFH (*collier de perles, foulard Hermès* – pearl necklace, Hermès scarf). Like their British and American counterparts, a profound conservatism, adherence to classicism and traditional values and a marked dislike of anything new or trendy are the dominant

the wonderful eclectic jumble of jazz, rap, soul, blues, reggae, African, French and international sounds. Mixed culture aside, however, there are certain recognisable types.

City sorts: The *bcbg* (*bon chic bon genre*), the French equivalent of the British Sloane Ranger or the American preppie, can easily be spotted in their main stamping grounds of Neuilly, Auteuil and Passy, the rich suburbs of the 16th and 17th *arrondissements* to the west of the city, collectively known as NAP.

Left, trendy is not necessarily chic. **Above**, doorman at the Hotel Crillon.

traits of this species of Parisian. To see them in their natural habitat, try the VIP enclosure at Chantilly race course. They can also be spied sipping "chocolat africain" with pet poodle in tow at Angelina's *salon de thé* on Rue de Rivoli or, for the more *branché* (literally, "plugged in") of the species, dancing the night away at Les Bains Douches, Paris's perpetually "in" nightclub located in an old swimming baths.

For a glimpse of a world as totally removed from that of the *bcbg* as it is possible to get, travel on RER commuter line B north from Châtelet with "les rappeurs", the second or third generation descendants of African and Caribbean immigrants. With shaved heads, baseball caps set backwards at a jaunty angle and "baskets" by Nike or Reebok, the names of American basketball and football heroes emblazoned across their chests, the style and philosophy of "*les rappeurs*" is imported direct from New York. American rap (of which a greater and less censored variety is to be found on French rather than on American radio) is popular, as are African stars such as Youssou N'Dour and home-grown rap heroes like MC Solaar. Disenchanted with a life which offers few prospects in the grim housing estates which ring

Paris, "*les rappeurs*" are nevertheless mostly a gentle and graceful group in comparison with their often more aggressive American counterparts. In between these groups are the average Parisian – the *beaufs* (short for *beau-frère* or brother-in-law). A *beauf* is generally someone you are associated with by obligation rather than by choice, but good for a laugh, anyway.

To discover the city's Asian community head for Belleville in the 20th *arrondissement* or to Chinatown in the 13th, home to the majority of the capital's 35,000 Vietnamese, Cambodians, Laotians, Chinese and Japa-

nese. Here, green tea, hundred-year-old eggs and *dim sum* compete for space with the traditional French *baguette* and *grand crème*. Alternatively, for a taste of Africa, visit the area around the Marché Dejean (Metro: Barbes-Rochechouart) in the 18th *arrondissement*. Mangoes, yams and plantain spill onto the street from tiny shops as African women in bright batik prints, babies slung papoose style around their waists, sway gracefully among the stalls, picking out salt fish and papaya for the evening meal.

Problem areas: The city's problems seem small compared with most modern cities. The roughest parts of Paris are probably as safe as the safest parts of most American and many British cities; traffic congestion is the Parisians' most oft-cited worry. Homelessness in the capital is an increasingly visible problem, but the city's tradition of romanticising the *clochards* (tramps) who sleep rough along the Seine keeps it from coming too high on the list of most Parisians' main concerns.

In the winter however, with temperatures often plunging below zero, there is nothing romantic about life for the capital's 15,000 homeless. The government and various private organisations provide 60 shelters where they can receive six months' free room and board, medical care and job training. Attendance is voluntary but in winter the police will often round up those sleeping rough to protect them from the cold. Two newspapers, *Le Réverbère* and *Macadam*, Parisian equivalents of London's *The Big Issue*, endeavour to give the capital's homeless a measure of financial independence and self respect.

But these are not huge problems. One American resident recalls that, on her way home from the market one summer evening she passed two good-natured *clochards* who lived on a nearby grating. They were cooking up an omelette on a small spirit stove, had just opened a bottle of wine and were listening to jazz on their battered transistor. *"Bon appétit!"* they called out, raising their glasses as she passed laden with groceries. For her, that really said something about Paris.

Left, dressed for the mosque. **Right**, for some, every pavement is a catwalk.

If the name of Toulouse immediately evokes a famous bean dish (*cassoulet*), Marseille a celebrated fish stew (*bouillabaisse*), and Strasbourg steaming sauerkraut (*choucroute*), ask a Frenchman to name a typically Parisian dish and you will usually receive a blank stare in return. After several minutes, and some coaxing, he might raise his eyebrows and hesitantly suggest "*steack frites*" (steak with French fries), before declaring that Paris is a city without any specifically regional fare. He would, of course, be wrong.

Local products: One of the finest French cheeses, Brie, is produced within 50 km (30 miles) of Notre Dame, the windows of pastry shops are crowded with Parisian specialities (*Paris Brest, L'Opéra, Saint-Honoré, Puits d'Amour, Amandines*) and the elongated *baguette* which was perfected in Paris is no longer considered specific to this city but simply "French bread". In short, Parisian foods are so frequently found throughout the country (and the world) that they are not thought of as "local" at all, and a list of typically Parisian bistro dishes reads like a *Who's Who* of French favourites: smoked herring marinated in oil and served with warm potatoes (*hareng pommes à l'huile*), calf's head with a mustardy-eggy *vinaigrette* (*tête de veau, sauce gribiche*), steak with red wine sauce (*entrecôte marchand de vin*), roast leg of lamb with kidney beans (*gigot rôti, flageolets*), chocolate mousse (*mousse au chocolat*), caramel custard (*crème caramel*) and floating island (*île flottante*), to name but a few. Such a listing, however, provides only a partial picture of what awaits the gastronomically curious in the French capital. Indeed, pavement vendors, café terraces, and elegant restaurants all offer different, but equally specific, "Parisian fare".

Street food: For centuries, Parisian streets echoed with the cries of vendors carrying baskets of food ranging from fresh fish to pastries. Today, that tradition survives in the

heart of the Latin Quarter (Boulevard St Michel) and on the big streets surrounding the department stores behind the Opéra. There, chestnut vendors improvise stands during the winter and tempt passers-by with the irresistible smell of chestnuts roasting over a bed of coals. Other street vendors cook paper-thin crêpes on hot griddles and will stuff them with your choice of either a sweet or savoury filling. But for anything more substantial and varied you must go

indoors – but not necessarily to a restaurant.

Everything from quiche to salad, and daily specials like *poulet basquaise* (chicken with tomatoes and bell peppers) or salt cod puree (*brandade*), can be taken-out from any of the many Parisian *charcuterie*s. A slice of pâté or ham can transform a crisp *baguette* from the neighbouring bakery into a sandwich, a delicious and simple meal nicely finished off with a wedge of cheese from the *fromagerie*, or pastry from the *pâtisserie*.

Café meals: When one's feet are sore and queues in shops are long, the marble-topped tables of pavement cafés may be more allur-

Preceding pages: plenty of choice. **Left**, street food. **Right**, Paris takes its time over dinner.

ing to someone in search of a midday meal. All cafés offer a variety of sandwiches (ham, cheese, pâté) which are notoriously short on filling and long on bread. This said, for a modest supplement, butter or pickles (*cornichons*) can be added and Dijon mustard will be supplied free. Since the bread is generally freshly baked and the butter excellent, you can begin to overlook the paper-thin slices of ham or cheese.

Crôque Monsieur and *Crôque Madame* are two other popular on-the-run café lunches. The former, a grilled ham and cheese sandwich, is much more commonly available than the latter (grilled chicken and cheese)

than usual (*café-brasseries*) and grandiose restaurants serving Alsatian specialities in addition to more traditional French fare. The latter were introduced to the French capital in the late 19th century, about the time modern methods of brewing were being perfected. Cold draft beer was a novelty to Parisians then, as was Alsatian sauerkraut (*French choucroute*), and both quickly became as popular as the *baguette*. Surprisingly, given the distance of Alsace from the ocean, brasseries also specialise in shellfish platters of all sorts. Baskets of oysters, clams, cockles and mussels line the sidewalks in front of most of them and men in sailor's

and both make filling, if not particularly memorable, meals.

Cafés also serve omelettes, shirred (baked) eggs (*oeufs sur le plat*) and cold hard-boiled eggs (*oeufs durs*). A plain omelette (*omelette nature*), slightly runny inside and perfectly brown outside, with a green salad (*salade verte*) and a little basket of freshly sliced *baguette* makes for a typically Parisian lunch, good value and brimming with flavour.

Brasserie and bistro meals: One step up from the café is the brasserie. This term, which literally means "brewery", designates both cafés that serve a wider variety of food

caps deftly open oysters under the admiring gaze of passers-by.

One can make a meal of shellfish (during the "R" months of the year – September to April) in any of the many brasseries, or simply sample the seafood as a prelude to the sauerkraut piled high with pork and sausages that attracts hungry Parisians on cold winter nights. In either case, Alsatian wine (probably a Riesling) is a necessary accompaniment, as is a wedge of Munster cheese served before – or instead of – dessert with a glass of the very same wine.

If brasseries are generally spacious, festive and slightly "exotic", bistros are traditionally small, modest and *very* French. Today, the term is used more freely than in the past and is no longer limited to family-style establishments where simple food is served. The origin of the name "bistro" supposedly lies in the days of Russian occupation of Paris in 1814. The Russian military were forbidden to drink, so whenever they dived into a bar they demanded their refreshments urgently – *bistro* – lest they should be caught in the act.

In fact, any restaurant with a more or less relaxed atmosphere might call itself a bistro these days (seafood restaurants are often

very rare with French fries (*steack frites*), calf's kidneys, also cooked rare, often in a mustardy sauce (*rognon de veau à la moutarde*), roast chicken (*poulet rôti*), tripe sausage (*andouillette*), green salad, cheese, fruit tarts, custards and *mousse au chocolat*.

Today, bistro food is also to be found in wine bars or *bistro à vins*. Though some more fashionable establishments offer smoked salmon and *foie gras*, most serve the kind of hearty food that Parisians call their own: cold plates of ham, sausage and pâté (*assiette de charcuterie*), lentils with salt pork (*petit salé au lentils*), rabbit with mustard sauce (*lapin à la moutarde*) not to men-

called *bistros de la mer*). Nor is the term necessarily associated with moderate prices, so many a bistro meal will cost as much as one served in a starred establishment. Nonetheless, traditional bistros do exist and continue to serve a repertoire of dishes which has varied little in the past hundred years, offering (among other things) home-made pâtés, herring marinated in oil (*hareng pommes à l'huile*), leeks with vinaigrette (*poireaux vinaigrette*), tasty steaks cooked

Left, **kosher takeaway in the Marais district**.
Above, **irresistible patisseries**.

tion excellent cheeses and, of course, remarkable wines. In most wine bars, contrary to bona fide restaurants, one can either eat an entire meal or simply order one dish. Wine tends to come from the Beaujolais region or the Loire Valley and is served by the bottle or the glass to accompany the kind of *bonne cuisine* (good cooking) that Parisians crave when they hunger for a light lunch or a simple evening meal.

Chefs and haute cuisine: Staff who prepare food in a traditional bistro are simply cooks (*cuisiniers*), not chefs. Generally speaking, a chef is more ambitious than a cook and places greater importance on innovation and technical prowess. Bistros pride themselves on serving well-executed versions of traditional fare.

On the other hand, chefs run restaurants where the food reflects both changing fashion and/or personal taste. They labour in the hope that one day they will be recognised as talented, which in France is synonymous with creative. This trend has been greatly accentuated in recent years with the rise of *nouvelle cuisine,* whose supporters applaud unorthodox combinations of taste and encourage a break with routine. "*Les chefs*" everywhere listened to the message and,

"classics" is now being served not only throughout Paris but throughout France. This said, today's chefs are not all slavishly reproducing dishes that resemble each other – at their best, they are providing meals that are fresher, lighter and generally more adventurous than they were in the past.

Whatever the cuisine, however, few chefs are great chefs. But Paris is fortunate in having an exceptionally high concentration of restaurants and the largest number of great chefs in France. Of the 19 restaurants in France that earned the coveted three-star rating in a recent Michelin Guide, five were in Paris (more than a quarter of those with

today, flourless butter sauces (*beurre blanc*) have replaced the *béchamel* of yore, *feuilletés* (thin layers of puff pastry) have supplanted the once popular *bouchées* (puff pastry shells), fish fillets have ousted whole fish from menus, duck steaks (*magret de canard*) have displaced beef, raw fish (*tartare de poisson*) is no longer scandalous and exotic food combinations or tastes (fruit with meat or fish, the use of spices such as ginger or unusual herbs like fresh coriander) no longer shock but are accepted as bold touches on the part of the chef. In short, *nouvelle cuisine* has simply become *cuisine*, and a series of new

two stars were in Paris as well).

Food served by a master chef only incidentally satisfies one's hunger; it is more of a dining experience than a meal. Chefs are less interested in filling the belly than in stimulating taste buds and making one pause and think. Such a dinner should provide a glimpse of an individual chef's style or attitude toward food and be as plentiful in ideas as in flavours. Anyone seeking an aesthetically sensual experience has come to the right place in seeking out a great chef and a starred restaurant, but ravenously hungry sightseers might well prefer bistro fare.

Provincial food in Paris: Unlike other big cities in France, Paris offers a varied and changing spectrum of foreign cuisines as well as its own local fare, making it possible for the curious to sample not only the regional cuisines of France but specialities from around the world.

The oldest and largest immigrant community in Paris is the rural French. Many a Parisian will tell you that grandmother came from the Auvergne, Brittany or some other distant corner of France. Numerous provinces were autonomous kingdoms in the past and, in some areas, even as recently as a century ago many people spoke dialect rather

Bastille station, traces of an Auvergnat community are still to be seen.

Today, however, the regional cuisine most popular with Parisians is that of Gascony, broadly referred to as the "Southwest". Throughout the city, speciality shops sell *foie gras* and even traditional Parisian bistros now offer *confit de canard* (preserved duck) and *magret* (duck steak), both literally unknown in Paris 50 years ago but adopted as enthusiastically and as quickly as sauerkraut was roughly a century earlier.

Couscous and other exotics: Of all the foreign cuisines to be found in the French capital, two might be called favourites: North

than French. To accommodate these displaced communities, restaurants often sprang up around the spot where these newcomers first touched Parisian soil – the train stations.

The Gare Montparnasse is surrounded by bars proudly draped with the flag of Brittany and *crêperies bretonnes* line the side streets leading to the station. The Gare de l'Est is flanked by Alsatian restaurants (and a famous Alsatian *charcuterie*), whereas, not far from the Gare de Lyon and the now-vanished

Left, would-be chefs. **Above,** bistros take pride in serving good value traditional fare.

African and Vietnamese. Simplified and modified to suit French taste, both boast emblematic dishes: *couscous* (steamed semolina served with a spicy meat and vegetable stew) and *phô* (beef and noodle soup) respectively. Though the French do not consider any cuisine a rival to their own, they do consider *couscous* a welcome change and students, in particular, are happy to find a source of inexpensive meals in the many Vietnamese restaurants so popular with the younger crowd. Restaurants offering these cuisines are found throughout the city although a large Asian community has developed near the Porte d'Italie (between Avenue Choisy and Avenue d'Ivry).

An Indian community has grown up in the north of the city (Passage Brady just north of the Porte St Denis and the streets bordering the Rue du Faubourg Saint Denis behind the Gare du Nord might be called "little India"). Several excellent Lebanese restaurants are grouped on the Avenue Marceau, and two ancient Jewish communities offer kosher meals in the Marais district (Rue des Rosiers) and in the 9th *arrondissement* of the city around the Rue Richer.

In a word, Parisian fare is as cosmopolitan as the city itself. Regional produce is shipped

are frog's legs, many an innocent tourist has unwittingly ordered calf's head (*tête de veau*) or calf's kidney (*rognon de veau*) thinking they were ordering veal (*veau*) or knowingly pointed to *andouillette* believing that some pork sausage would appear, only to discover a pungent tripe-filled creation instead.

The reader should not fear the above-named specialities – after all, 50 million French (and many a foreign visitor) relish their taste – but those with a meat and potatoes upbringing may well be shocked by the French penchant for the organs or offal (*les abats*) and animals that tend to hop or crawl.

Even certain favourite French fish are not

daily to Paris and nowhere else will you find as many French cheeses, wines, sausages or hams on display. Parisians are used to this concentration of resources and take the exceptional variety of foods made available to them for granted. "Their" food is the nation's finest. Marketing in the French capital is like taking a survey of France's agricultural wealth, while dining in Paris provides a glimpse of French cuisine at its best.

Frightful foods: Not all visitors to Paris are as enthusiastic about certain classic dishes as the French. If almost everyone knows that *escargots* are snails and *cuisses de grenouille*

to everyone's taste. Eel (*anguille*), a speciality in both the northern provinces and the southwest, is rarely served in Paris though sea urchins (*oursin*), an equally strange creature for some, are a standard feature of most Parisian *plateaux de fruits de mer* (raw shellfish platters). Mussels (*moules*), generally cooked with a little white wine and eaten with french fries, are served in many modest *café-brasseries* and are as Parisian as *steack frites*. And most Parisians prefer their herring smoked, filleted and left for several weeks with carrots and onions in a bowl full of peanut oil (this many sound terrible but, drained and served with a warm potato salad, they make an appetizing first course).

Some familiar foods are presented in ways that have surprised more than one conservative diner. Steaks, lamb and duck, for example, will always be served rare (*saignant*) and those who prefer their steak medium are generally better off asking for it *bien cuit* (well done). *Confit de canard* (preserved duck) is a specialty that must be tasted to be understood and generally becomes a favourite with those who discover it. Squeamish visitors sometimes feel faint when they learn how this great southwestern delicacy is made (ducks, force-fed to fatten their livers into

strange food habits make eating-out a source of anguish rather than pleasure. Raw vegetable salads (*crudités*) are as common as smoked herring, roast lamb more frequently served than calf's head and mild cheeses as plentiful as strong.

Eating etiquette: Regardless of your budget, some basic rules apply to all French meals and respecting them will increase your pleasure and help you avoid awkward situations.

Before any large meal one is offered an *apéritif*. In a French home this can be anything from Scotch to Port but in restaurants a glass of Champagne, white wine, or a *kir* (white wine with blackcurrant liqueur) are

foie gras, are salted for several days, then simmered in their own fat for hours).

Lastly, though French cheeses deserve their international reputation and are nowhere as good as in France, timid first-time visitors reel from some of the more pungent ones. More specifically *Epoisses, Munster, Boulette d'Avenes,* and *Vieux Lille* are not for those who eat only mild Cheddar.

With all this in mind, don't consider France a country where bizarre food items and

preferred. Don't feel obliged to order an *apéritif* if you are on your own but if your French host offers you one, it can be taken as a (minor) insult to refuse.

Wine is, of course, the perfect accompaniment to French food. Alternatively, or additionally you can order mineral water, sparkling or not (*pétillant* or *plat*, respectively). Beer is drunk only with sandwiches, with very simple meals like steak and French fries, as a thirst quencher or with Alsatian meals.

Even in extremely modest restaurants, a meal is composed of three courses: starters/

Left, traditional zinc-topped bar. **Above**, seafood will be good but not cheap.

salads (*entrées/hors d'oeuvres*), a main course (*plat*) and dessert (*dessert*). Americans used to referring to their main dish as an entree should beware – an *entrée* (as its name implies) is a first course in France.

Though an *hors d'oeuvre* may be a salad, a green salad (lettuce with vinaigrette) is never an *hors d'oeuvre*. Grated carrots or boiled leeks with vinaigrette are typical *hors d'oeuvre* "salads". Green salad (*salade verte*) is served after the main course and before cheese. Though fewer and fewer restaurants offer a green salad as a matter of course, most will be glad to prepare one and it makes a refreshing break midway through the meal.

Many Parisians prefer to end a meal with cheese rather than something sweet, so it's extremely common for moderately priced restaurants to offer fixed-price menus that include a starter, a main dish and cheese *or* dessert. When ordering cheese in a restaurant, a cheese platter will be presented. Don't hesitate to try a small slice of several cheeses (in private homes three is the polite number to try) and keep in mind that a cheese platter is almost never offered a second time.

Bread is an indispensable part of every meal. It should be on the table virtually from the time you sit down until the moment dessert is to be served. Bread is almost never eaten with butter, though a little butter might be on the table in fancier restaurants to accommodate tourists; butter *is*, however, served with radishes, country hams, sausages and Roquefort cheese.

Dogs are so loved in France that few restaurants refuse them entry. Don't be surprised, even in the finest establishments, to see them under tables or in laps sharing meals with their masters. This said, "doggy bags" are virtually unknown (there is no French equivalent).

Good value fixed-price menus are common in fine restaurants and in simple eating places alike, but better restaurants tend to offer them only at lunch. If you plan on ordering the fixed menu in the evening, read it carefully to make sure the words *déjeuner seulement* (lunch only) do not appear.

Some better restaurants offer a *menu dégustation* (tasting menu) and usually everyone at table must order it or no one can have it at all; it involves serving numerous courses and is difficult to orchestrate when some people at the table have ordered a simple three-course meal.

Coffee is never served with milk after a meal in France. *Café au lait* is considered hard to digest whereas black coffee is a stimulant that wakes you up. This said, decaffeinated coffee (*café décaféiné*, or *déca* for short) is available everywhere – it is made and served like expresso and can actually be quite good.

Lastly, a wide range of *digestifs* (after-dinner drinks) is available in even the simplest of cafés. They range from the roughest of rough brandies ("grappa") to the smoothest of Cognacs. Fruit brandies are particularly good. Pear (*poire*) and plum (*mirabelle*) are two favourites. Brandies are never mixed with anything else and always served at the end of a meal.

Voilà! You are now ready to confront your waiter. Speak slowly, listen attentively, relax and... *bon appétit!*
See Travel Tips at the back of this book for specific restaurant recommendations.

<u>Left</u>, most fixed-priced menus offer at least three courses. <u>Right</u>, eating al fresco.

Or, How to Get the Most out of Paris without Bothering about the Sights.

The secret of appreciating Paris is to love life. The surest way to seize the city for yourself is to forget its quicksand of historical facts and its overwhelming pomposity. Instead you should wander about the city, down shady boulevards, or by the quiet and gritty pathways in the parks, alert for those telling details that make this city unique.

Indeed, the best way to start may be to stop. Watch Paris breathe – heave, rather, with an endlessly fascinating mixture of energy and relaxation, passion and disdain. Find a bench, better still find a café, read nothing, but look at the strangers struggling with their map, the old woman struggling with her shopping, the motorist with the slow-coach in front, the lovers with each other. Against the background of traffic noise rises the chirp of birds, the chatter of conversation and the chink of glasses at the table.

All the pavement's a stage: The beauty of Paris is that it is lived in, right at the very heart; downtown London is worked in by a tide of commuters, who ebb back to their suburban gardens at the end of the day, but the Parisian pavements are workplaces by day and places of recreation by night. In this grand theatre every pavement is a stage: watch out for the fashionable ladies with their tiny yapping dogs; and definitely watch out for the pavement pictograms where these dogs do their business; watch out too for the Parisian street-cleaning machines, which look like a cross between a golf cart and a toothbrush; and wherever you go watch out for the Eiffel Tower, which standing amongst all this dignified architecture looks as out of place as a nude at a dinner party.

Paris can be one of the most daunting cities of all. So many expectations are heaped upon it – and upon you, especially as a first-time visitor, by the buffs and bores that claim to

know it backwards. You shouldn't be afraid to admit it if the sense of duty – you must see all the sights, the monuments, the museums, the galleries – is at odds with your inclination, your timetable, and even your energy on what is supposed to be a holiday. Take it easy. Just as *Hamlet* is more than a sequence of quotations, so Paris is more than a catalogue of sights.

Sights were scarcely ever built as sights, in any case. Even the Eiffel Tower, built to

vaunt French technology at one of the Universal Exhibitions a century ago, was to be dismantled thereafter – and was saved because of its function as a military and civil communications mast. Given that also at that time Paris was at its most stylishly frothy, naughty and bawdy, it seems a perfect touch that Eiffel, the designer of a tower both serene and phallic, was also the inventor of the garter belt (imagine the Eiffel Tower upside down and you'll see the connection).

Connoisseurs of this city often say that Paris is still in essence a medieval city. Some of its monuments are medieval; its undying

Preceding pages: one way of going around. **Left**, and right, soaking up the atmosphere.

taste for bawdy high-living is medieval; and the fact that on any given walk you are quite likely to squelch your foot on fresh fruit (hopefully) is also medieval. Paris, it should be said, is not now a dirty city – and an army of garish-green uniforms sweeps and washes streets endlessly – but it is an *everyday* city, briskly mundane in the midst of the breathtaking grandeur. The squelched fruit clinches the excellence and excitement of Paris more than a dozen museums and dutiful facts can. Balzac, the great novelist of Paris, thought of the place as a city of ideas, but of ideas that smile at you at street corners or splash you with mud from carriage wheels.

benefits of traffic, but for better control of a restive civilian population: narrow streets lend themselves nicely to barricades, whereas boulevards are better for baton charges.

Parking problems: The most conspicuous blockade these days is the parked car. Paris is the centre of that continental sport, the nudging forwards and backwards of the cars that prevent you having space to park. Among the signs you may notice on the street is the one which warns of the risk of towing away – yet all it says is that you may have your car towed away if your parking is *gênant*, a word meaning mildly annoying. Throughout the streets you will also come upon evidence of

New York, in compression and excitement so comparable to Paris, nonetheless gives the stroller the impression of being built from the sky down; Paris was built from the pavement up. Balzac also compared Paris to an ocean, with uncharted depths ever-yielding new pearls and monsters.

Even the traffic of Paris has its pace in the history of France. In 1610, two dozen or so attempts on his life having failed, King Henry IV was stabbed to death as his carriage was trapped in a traffic jam in Rue de la Ferronerie. Moreover the great sweeping grand boulevards of Paris today were not built for the

the essentially Napoleonic taste for edicts and statutes, simple instructions backed up by the date of the relevant law. For example, the sinister and frequently encountered citation of a law preventing sticking posters: it is dated April 1943 – when Paris was occupied by the Germans. Or even the prohibition against drunkenness displayed in those tobacco-yellowed announcements in every bar, "Protection des mineurs et répression de l'ivresse publique".

The architect of the way Paris looks today is Baron Haussmann. Appointed Prefect of the Seine, Haussmann had orders midway through the 1800s to rebuild the city. Boulevards had been popular for a hundred years, but in Haussmann they found their champion. He set to his task like a boy with a train-set – and blank cheque – modelling boulevards, squares, streets, avenues, lanes, parks, bridges and sewers all with a peculiar blend of French quirk and German system (he was of German descent). He also pulled a great deal of old Paris down – the Marais was next in line to go – buying up old property like a bulldozer. His prices were such that people would readily give up their homes:

"How d'you afford your carriage, those clothes?"

to see Haussmann's drama unfurl behind you – a tremendous vantage point upon the world's busiest stage.

Explore on foot: Paris is a compact city, worth a good walk – just as your feet tire, your soul gasps. Large maps are at most street corners and street-names are well displayed. Curiously, the name plates have been designed to look as if they are in relief, with something like a shadow marked on the borders: this is Paris seeking to "present" or thematise itself.

It is easy enough to get lost in Paris, even in Haussmann's scheme – possibly even more so, since his passion for vista gives rise

"Oh, I've been dispossessed!"

Never so hugely was a city map redrawn. Climactic views and sweeping carriage-trots this way and that across the city are achieved by a splintering geometry of long avenues that meet in star-burst junctions (Place de Ternes, Place Victor Hugo) or round a great building like an exuberant but organised dance (the Opéra, the Madeleine, even the Gare St Lazare). This is a city also to be seen on the move. Try one of the buses that still has an open balcony at the back, and lean out

Left, walking the lunch. Above, time for a beer.

to a great quantity of extremely sharp-angled street corners, which can make you feel lost like a mouse in a mosaic of slabs of cheese, but can also hide small shifts of direction in the pattern, leading you off course. And where better to be off-course than Paris?!

We expect old buildings to be skew or awry. Those tall old houses on the south bank of the river, by Notre Dame, clutter and lean in on each other like drinkers over-filling a bar, not quite all falling over. Even today this quirkiness continues. Out just beyond the city limits, in the downtown area known as La Défense, the Grand Arche that is the focus of the central avenue – itself a perfectly straight continuation of the line constituted by the Champs-Élysées and the Avenue de la Grande Armée passing through the Arc de Triomphe – is squint, skew to the straight. To catch the sunset? No: to avoid the railway tracks that run through its foundations.

La Défense itself is a phenomenon: whereas most cities could do with a dose of old Paris, new Paris wanted its own high-rise area: La Défense expresses the Parisian taste for high-rise technology just as the Eiffel Tower before it – and Notre Dame before that.

Once your eye has acquired the habit, there is plenty to notice: the grills round

scale of the great student riots of 1223 in which hundreds were killed – there was a rebellious slogan to the effect that under the paving lay the beach – *sous les pavés la plage*. The gist of this was that freedom, symbolised by the beach, was represented by the sand typically to be found immediately under the cobblestones; and that such freedom could therefore be won by hoisting the cobblestones at the police. After the riots most of the pavements were replaced by unlobbable tar. And recently the slogan has been used by a car manufacturer, substituting "on" for "under", to advertise the easy ride of a new model.

trees; the stray café chairs that block all but the narrowest passageway; the indentations marked with pictograms to encourage dog-owners to get their dogs to do their doggy business in special reserves in the gutter; the rolls of old carpet used to divert the morning rivers that flow down these gutters; and as for the gutters themselves, there are frequent, alarmingly gaping mouths of drain-holes which can be visited: the sewers of Paris are a popular tourist attraction.

The pavements have played their part in the city's history too. During the student riots of 1968 – violent enough but not on the

For artists, this city's centre is Montmartre; for students, the university quarter south of Notre Dame. It is known as the Latin Quarter as a result of the long tradition of servants having to speak Latin. The Sorbonne is the oldest university in the world, and whereas in other capital cities learning may be tucked away, here in Paris it has spread a shadow over a whole central district. Student life is conducted in the street. And along the Boulevard St Germain especially, there is something like the graduate equivalent – in the cafés that were once frequented by Jean-Paul Sartre and Albert Camus, by Ernest

Hemingway and Henry Miller. Every nation's literature seems to have its writer who has adopted Paris.

Café life: Parisian cafés manage to accommodate everyone from the dandy – the *flâneur*, a word meaning literally one who strolls – to the bohemian poets and painters doing their best to escape the landlord's reckoning. The dandy seeks to see and be seen, but it suits him just as well as it does the penniless bohemian to indulge in the habit of holding on to his café table for a long stretch, no matter how long ago he drank his already tepid coffee. Almost every café has the paragon of fashion and the scallywag reading

Nietzsche, their attention momentarily caught by the smartest of businessmen making a brief call for a snatch of coffee and a private word to each other on their way, or by old cronies arguing over politics or *pétanque*. All to the music of a flipper machine, and the roar of the traffic.

In the Marais, one of the most characteristic and varied quarters of Paris, the ancient contrast between artisan and aristocrat can still be sensed today. In the boulevards, so-

cial standing was measured vertically, the finest apartments on the first floor, the most rudimentary on the topmost. (Carbon monoxide may have reversed this order.) In the Marais (the web of streets to the east of the Pompidou Centre) however, the jumble is a horizontal one, your standing more likely to be defined by the width of the property than its height, and an aristocrat's neighbours are as likely as not to be a carpenter or shoe mender. Amidst the old aristocratic mansions and workshops you can buy vegetables in one shop or the rarest of fashionable high-tech accessories next door.

The Marais streets mish-mash, never quite at right-angles, almost as if the better to hide the Place des Vosges, one of the finest, most serene town squares in Europe, of great understated symmetry and refreshing in its arcades and parks. This was the last duelling-ground of Paris.

Most cities have a contrast between seedy and splendid: in Paris the mixture is like a chemical reaction whose by-product is energy, sheer energy. A hundred years ago, Montmartre was a seedy quarter that became the genuinely creative crucible of Europe, a shanty town that gave birth to cubism and a gossip madhouse of chattering poets.

You will not find much of the same energy now – and the seediness lies tucked away from a rather too presentable, model village neatness – but if you take in the unique view across the whole of Paris, a swordfight splatter of roofs shimmering beneath, a capital at your feet, you may understand the vaunting, almost arrogant fertility of that creative world: to the artists of the time it made sense to live in a shack but to look down on a quilt of palaces and boulevards.

There is a street, side-street or square in Paris for every mood – and for all weathers. Paris has shifting weather, blue, fluffy-white or damnably grey. It can look its best shimmering after a downpour, or in the lazy early light before breakfast, when the smell of fresh bread and coffee lurks behind every café front. So, take a seat. Breathe in, keep your eyes open. Mind the traffic, don't trip over a dog. If the coffee is terrible, that is history, because Casanova made *exactly* the same complaint. And that is historical fact.

ARCHITECTURE
THROUGH THE AGES

Two thousand years of history and seven centuries of artistic brilliance have made Paris a city rich in architecture. Yet invasions, sieges and insurrections have irreparably destroyed a great number of architectural masterpieces.

In 1944, as Allied troops approached, Hitler gave General Dietrich von Choltitz, Governor of Paris, the order to blast every single historical edifice to pieces, so that the Allies' triumphant entry would be greeted by a field of smoking ruins. Charges of dynamite were laid under the Invalides, Notre Dame, the Madeleine, the Opéra, the Arc de Triomphe and even at the foot of the Eiffel Tower. But at the last minute, unable to perpetrate such sacrilege, von Choltitz refused to give the order and ultimately surrendered the city intact to General Leclerc, liberator of Paris.

Despite the various devastations in its history, Paris has retained examples of all France's architectural styles, especially from the 12th century and the beginnings of the Gothic era onwards. The city is a veritable textbook of architectural history, a living museum. It requires little imagination to conjure up a sense of the past. This explains the extraordinary juxtaposition of different styles of architecture, complementary or contrasting.

These juxtapositions are seldom jarring or in bad taste. The architectural landscape nearly always appears elegant and harmonious. The reason is that Paris has traditionally attracted the best architects, sculptors, masons and painters.

Roman remains: Nothing remains of the wooden huts occupied by the Gauls on the Île de la Cité. However, thanks to the Romans' development of an extremely durable concrete, their ruins can still be found in the Latin Quarter, the site of their settlement. Several streets, such as the Rue St Jacques and the Boulevard St Michel are built on ancient Roman roads. Lutetia (the Roman

Preceding pages: la Gare de l'Est. **Left**, the Sainte-Chapelle, Gothic at its most flamboyant.

settlement that preceded Paris) was not an important city at the time, but it nonetheless boasted all the buildings necessary to Roman civic life – palace, forum, theatre, arena, baths and temples. The vestiges of one of these baths can be found in the garden at the Cluny Museum and the ruins of the arena have also survived. It is possible that early Christians were thrown to the lions in both the theatre and the circus here.

Prior to the birth of Gothic: Unfortunately, nothing is left of the Merovingian and Carolingian eras (6th–9th centuries), because the Vikings burnt and pillaged Paris on three occasions during this period.

use of ribbed vaults with flying buttresses, a technique that allowed windows to replace walls and walls to soar towards the heavens.

The most beautiful religious edifice in Paris, Notre Dame cathedral, epitomises the perfection of this style. The cathedral was constructed on the site of a Romanesque church, which had been built on the foundations of a Carolingian basilica, which in turn had been built on the site of a Roman temple. In fact, people have prayed here for at least 20 centuries.

Work on Notre Dame began in 1163 and it took 200 years and several generations of architects and craftsmen to finish it. The

Romanesque, with its ponderous and gloomy structures, hardly left a mark either. The only remnant of this artistic and religious movement that spread throughout France at the turn of the first millennium is the steeple of the St Germain-des-Prés church.

From a very early date, Paris and the Île de France turned to the newest rage in religious architecture: Gothic. Lighter, more slender and luminous than what had gone before, Gothic coincided with the strengthening of the French crown and a fresh religious fervour inflamed by the Crusades. Gothic architecture is distinguished by the combined

building began to decay during the 17th century. During the 19th century, its restoration was undertaken by Viollet-le-Duc, which was a brave effort in keeping with the cathedral's spirit, if not with its form.

Notre Dame, like all medieval churches, was completely painted on the inside. The statues over the triple front doors were once multicoloured on a gold background; the use of colour was meant to glorify God and breathe life into the sculptures. These early paintings were the way medieval man learned the Bible stories.

Gothic's golden age, the flamboyant style,

is represented by a famous and fragile-looking church, with all windows and stained glass (the oldest in Paris) supported by a thin framework of stone: nestled within the walls of the Palais de Justice, the Sainte-Chapelle was built by Saint Louis (King Louis IX) to shelter the crown of thorns and a fragment of the Cross.

The Renaissance: Imported from Italy in the 16th century, the Renaissance style is characterised by contempt for Gothic forms, a rediscovery of antiquity and the development of a taste for the profane. In architecture, the ribbed vault disappeared in favour of flat ceilings with wooden beams. Medi-

beautiful example of Renaissance sensuality jubilantly rejecting the sacred hierarchy of figures imposed by the Middle Ages.

Classicism: At the end of the 16th century, while the Renaissance had succumbed to the baroque movement in the rest of Europe, French architects looked towards sobriety and classicism. A desire for strength and clarity, born of rationalism, dominated architecture. The classical style is based on symmetry, simplicity of line and wide open perspectives. Constructed in this style in 1606, the Pont Neuf (now the oldest bridge in Paris) was the first one to be built without houses on it. Thus, a view of the Seine was

eval fortresses gave way to genteel palaces and the Greek column of the earlier days made a comeback.

Among Paris's main exponents of the Renaissance were architect Pierre Lescot and architect/sculptor Jean Goujon, who constructed the Hôtel Carnavalet in 1544 (now the Museum of Paris at 23 Rue de Sévigné, in the Marais district), then the west wing of the Louvre. Goujon also sculpted the bas-reliefs on the Fontaine des Innocents, a

finally revealed – and today no bridges with houses remain.

To lighten the urban atmosphere, the first squares were laid, ringed by uniform buildings and with a statue of the king in the middle. The Place des Vosges, with its graceful arcades, was the first and most elegant of the royal squares. A cool summer haven, it was created at the behest of Henri IV.

Another example is the Place de la Concorde, designed by Gabriel in 1757. A statue of Louis XV first graced its centre, but this was replaced during the Revolution by the guillotine. Finally, in 1836, an Egyptian ob-

Left, Place des Vosges dates from 1612. Above, Notre Dame, built on the site of a Roman temple.

elisk from the temple of Luxor came to rest here after travelling for four years since leaving Egypt. The Louvre has been a continual construction site since the Middle Ages, and looks nothing like its origins – a 13th-century keep. This is especially so since the birth of the so-called "New Louvre" or Le Grand Louvre, the most recent restructuring of the huge palace and museum inside.

The Chinese-American architect I. M. Peï was employed to come up with a new entrance and orientation centre for the museum. His solution, the pyramids, an illusionistic "landscape" in stainless steel and specially created polished glass, in the Cour

Napoleon, are already world-famous. Generally lauded for its beauty and efficiency as the museum's main entrance, the largest, central pyramid has entered the architectural legend of Paris.

Starting in 1760, the neoclassic movement turned to forms lifted directly from antiquity, taking the utmost care to reproduce what recent progress in archaeology had brought to light. Soufflot designed the Panthéon, originally a church and today a secular temple where great patriots are buried. Copied from the ancient architectural repertory, the single column came into vogue

(witness Place Vendôme and Place de la Bastille), as well as colonnades (for example, the Madeleine church), and the triumphal arch (Arc de Triomphe du Carrousel and Arc de Triomphe).

Baron Haussmann's legacy: With the exception of a few elite neighbourhoods, Paris was a squalid city during the 19th century. Poverty-stricken communities, with their filthy, narrow alleyways and miserable, overpopulated shacks, were constantly on the brink of revolt. For obvious sanitary reasons, but also to circumvent the risk of riots, Napoleon III and the Prefect Haussmann began a sweeping urbanisation programme in 1850.

Medieval Paris all but disappeared. Whole quarters were razed and wide, tree-lined avenues, more difficult to barricade as insurgents were wont to do, took the place of grimy backstreets.

The city of Paris today is still strongly stamped with Haussmann's ideas. After clearing out slums and opening up the area around the Louvre, he concentrated on creating the *Grands Boulevards* through the city centre. A small hill then known as the Butte Saint-Roche, occupied by windmills, a gallows and a pig market, was intended to be their centre. Joan of Arc led an attack on the city from that vantage point. It is hard to imagine all that today as you stand on the level, busy Place de l'Opéra.

The Second Empire's most sumptuous construction was the Charles Garnier Opéra House, with its monumental staircase, its lavish auditorium almost dripping with red and gold, the ceiling by Chagall (painted in 1964) and a six-ton chandelier.

Mr Eiffel's Tower: The second half of the 19th century was very rich in creativity. Wrought-iron architecture made its début with the Grand Palais, the Pont Alexandre III and, of course, the Eiffel Tower. Panned by the architectural critics during its construction in 1889, the Tower is now the universal symbol of Paris. It was orginally designed to be a temporary exhibit at the World Fair of 1900, along with "a grotesque city of plaster, staff and pasteboard... buildings from an Asian temple to a Swiss chalet, from Kanaka hut to medieval Paris, Chinese pagoda to Montmartre cabaret," as one contemporary visitor remarked on a trip to the city. As Eiffel's controversial creation, symbolising the uneasy relationship between science, industry and art, rose higher and higher, bets were placed on when it would topple over.

When Gustave Eiffel himself climbed up to plant the French flag atop his iron latticework fantasy, the cheering crowds comprised ordinary Parisians who admired his vision; snobbish aesthetes stayed away. Finally, it was wireless radio that saved the Tower from demolition and it is still used as a transmission station today.

This was also an eclectic period. The Hôtel de Ville (city hall) was rebuilt Renaissance-

buildings in the 16th *arrondissement*, including the Castel Béranger (14 Rue de la Fontaine) and also some lovely Metro entrances – Porte Dauphine and Abbesses.

Both the modern movement of the 1920s and 1930s and art deco were born in the 16th *arrondissement*. Mallet-Stevens (Rue Mallet-Stevens) and Le Corbusier (Maison Jeanneret, 8 Square du Dr Blanche) were the main artisans of this cubic style, all pure line and concrete. The Palais de Chaillot is a typical example of an architectural style that left its mark particularly on the Third Reich and on Soviet Russia.

Paris has kept up with technical advances

style, while the Sacré-Cœur basilica was done in the antique tradition, and numerous churches along Gothic lines. Reacting against these academic approaches and inspired by Japanese art, Hector Guimard launched the art nouveau movement, now most visible in the Metro entrances and signs.

The sinuous plant forms and curving lines, natural and baroque at the same time, were decried by the new trend's detractors as "noodle style". Guimard designed several

in architecture, building upwards (La Défense, Montparnasse Tower, for example), expanding indoor space (the Pompidou Centre, La Villette, Bercy), and experimenting with new materials that capture, reflect and admit light. The new Opéra de la Bastille, like Peï's pyramid or the Géode at La Villette, exemplifies the harmony of modern architecture in Paris by reflecting the neighbouring buildings and the changing Parisian sky. Gothic architecture, in its time, held a mirror to society in much the same way. But today's cathedrals generally serve a cultural, not religious, purpose.

<u>Left</u>, the dome in Galeries Lafayette. <u>Above</u>, art nouveau Métro entrance.

For the Russian painter Marc Chagall, Paris was "my heart's image – I should like to blend with it and not be alone with myself". In many paintings, especially those depicting lovers sky-high in serene embrace, he did just that, wrapping the couple in warm colours as if in the evening air over Paris, giving flight to their calm passion across the rooftops of the capital.

Paris may be the city of lovers – if lovers need any city in particular – but it is certainly

bearing. In an Italian capital it may be difficult to escape the artistic traditions of the past; in Paris the artist thinks most of all of escaping tomorrow's bar bill.

In the 19th century, however, the young artist's greatest ambition was to win the *Prix de Rome*, with the long study in the city that that prize brought with it. Yet few of the names of the winners mean much to us today. This is the discrepancy between the official, sanctioned, opinion of the establishment,

the city of painters. Apart from the obvious justification – that it is itself a lovely place to paint – there are special reasons for this. For one thing, perhaps no other capital city has so greatly, or for so long a history, been the centre and focus of its whole nation's identity. Nor has any comparable country quite so unique a divide between "town" and "country" as exists in France, which is essentially a rural, provincial country, whereas its city is sophisticated and worldly-wise.

Nor, by comparison especially with Rome, Florence or Venice, is the creative history of the city so ever-present that it becomes over-

and the verdict of history. In France, the establishment is rooted to Paris, epitomised by the annual "salon" exhibitions of the 19th century. These exhibitions were all-powerful; sometimes an artist who had sold a given picture to a customer shortly before the opening of a salon, would be obliged to take the picture back if it failed to be selected for the exhibition. The salon overlooked many great talents: Cézanne was never accepted by the Salon jury.

Though many of the greatest artists of history are inextricably linked with Paris – think of Corot, Courbet, Degas, Delacroix,

Géricault, Manet, Monet, Renoir and so on – the capital nevertheless displayed an infuriatingly persistent philistinism. If on your walks in contemporary Paris you glance in gallery windows showing paintings fresh from the studio, you may well not be too impressed. There certainly seems to be something missing, a lack of spark in the work.

In today's Paris there is nothing like the system of studios of the 19th century, in which painters were apprentices to masters, Courbet gave up bothering to have a studio.

Manet yearned for the country for different reasons: of the studio to which he was attached he complained, "I don't know why I come here, everything that meets the eye is ridiculous – the light is wrong, the shadows are wrong. I am perfectly aware you can't undress the model in the street but there's always the country; in summer at least one could do studies from life, in the fields". Drawing was at the centre of the training, the

learning in an atmosphere sometimes deeply serious to the point of stuffy, or hilarious to the point of bawdy. Commonsense did not always mix with high principles: Courbet thought that life classes should extend beyond the human nude, to take in animals as well, but instead of making excursions to the country, he had the animals brought to the studio – horses, cattle, the lot. The landlord had other ideas and, after less than two months

nude the central subject of the draughtsmanship. Mythological and generally heroic subject matter was emphasised to such an extent that we may wonder that anyone bothered to turn out a simple view of a Paris street. Indeed, it was later in the century and into the 20th century that French painting – and the paintings of the many foreigners who came to live and work in Paris – became so domestic, be it rural or urban.

Whereas the history of the depiction of Paris in earlier centuries is much along the lines of any similar city such as Vienna or London, in the past 200 years or so artists'

Preceding pages: art on the Pont des Arts. Left, Manet painted Parisian ballerinas, while Monet (above) painted trains at Gare St Lazare.

awareness of Paris has seemed to have gone through a subtle but distinctive shift, probably as a result of the French Revolution. Montgolfier's balloons also had some impact. Paris was the first city to be seen from the air in the early 1780s, and indeed the first city to be photographed from the air, by Nadar, some three-quarters of a century later. Moreover, with the reshaping of the city, still within compact limits but along star-burst lines of avenues and junctions, an artist in Paris a hundred or so years ago would have felt that, as he created his Paris on the canvas, Paris itself was being created on the ground.

This of course goes hand in hand with the

seen to have had a surreptitiously liberating effect on all sorts of styles of art we associate with Paris, be it Cubism, Vorticism or Futurism. The fact that Eiffel was also the inventor of the garter belt seems perfectly Parisian (imagine his tower upside down; does it not look like a stockinged leg?)

At the turn of the 20th century, all artists flocked to Paris, a city of taste and filth, style and vulgarity, romance and prostitution – a city of energy. Talking of the 1890s, one writer described the successful artist's lot: "At the present time a painter becomes established more quickly than a notary's clerk: he does watercolours in albums, dresses like the

French fascination with technology, first with railways and then as epitomised by the Eiffel Tower, itself a subject for painters but also one that afforded an easily accessible aerial view as in no other city. For the Impressionists the railways were important, partly because they might take the train from the Gare St Lazare up the Seine, but partly also because steam makes such a splendid haze of one's field of vision. The Eiffel Tower, placed beside all the other palaces and avenue apartments of Paris, was like a nude at a dinner party, and the sight of so blatant and jagged a thing that was yet so characterful can be

Prince of Wales, paints slick portraits of ladies, leads the dancing. He pays his colour merchant in cash in order to get a discount, invests his money in the railways and, as soon as he is *hors concours*, marries the daughter of a wealthy if unscrupulous banker." In the shanty-town of Montmartre life was not like that, but Montmartre was crowded with artists brought there by the attraction of this sort of existence as the focus of their ambition.

So obvious was Paris as the place to be, that Pablo Picasso used to claim that his journey there in 1900 was in fact a halt on the way to London; it was as if he could not dare to admit to something as *obvious* as the lure of the French capital.

Though neither Picasso nor to a lesser extent Matisse, the greatest painters of the 20th century, were known for landscape painting, their output being concentrated on line and the human form, they could not resist Paris as a subject, and Notre Dame especially. Both artists' works tackle something of the intimate grandeur of the building, which is imposing not by size but by detail, not by scale but by rhythm. Clearly, this fascinated Matisse as he looked out on it from a studio facing the Sureté on the Île de

dominating an island. He evokes not only the intimate image of a woman but also the inviolable heart of a nation.

Raoul Dufy's vision of Paris is perhaps the most charming of all, for with deft simplicity he is able to conjure up the sheer jumble of impressions that is Paris. It is a touch as brisk as the traffic but as certain as the *joie de vivre* peculiar to the place. It seems typical that while Picasso travelled all the way from Barcelona to Paris for the Universal Exhibition of 1900, Dufy did not even bother to stroll down the street to it. His pictures saunter in the shade, bask in the sun; his may be a lazy understanding, but it is an understand-

la Cité, and he produced one of his most abstract works, lush in its austerity.

Picasso, on the other hand, painted a number of pictures of Paris, mostly during World War II, in tones and moods reflecting either the grey quality of life under an occupying army or the frantic relief of hope or news of victory. In the pictures of Notre Dame and the Île de la Cité we can detect his sensitivity to the church's unique position

Matisse painted Notre Dame, far left, while left, Toulouse Lautrec focused a sharp eye on Parisian society. Above, Raoul Dufy's vision of Paris.

ing for all that, and perfect for this city.

The most popular artist associated with Paris seems to be Toulouse-Lautrec, 1864–1901, whose short life saw Paris blossom as never before. He was an aristocrat – with him died the younger line of counts of Toulouse-Lautrec-Monfa – but his eye was a street eye, sharper than any in cafés, theatres, bars and brothels. It is the perfect Paris cocktail. And where was his art seen most of all? In the street. His posters led the way as layers of print were replaced by swathes of lithographic colour wrapping the ventilation shafts – and urinals – of the capital.

Topographically, it is central to France. In terms of urban sprawl, it is, in Europe, second only to London. Where matters of French administration, politics and cultural life are concerned, it plays an absolutely dominant role. It is also the world capital of chic. For all these reasons and more, Paris is so unlike much of the rest of its own country that it has been described as virtually a city-state in its own right.

Largely undamaged by two world wars, its centre dates back to the days of Napoleon, with grand boulevards and elegant city mansions displaying a remarkable uniformity. Its street corners reek of history, its monuments and museums are instantly recognised all over the world, and its people are an endless source of controversy. In Paris, every pavement is a theatre on which daily life is played out.

Perfectly preserved though it is, this is also a city of planners and a city which is unafraid of change. I. M. Pei's pyramid in front of the Louvre and the massive development at La Défense are evidence of that. But there are regrets in this continual process of change: in the city where Voltaire was reputed to drink 40 cups of coffee a day at La Procope, the café culture is threatened by the fast-food invasion, and the number of Parisian cafés has drastically fallen from 12,000 at the beginning of the 1980s to fewer than 5,000.

This is also the city of lovers, and the city of arts *par excellence*. There's endless entertainment here for the observant, who will learn as much about Paris and the Parisians from walking the streets as from visiting the great museums.

The chapters that follow cover the key destinations on both banks of the Seine, as well as venturing further afield to outlying parks and markets, to Euro Disney and La Défense, and to destinations that can easily be reached in a day from the city, such as the palace at Versailles, Monet's house at Giverny and the cathedral at Chartres.

This is a city which can easily be discovered on foot. But help is at hand for the weary: one of the beauties of Paris is a superb public transport system, and it is thanks to the RER and SNCF that the region surrounding the city is so easily accessible.

Preceding pages: La Madeleine by night; the view from Montmartre; village Paris; Shakespeare and Company, booksellers. **Left**, the Arc de Triomphe and the Champs-Elysées.

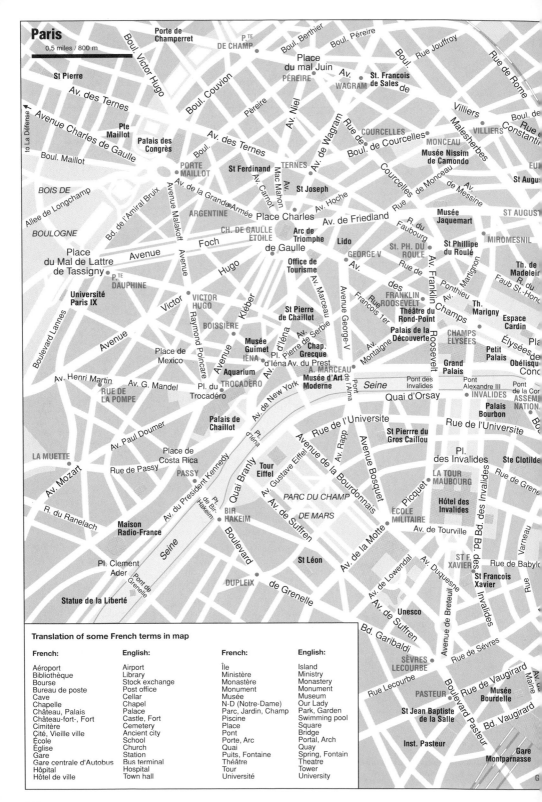

Paris

0,5 miles / 800 m

to La Défense

Porte de Champerret
P.TE DE CHAMP
Boul. Berthier
Boul. Péreire
Boul. Péreire
Rue Jouffroy
Boul.
Rue de Rome

Boul. Victor Hugo
St Pierre
Av. des Ternes
Boul. Couvion
Péreire
Place du mal Juin
PÉREIRE
Av. de Wagram
Av.
WAGRAM
St. Francois de Sales
de
Villiers
Boul. de
VILLIERS
Constantin

Avenue Charles de Gaulle
Pte Maillot
Palais des Congrès
Av. des Ternes
Boul.
Av. Niel
Rue de Courcelles
COURCELLES
Boul. de Courcelles
MONCEAU
Musée Nissim de Camondo
Malesherbes
EU

Boul. Maillot
PORTE MAILLOT
St Ferdinand
Av. Mac Mahon
TERNES
Courcelles
de Monceau
Av. de Messine
Musée Jaquemart
ST AUGU
EU
St Augu

BOIS DE
Avenue Malakoff
Av. de la Grande Armée
Av. Carnot
St Joseph
Av. Hoche
Rue
R. du Faubourg

BOULOGNE
Allee de Longchamp
Bd. de l'Amiral Bruix
ARGENTINE
CH. DE GAULLE ÉTOILE
Place Charles
Arc de Triomphe de Gaulle
Av. de Friedland
Lido
GEORGE V
St. PH. DU ROULE
St Phillipe du Roulé
MIROMESNIL
Th. de Madelei
R. de Faub St.-Hono

Place du Mal de Lattre de Tassigny
Avenue Foch
Avenue
Hugo
Office de Tourisme
Av.
Rue de
des
FRANKLIN ROOSEVELT
Ponthieu
Av.
Champs
Th. Marigny
Espace Cardin

Université Paris IX
P.TE DAUPHINE
Victor
VICTOR HUGO
Kléber
St Pierre de Chaillot
Av. Marceau
Avenue George-V
Francois 1er
Théâtre du Rond-Point
Palais de la Découverte
CHAMPS ELYSEES
Élysées
Petit Palais
Pla
de

Boulevard Lannes
Avenue
Raymond Poincaré
Place de Mexico
Musée Guimet
IÉNA
Av. d'Iéna
Pl. Pierre de Serbie
Chap. Grecque
Av. du Prest
A. MARCEAU
Av. Montaigne
Av. Roosevelt
Grand Palais
Obélisqu
Conc

Av. Henri Martin
Av. G. Mandel
Aquarium
Pl. du TROCADÉRO
Trocadéro
Av. du Prest d'Iéna
Musée d'Art Moderne
Pont de l'Alma
Seine
Pont des Invalides
Pont Alexandre III
Pont de la Cor
INVALIDES
ASSEM
NATION.

RUE DE LA POMPE
Pl. d'Iéna
Av. de New York
Quai d'Orsay
Palais Bourbon

Palais de Chaillot
Av. Paul Doumer
Palais de Chaillot
Pl. d'Iéna
Rue de l'Université
Avenue de Rapp
St Pierrre du Gros Caillou
Rue de l'Université

LA MUETTE
Place de Costa Rica
Rue de Passy
PASSY
Pl. du Président Kennedy
Tour Eiffel
Avenue de la Bourdonnais
Avenue Bosquet
Pl. des Invalides
Ste Clotilde
Rue de Grene

Av. Mozart
Quai Branly
Av. Gustave Eiffel
PARC DU CHAMP
Picquet
LA TOUR MAUBOURG
Bd. des Invalides

R. du Ranelach
Pl. de Bir Hakeim
BIR HAKEIM
Av. de Suffren
DE MARS
Av. de la Motte
ÉCOLE MILITAIRE
Hôtel des Invalides
Varneau

Maison Radio-France
Boulevard
Seine
St Léon
Av. de Suffren
Av. de Tourville
ST F. XAVIER
Rue de Babylo
St Francois Xavier
Rue

Pl. Clement Ader
Pont de Grenelle
DUPLEIX
de Grenelle
Av. de Lowendal
Av. Duquesne
Av. de Breteuil
Avenue de Breteuil
Rue des Invalides

Statue de la Liberté
Unesco
Bd. Garibaldi

SÈVRES LECOURBE
Rue de Sèvres
Rue de Vaugirard
Av. de Maine

Rue Lecourbe
PASTEUR
Boulevard Pasteur
Bd. Vaugirard
Musée Bourdelle

St Jean Baptiste de la Salle
Inst. Pasteur
Gare Montparnasse

Translation of some French terms in map

French:	English:	French:	English:
Aéroport	Airport	Île	Island
Bibliothèque	Library	Ministère	Ministry
Bourse	Stock exchange	Monastère	Monastery
Bureau de poste	Post office	Monument	Monument
Cave	Cellar	Musée	Museum
Chapelle	Chapel	N-D (Notre-Dame)	Our Lady
Château, Palais	Palace	Parc, Jardin, Champ	Park, Garden
Château-fort-, Fort	Castle, Fort	Piscine	Swimming pool
Cimitère	Cemetery	Place	Square
Cité, Vieille ville	Ancient city	Pont	Bridge
École	School	Porte, Arc	Portal, Arch
Église	Church	Quai	Quay
Gare	Station	Puits, Fontaine	Spring, Fontain
Gare centrale d'Autobus	Bus terminal	Théâtre	Theatre
Hôpital	Hospital	Tour	Tower
Hôtel de ville	Town hall	Université	University

CIMITIÈRE MONTMARTRE

Rue Lepic   St Pierre
Av. de Clichy   Rue Caulaincourt   Rue Curtain   R. Lamarck

Moulin Rouge   Place de Parvis du Sacré Coeur   R. de Clignancourt
Pl. Blanche   St Jean de Montmartre   Théâtre de l'Atelier   BARBES ROCHECHOUART   LA CHAPELLE
L. DE CLICHY   BLANCHE   PIGALLE   Boul. de Rochechouart   Boulevard de la Chapelle   Théâtre des Bouffes du Nord   Place de Stalingrad   STALINGRAD
tignolles   Rue Fontaine   Rue Pigalle   ANVERS   Av. Trudaine   Boulevard de Magenta   R. Denis   JAURES   la Villette
Rue de   ST GEORGES   Rue des Martyrs   R. de   Gare du Nord   GARE DU NORD   Rue du Faubourg St Martin   St Georges
Th. de Paris   Rue Moncey   Rue la Bruyère   Rue de Rochechouart   R. de Dunkerque   Rue Lafayette   Place du Colonel Fabien   COLONEL
Casino de Paris   Ste. Trinité   Pl. Franz Liszt   Gare de l'Est   Saint-Martin   FABIEN
Rue de Londres   ST-LAZARE   N.-D. de Lorette   CADET   Rue Bleue   Pl. de Valenciénnes   R. du 8 Mai 1945   Gare de l'Est   Av. Claude Vélléfaux   Boul. de la Vilette
Gare St-Lazare   TRINITÉ   Rue de Châteaudun   Rue Lafayette   GARE DE L'EST   Boulevard Haussmann   LE PELETIER   Folies Bergère   Rue de Paradis   St Laurent   Av. Parmentier
Galeries Lafayette   Musée Grévin   St Eugéne   Boul. de Strasb.   JACQUES BONSERGENT   GONCOURT
CHAUSSÉ D'ANTIN   RUE MONTMARTRE   Th. des Nouveautés   Porte St Denis   Th. Antoine   St Martin   Rue de Faubourg du Temple   St Joseph
Th. Athénée   Opéra   Bd. Montmartre   Bd. Poissonnière   St Denis   Ptc. St Martin   GONCOURT   St Joseph
Th. Edouard VII   OPÉRA   Opéra Comique   BONNE NOUVELLE   STRASBOURG   Th. de la Porte St Martin
Olympia   Quatre-Septembre   R. du DOUSSE   Bourse   Th. de la Renaissance   Conserv. Nat. des Arts et Métiers   RÉPUBLIQUE   OBERKAMPF
MADELEINE adeleine   de l'Opéra   QUATRE SEPTEMBRE   Bibliothèque Nationale   Rue Réaumur   TEMPLE   Place de la République   Av. de la République
R. St Honoré   Place Vendôme   R. Étienne Marcel   N.-D. des Victoires   RÉAUMUR SÉBASTOPOL   ARTS ET MÉTIERS   Bd. du Temple   Boulevard
CORDERIE u de Paume   PYRAMIDES   Palais Royal   St Eustache   É. MARCEL   St Nicolas des Champs   R. de Bretagne   FILLES DU CALVAIRE   St Ambroise
angerie   TUILERIES   Comédie Française   LES HALLES   Rue de Turbigo   St Leu   RAMBUTEAU   Rue Vieille du Temple   AMBROISE   Voltaire
ine   JARDIN   PALAIS ROYAL   Rue de Rivoli   Bourse   Centre Nation. d'Art et de Culture G. Pompidou   Archives Nationales   St Denys du St Sacrement   Boulevard Richard Lenoir
gny   DES TUILERIES   LOUVRE   R. des Petits Champs   St Germain l'Auxerrois   St Merri   N.-D. des Blancs Manteaux   Musée Carnavalet   BRÉGUET SABIN
Musée du Louvre   Palais du Louvre   Th. du Châtelet   HÔTEL DE VILLE   PONT NEUF   CHÂTELET   Hôtel de Ville   Cité Int. des Arts   R. des Francs Bourgeois   Place BASTILLE
Musée d'Orsay   Quai   du Louvre   Pont Neuf   Conciergerie   ST PAUL   Colonne de Juillet
St Thomas d'Aquin   École Nationale Supérieure des Beaux-Arts   Institut de France   Palais de Justice   Q. aux Fleurs   Q. d. l'Hôtel de Ville   St Paul   Temple Ste Marie   la Bastille   Centre d'Exposition
Germain   Rue Jacob   Ste Chapelle   CITÉ   Pt. L. Phillipe   PONT MARIE   Bd. Henri IV   Bibliothèque de l'Arsenal
RUE DU BAC   St Germain des Prés   R. St. André Arts   Notre-Dame   Pl. St-Michel   Pt. St Louis   Pt. St Louise en l'île   Quai Henri IV   Rue du Faubourg
SÈVRES BABYLONE   Boulevard St. Germain   ODÉON   St Séverin   Pt. de la Tournelle   St-Louis en l'île   SULLY MORLAND
Boulevard Raspail   Rennes   Théâtre Nat. de l'Odéon   St Julien le Pauvre   M. MUTUALITÉ   St Nicolas du Chardonnet   Quai   Bd. de la Bastille
ST-SULPICE   St-Sulpice   CLUNY LA S.   Musée de Cluny   R. de École   Univ. Paris VI et VII   Bd. Diderot
Petit Luxembourg   Vaugirard   Sorbonne   St Étienne du Mont   QUAI DE LA RAPÉE   Pont d'Austerlitz
RENNES   ST PLACIDE   Palais du Luxembourg Sénat   JARDIN DU LUXEMBOURG   JUSSIEU   Saint Bernard   GARE D'AUSTERLITZ
N.-D. DES CHAMPS   Th. du Lucernaire   Panthéon   CARDINAL LEMOINE   Arènes de Lutèce   JARDIN DES PLANTES   Gare de Lyon
N.-D. des Champs   St Jacques du Ht Pas   École Normale Supérieure   MONGE   Musée Nationale d'Histoire Naturelle   Gare de Lyon
Boul. du Montparnasse   Rue d'Assas   Rue Lussac   Institut Musulman et Mosquée   Rue Buffon   Gare d'Austerlitz
tparnasse   Edgar Quinet   Pl. E. Denis   Institut National Agronomique   St Médard   Bd. de l'Hôpital   Quai d'Austerlitz   Seine
Th. Montparnasse   RASPAIL   Boulevard de Port Royal   Bd. Saint-Marcel   St Marcel
CIMITIÈRE DU MONTPARNASSE

THE LOUVRE AND THE BOULEVARDS

From Louvre to L'Opéra, along the Champs-Elysées to L'Arc de Triomphe, the west of Paris is an area of refinement, glamour and excess, comprising the 1st, 2nd and 8th *arrondissements*. Elegant expanses of gardens stretch into ostentatious squares, wide boulevards overflow with designer boutiques and department stores, whilst in the ornamental parks serious businessmen mingle with playful children, and boys and girls study each other with crafted disinterest from park benches.

Here is the world's most famous museum, a handful of palaces, an opulent opera house, and the lairs of the most fashionable of fashion houses. The buildings cry out to be admired, whilst the broad open-spaces laid out by Baron Haussmann engulf the visitor in 19th-century grandeur.

In this self-contained world, you can buy your luxurious outfit to wear to the luxurious restaurant which serves food bought from luxurious shops. At night, however, apart from the expensive sparkle of the Champs-Elysées, this area is empty and strangely forlorn.

Palace of art: Once the seat of royalty, the **Louvre** has been the home of art for 300 years. The palace, which is the biggest in Europe, was built by King Philippe-Auguste in 1200, to protect a weak link in his city wall. With the extension of the walls by Charles V, the fortress became a chateau, and the King established his extensive library in one of the towers. Successive monarchs added and destroyed until 1672, when Louis XIV, wary of Paris, moved to Versailles. The Louvre fell into disrepair until the Academy of Art chose its empty halls for painting "salons" in 1725. During the Revolution, in a rare moment of creative fervour, the rebels decided to inaugurate the palace as a museum, ironically fulfilling the plans of Louis XVI, whom they had just be-

headed. Opened in August 1793, the museum benefitted greatly from royal treasures (including Leonardo da Vinci's *Mona Lisa*), and from Napoleon's subsequent efforts to relocate much of Europe's artistic wealth, following victories in Italy, Austria, and Germany. After Napoleon lost at Waterloo in 1815, however, many of the stolen masterpieces were reclaimed.

Most recently, the Louvre Museum has been extensively renovated for its 300th birthday. Since President Mitterrand moved his Finance Ministry to Bercy, the north **Richelieu Wing** has opened, doubling the size of the already enormous museum to make it unquestionably the world's biggest. In 1989 the controversial **Louvre Pyramid** appeared, quickly becoming more infamous than its maternal neighbour. The glass pyramid, designed by the architect I. M. Pei, is a celebration of angles, contrasting with – and, to some minds, complementing – the ancient curves of the main building. Practical as well as

shiny, the pyramid leads to a large underground entrance from which escalators whisk visitors to various parts of the building. In its first year, the pyramid was cleaned by teams of specially-trained alpine climbers, attached with ropes. This precarious system has been replaced by small window-cleaning robots, which roam the glass at night.

To avoid clamouring crowds (particularly on Sunday when entrance is half-price) visit the Louvre on Monday or Wednesday, when it remains open until 10pm. In case of congestion at the pyramid entrance, head right, to the south-west tip of the museum, and **Porte Jaujard**, a lesser-known entry point.

The Louvre is seemingly infinite, a maze of corridors, halls, staircases and galleries, although star attractions are well signposted (the free map is essential). Begin with the History of the Louvre, and the newly discovered remains of Philippe-Auguste's fort and dungeon. Traverse the Sully Wing, admiring French painting up to the early 19th-century, including David's epic canvases. In the East Wing are the wonders of Ancient Egypt; in the South Wing, those of Greece, including *Venus de Milo*, purchased by the French government for 6,000 francs in 1820. From here, head to the Denon Wing, and Italian art, including Leonardo da Vinci's small painting of a Florentine noblewoman called Mona Lisa (*La Joconde* in French). The enigmatic smile, described by Lawrence Durrell as that "of a woman who has just dined off her husband", has fascinated art-lovers since the 15th century. The painting was stolen in 1911, and the police arrested Pablo Picasso and poet Apollinaire on suspicion of the crime, after they were caught in possession of statues stolen in the same robbery. Later the *Mona Lisa* was discovered in Italy, with a former employee of the museum and, after a short spell in Florence, the painting was returned to the Louvre in 1913. Picasso and Apollinaire had long since worn out their jailors and been released.

Below, *Mona Lisa* and her gallery.

From the Italians, proceed to the Spanish School, with masterpieces by El Greco and Goya. Across the courtyard, the new Richelieu wing contains oriental art, and Northern European paintings, including numerous Rembrandts.

Addicts of executive toys will marvel at the **Musée des Arts Décoratifs**, in the Rohan Wing. This exhaustive exhibition of interior design develops from medieval tapestries to the plastic "man-chair" of the 1970s. Next door, the **Museum of Fashion Art** houses temporary exhibitions revering Dior, Yves St Laurent, Chanel and the gang.

Peace and quiet: For the sufferer from a surfeit of museums, the **Jardin des Tuileries** offers shade, statues and fountains; the place to sit, sip Perrier, and pretend to read *Le Monde*. Once a rubbish tip, then a clay quarry for tiles (*tuiles*, hence the name, the Tuileries), the garden was created for Catherine de Médicis, along with a palace, to remind her of her native Tuscany. In 1664, Le Nôtre, whose family had been garden-ers in the Tuileries for three genera-tions, re-sculpted the park with his pre-dilection for straight lines and clipped trees. The garden then became public, and the first deckchairs were invented to seat elderly ladies. Surrounding its walls ran dense streets, passages, broth-els, inns and carriage houses, and it was here, in 1791, that Marie-Antoinette became separated from her bodyguards as she attempted to escape Paris. Unac-customed to the narrow squalor of the streets, she wandered for two hours, until discovering the royal carriage on Rue de l'Echelle. In the garden, 600 Swiss guards were chased by a revolu-tionary mob and stabbed to death in 1792, as the Royal Family ran to seek refuge in the National Assembly. The Tuileries Palace, which had housed Louis XIV, Napoleon Bonaparte, Louis-Philippe, and finally Napoleon III, was burnt down by supporters of the Paris Commune in 1871, when three centu-ries of art went up in smoke.

At the Louvre entrance to the Tuileries

stands the **Arc de Triomphe du Carrousel**, the smallest of the three arches on the Voie Triomphale, the Triumphal Way that leads all the way from the Louvre to the Grande Arche de la Défense several kilometres to the west. Erected in 1808 by Napoleon, to commemorate his Austrian victories, the Carrousel arch is a garish imitation of Roman arches; the four horses galloping across its summit are copies of four gilded bronze horses stolen by Napoleon from St Mark's Square in Venice to decorate his memorial. The original horses were returned to Italy in 1815. Wander through the arch, past the Maillol Statues, sensuous nudes that adorn the pools of the garden. Follow the riverside walkway, where Napoleon's children played under the watchful gaze of their emperor father. At the west end of the gardens, the hexagonal pool is a favourite for children with boats, and ducks with attitudes.

Here the twin museums of the **Jeu de Paume** and the **Orangerie** face each other across the wide sweeping steps leading to Place de la Concorde. The Jeu de Paume now houses temporary modern art exhibitions, following the Impressionists' migration to the Musée d'Orsay. The Orangerie is one of Paris' hidden gems, a beautifully harmonious museum, containing some of the world's finest paintings. If the big museums are full, come here for peace, quiet, and exhilaration.

The list of canvases is impressive; 22 Soutines, 14 Cézannes, including one of *The Bathers* which was cut in three, then re-stuck (look for the joins), 24 Renoirs, 28 Dérains, a pile of Picassos, Matisses and Utrillos. Yet the masterpieces of the museum are, undoubtedly, Monet's *Waterlilies*. Eight huge canvases drown the spectator in colour and movement, subtly displayed in a room purposefully built for them after Monet's gift to the state at the 1918 Armistice.

The Tuileries closes at nightfall, after which it becomes the biggest gay pickup venue in Paris. On warm summer **Making friends in the Tuileries.**

days, G-strings are much in evidence along the Quai des Tuileries.

History at every turn: North of the garden, Anglophiles and tourists mingle at **WH Smith**, a familiar hunting ground for English books and newspapers. To the right, along Rue de Rivoli, the **Louvre des Antiquaires**, behind the Louvre Museum, contains numerous antiques shops. This area, once so congested, was cleared on the orders of Napoleon following the attempt on his life when First Consul in 1800, as he headed from the Tuileries. Two royalists planted explosives in a cart, but the bomb missed Napoleon's carriage; not wishing to repeat the experience, Bonaparte razed 50 houses when he became Emperor in 1806.

Further east, **Place André-Malraux** has been a focal point of Parisian life since the Middle Ages. It was here that Joan of Arc stood at the gates of Paris in 1429, attempting to win back the capital from the English. She was struck by a sniper's arrow, and taken to a nearby house (No 4 on the square) to be bandaged. Her quest was in vain; the English held on, and Henry VI was shipped in from England to be crowned in Notre Dame in 1431, whilst Joan was burnt at the stake in Rouen. On the square stands the illustrious **Comédie Française**, the French national theatre. Nearby was the site of the stage where Molière collapsed and died in 1673 at the age of 51, whilst acting the title role in his play *The Hypochondriac*, in which an old man feigns death.

The **Molière Fountain** stands at the end of Rue Molière, close to 40 Rue de Richelieu, where the actor/playwright lived. In 1680 his company was merged with that of the Hôtel de Bourgogne by Louis XIV, creating a united Parisian theatre for the first time. The Comédie Française moved to its present site in 1799. In 1812, Napoleon passed a decree, still applicable today, placing the company under state control, with a director nominated by the government – his interest was far from passive; the

On the Rue de Rivoli.

leading lady at the time, Mademoiselle Mars, was his mistress. Today the Comédie Française is one of Paris's top venues; a place to be seen, and to see. A tip: each evening, 45 minutes before curtain-rise, 112 tickets are sold at low prices at the booth just off the square on Rue de Montpensier. Democracy lives.

One of the Comédie Française's favourite play-wrights, Corneille, lies to the west in the harmonious **Church of St Roch**. Accompanying him are Le Nôtre the gardener and Diderot, the philosopher. On the steps of the church, royalist insurgents were shot dead on the orders of Napoleon in 1795. The bullet holes remain today.

Den of state: The **Palais Royal**, stretching its elegant columns and arcades away from the Louvre, is a place of repose and refinement. Built by Richelieu on the site of a Roman bath house, the palace became a den of debauchery in the 18th century when Philippe II of Orléans held his infamous "libertines' suppers" here. Suffering from his family's free spending, Louis-Philippe of Orléans built shops around the palace, to rent at exorbitant prices. Under the order of the Dukes of Orléans, police were forbidden to enter the palace precincts, and soon the arcades housed gambling houses and brothels. Despite Napoleon's attempts to clean up the Palace, suicides in the garden were commonplace by 1830 as gamblers sought certain escape from their huge debts. Prostitution was so rife that guidebooks were produced detailing the wares on offer. After the palace was almost destroyed during the Commune in 1871, renovation led to the area being cleaned up.

Today the palace houses the more sombre Ministry of State, and the gardens are a tranquil oasis populated by nannies, children and tourists. In 1986, 250 black-and-white striped columns of varying heights were erected in the Cour d'Honneur by artist Daniel Buren, providing the perfect tripod on which to place your camera for a self-portrait. The galleries house interesting shops, **In the courtyard of the Palais Royal.**

110

including Carmen Infante (Galerie de Montpensier – west wing), with an amazing collection of hats and masks, as well as 600 wedding dresses at bargain prices, and Anna Joliet (Galerie de Beaujolais – north wing) offering delicate music boxes. Opposite is the most beautiful restaurant in Paris, **Le Véfour**, hiding shyly under the arches. The decor is sumptuous, as is the food, which merits two Michelin stars. It opened in 1784, and has greeted the likes of revolutionary Camille Desmoulins, and writers Lamartine and Sainte-Beuve.

Arcades: North of Rue de Beaujolais, beyond the crumbling, alluring facade of the Théâtre du Palais-Royal (specialising in bedroom farces much loved by the French), sits the **Bibliothèque Nationale**. This huge library, containing every book published in France since 1500, is one of the biggest in the world. Here are original manuscripts from Rabelais, Villon, Hugo and Proust, and Charlemagne's illuminated Bible. Take a detour north, up Rue de Richelieu to see the small **Square Louvois** and one of the most beautiful fountains in Paris, representing the four "female" French rivers – La Loire, La Seine, La Garonne and La Saône.

Next door to the Bibliothèque Nationale are the 19th-century **Galerie Colbert** and **Galerie Vivienne**, aristocratic covered arcades. Recently renovated, both galleries whisper of past grandeur, with their intricate brass lamps, graceful glass canopies and marbled mosaic floors. Sip a strong coffee at the expansive copper counter of Le Grand Colbert, an 1830s' brasserie, refurbished along with the gallery.

Tea addicts should head to the Galerie Vivienne, and A Priori Thé, a *salon de thé* which extends its serene tables into the gallery. At 6 Rue Vivienne, Jean-Paul Gaultier transposes the elegance of the area to his clothes, whilst at No 1, Chantal Thomass provides something to wear under them, with her modern, elegant lingerie. Away from the tourists, **Galerie Véro-Dodat**, to the south-

Galerie Colbert.

east (opposite Rue Montesquieu), is the most beautiful and atmospheric passageway in Paris, with polished mahogany facades, brass lamps, and musty sky-lights. Le Véro-Dodat Bistro serves wholesome dishes, expertly executed by Monsieur Gomond, and served by Madame Gomond.

From the Bibliothèque Nationale, Rue des Petits-Champs leads to the 17th-century crescents of **Place des Victoires**. This genteel square, guarded by Louis XIV and horse, is now home to the elite of the Parisian fashion world, boasting among its boutiques Kenzo, Stefan Kelian and Thierry Mugler. If too much style sticks in your throat, head to **Willi's** (13 Rue des Petits-Champs), and wash it down with the fine selection of wines and a slice of cheese.

From Place des Victoires, Rue Notre Dame des Victoires runs north, passing the Grecian columns of the Bourse (Stock Exchange), to **Boulevard Montmartre**. This wide avenue is part of the "Grands Boulevards", a 3-km (2 mile) stretch of road proceeding from the **Opéra** to **Place de la République**. Paris' strolling ground since 1705, the boulevards are tree-lined, bustling and endowed with huge department stores, cinemas and cafés spilling into the street.

The Boulevards have a colourful past. When the walls of Paris were torn down by Louis XIV, the King created open spaces, bordered with trees, for his subjects. A raised road was constructed, four carriages wide, which became known as the "Boulevard". By the 19th century, the west end of the thoroughfare was the reserve of the rich, and the east had become the playground of the workers of industrial Paris – vaudeville theatres, circuses, waxworks, bars and brothels competed side by side. By 1830 the theatres played so many tumultuous melodramas that the streets became known as the "Boulevard du Crime".

The seedy end: The east end of the boulevards maintains a nefarious reputation – the area around **St Denis** hosts 80 percent of the capital's prostitutes.

Place des Victoires.

Actress Shirley McLaine, perfecting her role for Billy Wilder's *Irma la Douce*, spent a week here, observing the life of a Parisian prostitute, amongst the neon sex shops and massage parlours. Paradoxically, **Rue St Denis** was the road taken by the Kings of France to Notre Dame for their coronation, as well as their route north, for burial in the St Denis Basilica.

Close to Sentier Metro, **Place du Caire** is rich in mementoes of Napoleon's Egyptian campaign, including hieroglyphics and sphinxes. It was here that the medieval Cour des Miracles was situated. By day, the handicapped, blind and deaf went out to beg on the streets; by night they returned, shed their wooden legs and eye patches, and embarked on riotous orgies, described by Victor Hugo in *The Hunchback of Notre Dame* – hence the ironic "miracles". Today, the district contains countless low-cost clothing shops, selling everything from gaudy underwear to handmade suits.

The Bourse (Stock Exchange).

Heading west to Boulevard Montmartre, one can find vestiges of popular 19th-century entertainment. **Musée Grévin** is a light-hearted waxwork museum, full of cheerfully incompatible figures – Marie-Antoinette, Michael Jackson, National Front leader Jean-Marie Le Pen, and a less charming display of revolutionary justice.

Opposite, **Passage des Panoramas** is a bustling arcade, lit by 100 lamps. Stop at the window of Stern, the engraver, whose decor has not changed since 1840. **Galerie des Variétés** still shrills to operatic tenors, reliving the golden years of the Théâtre des Variétés, and Offenbach's finest arias. **Passage Jouffroy**, across the boulevard, is a favourite haunt of stamp-collectors.

Shops and Opéra: The industrial revolution put money in pockets, which was then transferred to the newly-opened department stores (the *grands magasins*) a process vividly described by Zola in his novel *Au Bonheur des Dames*. South of the Seine Le Bon Marché was the first

such shop in 1852. Hot on its heels came **Printemps** and **Galeries Lafayette** on the right bank; these biggest of department stores were built, naturally, on the biggest road – **Boulevard Haussmann**, which is laden with shopping. The green domes of Printemps compete with the sparkling cupola of Galeries Lafayette; indeed the two giants seem to fight a constant battle for the title of "Most Parisian of department stores". Le Printemps' perfume department defies nasal capacity, whilst Lafayette has better clothes.

Nearby are a huge **Monoprix** and a **Marks and Spencer**, alongside the headquarters of French banks, housed in sumptuous temples to the franc.

From Boulevard Haussmann, Boulevard des Italiens descends to the Opéra, passing **L'Opéra Comique**, one-time home of Italian Commedia dell'arte (hence the street-name), now a centre for singers and musicians.

Place de l'Opéra is not just a setting for Garnier's massive building. Laid out by the hand of Haussmann, this is the intersection of six roads, a non-stop contest between pedestrians and traffic.

The **Opéra**, opened in 1875, is predictably resplendent, with gold leaf statues and monumental steps. Inside the decor is thickly ornate; if you cannot attend a performance, a tour of the interior will provide a glimpse of the pomp – Garnier's multicoloured marble, and the building's masterpiece of a ceiling painted by Chagall in 1964. Since the opening of the Bastille Opéra, this stage is predominantly reserved for ballet. Beneath the auditorium lies an underground lake, draining water from the foundations, where an Opéra employee has been raising trout.

Opposite the Opéra, **Café de la Paix** is one of Paris's most fashionable, most expensive and most crowded wateringholes. Avenue de l'Opéra contains innumerable boutiques offering perfume, scarves and Paris T-shirts.

Rue de la Paix, leading south from Opéra, is home to dazzling windows **Place de l'Opéra.**

Place de l'Opéra.

and fat purses. Here, Cartier rubs shoulders with airline offices and the Hotel Westminster. At Repetto (No 22), ballet dancers gaze in at the display of tutus and tiny shoes, whilst at No 5 Paloma Picasso continues in the family footsteps with innovative designs.

To the south lies the freshly renovated expanse of **Place Vendôme**. The wide square, dominated by Napoleon on top of his milky-green column, is ornamentally chic, resounding with every step of Italian shoes on polished marble. The 17th-century facades remained mere facades for half a century, following the construction of the square in 1685 as a display-case for Girardon's statue of Louis XIV. Like a film set, the walls had no building behind them, until gradually the rich and influential were persuaded to fill up the empty spaces.

The Napoleonic column replaced Louis XIV's statue, torn down during the Revolution. Napoleon melted down 1,200 cannon captured from the Battle of Austerlitz to make the column, placing himself as Caesar on top. Since then, he's had some ups and downs. The fall of the Empire brought the fall of the statue, and Louis XVIII hoisted a huge *fleur de lys* flag. Louis-Philippe restored Napoleon to his perch, only for him to be toppled by the painter Courbet into a carefully arranged pile of manure during the Commune. The Third Republic threw Courbet in jail, and his paintings were requisitioned to pay for Napoleon's re-instalment at the top of the column. Today the square exudes concentrated wealth. Here are jewellers Boucheron, Van Cleef and Arpels, and couturier Chanel. Here too are banks, including Rothschild's. After a quick purchase in the square, venture into **The Ritz** at No 15. Hemingway once hoped that heaven would be as good as the Ritz; his ghost still haunts the bar which is named after him (prices have risen since Ernest's day).

To the Faubourg: Close to Place Vendôme, the church of **La Madeleine** rises classically from the midst of roar-

Place Vendôme.

ing traffic and expensive shops. Its temple facade is Athenian, its interior gloomily Italian, and its history very French; commenced and destroyed twice, almost turned into a bank and a railway station, it was dedicated in 1842, and its priest shot in 1871 by the Commune.

Surrounding the foreboding church are the food-halls of the rich and famous; **Fauchon** has a range of fruits worthy of the Garden of Eden, its own coffee label, and an irresistible patisserie; **Hédiard** offers rival fruit and cakes; La Maison de la Truffe serves truffles; Caviar Kaspia specialises in Iranian Caviar. On the square, the impressive flower market provides less edible gifts.

Just south of the square, **Rue du Faubourg St Honoré** extends luxury westwards. A flock of fashion designers have their principal houses here; Christian Lacroix at No 73, Sylvia Rykiel at No 70, Yves St Laurent at No 38, and Japanese Ashida at No 34. For the best in scarves and leather goods, **Hermès** at No 24, is worth saving up for. Neighbouring streets entertain Karl Lagerfeld and Gianni Versace.

From La Madeleine, Rue Royale runs past Maxim's Restaurant, and its bulletproof obscurity, to Place de la Concorde. In the **Hotel Crillon** to the left, Benjamin Franklin signed the Treaty of Friendship between the newly formed United States of America and King Louis XVI in 1778. Appropriately the **United States Embassy** stands just to the west, not far from the **Elysée Palace**, home of the French President. Symbolically, the old enemy, in the shape of **The British Embassy**, lies in-between.

Place de la Concorde was originally marshland, offering the architect, Gabriel, much scope for grandeur. His square has been the site of grand events since its completion in 1763, most importantly, the decapitation of Franklin's ally, Louis XVI, on a cold day in January 1793. The guillotine stood near one of the statues of the eight largest towns in France, that of Brest, where, despite the onslaught of traffic and tourists, it

For luxury shopping.

RUE DU FAUBOURG SAINT-HONORÉ

EMAIL LABORDE

still is possible to imagine Louis' calm words as the blade was raised: "May my blood bring happiness to France". The square obtained its optimistic new name after the Revolution.

Standing majestically in the middle of chaos, the central obelisk was a gift from the Viceroy of Egypt in 1829, attempting to gain favour with Charles X. The column originated in the Temple of Thebes, and is 3,300 years old; 220 tons in weight, the gift took two years to ship from Egypt, and a further two to get up to Paris from Toulon. The monument has the distinction of being the most apolitical in the capital.

Elysian Fields: From Concorde runs the most famous street in the world – the **Champs-Elysées**. Since their recent facelift, with a new row of trees, underground parking and legislation banning the tacky facades of fast-food joints (they must now complement their more ostentatious neighbours), the Elysian Fields are looking more elegant again.

At the entrance to the avenue, the unruly **Marly Horses**, sculpted by Coustou, were "sold" to an American collector by a Parisian con-man in 1956. To the left, the unmistakable greenhouses of the **Grand Palais** and **Petit Palais** are remnants of the *Belle Epoque*, built for the 1900 World Exhibition. The big one holds conferences and exhibitions, and contains the **Palais de la Découverte**, Paris's less interesting science museum (what a laser can do to a brick is mildly amusing). The little one houses the **Musée des Beaux-Arts de Paris**, with paintings by Rembrandt, Cézanne, Renoir and Pissarro.

The Champs-Elysées was a bog until Marie de Médicis created a fashionable carriageway here in 1616. During occupation in 1814, the Russians pulled down all the trees for firewood. Napoleon III embellished the avenue, and its promenade became lined with cafés. In its parks people gathered to listen to the musician Sax, and his new invention – the saxophone – and successive world fairs drew the well-heeled from around

Dining out on the Champs-Elysées.

the world to its sprouting shops and restaurants. Crowds still converge here for the annual 14 July parade.

The far end of the avenue is dedicated to glitz and glamour – Le Fouquet's Restaurant greets film stars and singers, whilst the Lido offers a sparkling cabaret of naked women.

Fully clothed beauty can be found on **Avenue Montaigne**, where designers Celine (No 38), Chanel (No 42), Dior (No 30), Guy Laroche (No 29), Thierry Mugler (No 49), and Torrente (No 60) have main outlets. Fittingly, this was "Widows' Alley" in the 19th century, where young wives, recently bereft of elderly husbands, would come in their grieving finery, hoping to seek solace with a cavalryman.

Crowning the Champs-Elysées, the **Arc de Triomphe** is a memorial to megalomania. Envisaged and begun by Napoleon, the arch was completed after his death, and received his ashes before their transfer to the Invalides. The Prussians marched through the arch in 1871, as did the Allies in 1919 and 1944. One cold, deserted morning in 1940, Hitler gazed up at the *Marseillaise* frieze, admiring the vigour of the volunteers marching to Paris, and the ornately carved 2-metre (6-ft) figures.

The huge arch, 46 metres (50 ft) high, and 41 metres (135 ft) wide, is best seen from across the automobile stampede of **Place Charles-de-Gaulle** (take the underpass). Beneath the ample armpit of the arch, the Unknown Soldier was laid to rest in 1920, and in 1923 the eternal flame was lit for the first time. It is rekindled each evening, with a wreath-laying ceremony. In 1962, a man was arrested for frying eggs over the flame, but more daring deeds date back to 1919 when a bi-plane flew through the arch with just feet to spare.

From the top of the Arc de Triomphe, the view is breathtaking. Look out west to the futuristic sky-scape of La Défense, and east over the graceful parks of the Louvre. Paris stretches to the horizon, humming, sparkling and enticing.

The Arc de Triomphe.

THE MÉTRO

Deep beneath the streets of Paris there exists another city, a subterranean society with its own shops, cafés, market stalls, hairdressers, banking facilities, musicians, artists, beggars and pickpockets, even its own police force and its own micro climate. Temperatures here occasionally exceed 30°C (86°F), while wind speeds through the tunnels can reach up to 40 km (25 miles) per hour.

Luc Besson's 1985 thriller *Subway* gave audiences a glimpse of this surreal world, portraying some of the eccentric characters who have made the Métro their home. In real life it is a sad statistic that every night 1,000 people take refuge underground, most because they have nowhere else to go.

Construction of the Paris Métro began in 1898. The first line, 10.3 km (6.4 miles) long between Porte de Vincennes and Porte Maillot, was opened on 19 July 1900. Within a year the passengers carried numbered over 15 million.

Since then the Métro has extended its routes in every direction and today it is widely hailed as the world's cheapest, cleanest and most efficiently-run underground system, carrying over 3½ million passengers daily along 200 km (124 miles) of track to 370 stations on 15 lines.

The massive station at Châtelet Les Halles is the hub of the whole network. Four Métro lines and three RER commuter lines meet here, disgorging a quarter of a million passengers daily into its labyrinth of corridors. As you search this nightmarish warren for the exit you may wonder if you will ever come up for air. Trudging the 75 km (47 miles) of corridors and 60 km (37 miles) of platforms, it seems unsurprising that the Parisian's average body weight is among the lowest in the industrialised world.

Leaping out in front of a speeding Métro train long ago outstripped jumping off the Eiffel Tower as one of the most popular ways to kill oneself. There is, on average, one suicide attempt – what the RATP (the organisation which runs the Métro network and the above-ground buses) coyly terms "*un incident voyageur*" – every two days. Surprisingly, two-thirds are unsuccessful.

Other risk-takers are the fare dodgers, who the authorities estimate number as many as 450,000 a day, resulting in 300 million francs in lost revenue. But don't be tempted to jump the barrier: bands of uniformed and plain-clothes controllers patrol stations and trains, doling out on-the-spot fines of several hundred francs.

The average Parisian commuter spends a year and four months of his or her life underground. In an attempt to make this time slightly more bearable, the RATP organises a diverse programme of cultural events, from photography exhibitions to fashion shows, classical concerts to puppet theatre. Less organised are the musicians who roam the corridors, looking for the perfect acoustic. Tunnels boom with the beat of African drums or echo with the haunting notes of a jazz trio.

Back home in Birmingham, England or Knoxville, Tennessee, you may find yourself beginning to pine for a whiff of that distinctive aroma of gorgonzola and old socks, so redolent of the Métro. Then you will know that Paris has truly worked its way into your heart and that the time has come to plan your return. ∎

The Métro is distinctively art nouveau.

HEART OF THE CITY

In 250 BC as thick mists swirled around the marshland of the Marne, a group of fishing families lost their way on an unknown river and landed on a ship-shaped island. Members of the Gaulish Parisii tribe, the boat-people christened their new settlement *Lutetia*, or "home surrounded by water". By the time the Romans invaded, the main island in the Seine was a thriving community, and in the 4th century its inhabitants gave their name to the fully-fledged city – Paris. With the arrival of King Clovis in AD 508, Paris became the capital of the kingdom of the Franks.

The **Île de la Cité** is thus the birthplace and topographical centre of Paris, and has been its spiritual and legislative heart for over 2,000 years. Across the river the **Hôtel de Ville** has been the cauldron of political debate since the Middle Ages whilst, just to the north, the area of **Les Halles** has fed the city's stomachs since AD 1110. This is the core of the capital, an area which, in many ways, embraces the essence of Paris. Here are the historic edifices of Notre Dame and Sainte-Chapelle, the 17th-century mansions of Île St Louis, the revolutionary dungeons of La Conciergerie and the modern mayhem of the Pompidou Centre.

Our Lady: "The bells, the bells," shout crowds of giggling schoolchildren from the towers of **Notre Dame Cathedral**, echoing the cry of Victor Hugo's ever-famous hunchback, Quasimodo. Gazing up at the cathedral's finely sculptured facade, it is hard to imagine the building's poor condition when Hugo wrote the *Hunchback of Notre Dame*. The Romantics were so appalled at the state of the building that in 1841 they petitioned King Louis-Philippe, who appointed architect Viollet-le-Duc to

Preceding pages: the Conciergerie, Île de la Cité. **Right**, Notre Dame.

122

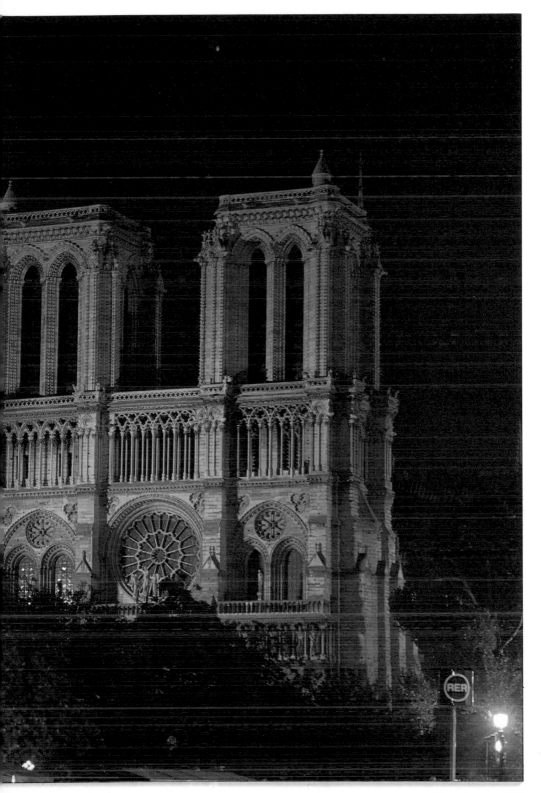

renovate the building, taking 23 years to restore Notre Dame to her former glory.

The church of "Our Lady" was built on the site of earlier pagan fertility worship venerating a black virgin. In the 6th century Clovis kicked out the pagans and erected a suitably impressive Christian basilica. By 1159 a young Bishop, Maurice de Sully, decided that Paris deserved bigger and better. The building of Notre Dame took just under 200 years following plans drawn up by Pierre de Montreuil, Sainte-Chapelle's architect. By 1345 it was complete.

Even before it was finished Notre Dame had become the venue for national ceremonies. In 1239 St Louis deposited the Crown of Thorns of the Lord in the cathedral, awaiting the completion of Sainte-Chapelle, and in 1572 the cathedral's strangest wedding took place. The bride Marguerite de Valois (a Catholic) stood at the altar, whilst the bridegroom Henri de Navarre (a Protestant) called in his vows from the doorstep. Later Henri was crowned in the cathedral, having decided to convert to Catholicism with the words "Paris is well worth a mass." Come the revolution, Notre Dame was ravaged by enthusiastic citizens, who lopped off the heads of the kings of Judah standing above the portal believing them to be kings of France. The heads were discovered in a bank cellar in 1977 and now reside in the Musée de Cluny. Viollet-le-Duc had replaced them with copies in 1850.

By the time Napoleon decided to crown himself emperor, the cathedral was in such a shabby state that bright tapestries were hung to cover the crumbling decor. Pope Pius VII attended with reluctant obedience, and as he hesitated at the altar Napoleon snatched the crown and placed it on his own head as the crowd cheered *Vive L'Empéreur!*

Above it all: Notre Dame is magnificent from any angle, but its Gothic facade is particularly impressive. Viewed from amidst the crowds out front on the **Place du Parvis**, the twin towers soar to the heavens with dramatic grace. The cathedral's three doors each have a distinct design – an asymmetry typical of medieval architecture. Originally the stone figures were finely painted, against a gilt background, and were designed to illustrate the Bible to an illiterate populace. On the left, the **Portal of the Virgin** depicts the ark of the covenant and the coronation of the Virgin. The middle **Portal of the Last Judgement** shows the Resurrection, weighing of souls and their procession to heaven or hell. The **Portal of St Anne** portrays the Virgin and Maurice of Sully. Above the doorways, the Rose Window is a miracle of engineering. Picture the rickety scaffolding with armies of stonemasons, who with simple measuring techniques constructed an intricate masterpiece that has held strong for 750 years.

The belltower of Notre Dame is a religious experience for those who love heights, and a taste of hell for claustrophobes with vertigo. From the top of 387 steps Paris stretches to the

The Rose Window, a star attraction.

horizon. "Emmanuel", the 13-ton bell of Notre Dame, is pealed only on state occasions. It dates from the 17th century, and legend has it that the purity of the bell's tone is due to the gold and silver jewellery cast into its heated bronze by the most beautiful women of Paris. Devilish gargoyles scowling down from the gallery are not medieval nightmares, but the playful inventions of 19th-century Viollet-le-Duc.

Inside, the cathedral is enough to inspire the most hardened atheist. Supported by a flying-buttress, the vault of the chancel seems almost weightless, stained glass windows distributing rays of coloured light into the solemn shadows. The exquisite **Rose Windows** are the transept's two star attractions. Each Sunday, at 5.45pm, the organ master fills the cathedral with classical music, soaring to paradise from 6,100 pipes. The cathedral's relics, the Crown of Thorns and the Holy Nail of the Cross, are shown to an adoring public on Sundays during Lent and on Good Friday.

Vaulted elegance.

Behind Notre Dame, at the east tip of the island, lies the **Memorial to the Deportation**. Within this rather bleak structure 200,000 crystals commemorate the 200,000 French victims of the concentration camps, overlooking the quays and river where many of them lived. To the north of the cathedral is the **ancient cloisters quarter**, home and study area for 12th-century monks. Here the scholar Abélard became tutor to Heloïse, niece of Canon Fulbert, and they fell in love, having a son. When Canon Fulbert discovered the defilement of his niece, he had Abélard castrated – Heloïse became a nun, and Abélard a monk at Ste Geneviève, where he philosophised until his death.

In medieval days the area around Notre Dame was a warren of houses, but in the 19th century Haussmann razed the brothels, pawnbrokers and taverns, moving 25,000 inhabitants to provide the present vista. Pass along Rue de la Colombe, noting the remains of the Gallo-Roman wall in the pavement, to the **Flower**

Market opposite Haussmann's **Hôtel Dieu** and **Préféecture de Police**. In contrast to these sullen structures, the market is a joyful array of small glasshouses selling flowers and plants underneath classical black street-lamps. On Sunday the stalls become a bird market and the jabbering of parakeets fills the air.

The island's other end: To the west rise the imposing walls of the Palais de Justice and La Conciergerie. At one time, the **Palais de Justice** was a Royal Palace: St Louis had his bedroom in what is now the First Civil Court. The courts are open to the public, and a wander around the hushed corridors, past fleeting black-robed figures, is a reminder of the tense days of the Revolution when Fouquier-Tinville sent thousands to the guillotine. The courts are closed at weekends.

Confined within the walls of the Palais de Justice, **La Sainte-Chapelle** stands like a skeletal finger pointing heavenwards – an ethereal counterpoint to the stones of the establishment. This miracle of Gothic ingenuity is an obligatory

pause on any visit to Paris. Completed in record time (33 months) by Pierre de Montreuil, and consecrated in 1248, the chapel was built to house the Crown of Thorns, bartered from the Venetians by St Louis. Although the thorns are now in Notre Dame, the elegance of the chapel remains. Seemingly constructed without walls, its vaulted roof is supported by a thin web of stone, from which descend veils of stained glass.

Enter through the lower chapel, which was designed for lower echelons of the court, and is consequently smaller and gloomier. From the shadows, climb the spiral staircase into the crystalline cavern of the upper chapel. The soaring windows catch the faintest of lights, creating kaleidoscopes of colour. The 13th-century colours are sharply vivid: 1,134 scenes from the Bible begin by the staircase with Genesis, and proceed round the church to the 15th-century rose window. Regular classical concerts in the chapel entertain the serene saints and apostles.

A corner of Sainte-Chapelle.

Viewed from the Seine's right bank, the **Conciergerie** looks like an intimidating castle, its four towers rising insolently above impenetrable walls. It isn't hard to imagine this fortress as a merciless medieval prison – which it was (although much of the pitiless facade is 19th-century). The right-hand tower is called "Bon Bec" (the squealer), for it was here that torture victims told all during the Revolution.

To the left is the 14th-century **Clock Tower** containing the first public clock in Paris, still ticking today. During the Revolution, 2,600 prisoners left the Conciergerie for the chopping block, including Marie-Antoinette whose cell has been restored to its former state, complete with waxwork figure. Ironically, her prosecutor Danton resided in the next cell before losing his head, as in turn did his nemesis, Robespierre. In the merry-go-round of retribution, 1,306 heads rolled in one month at Place de la Nation. To the west of the prison is the **Cour des Femmes**, a rough courtyard where the 12 daily victims bound for the guillotine said their fond farewells to their womenfolk.

Escape the shadows of the Revolution along **Quai des Orfèvres** (now home to the Police HQ), where goldsmiths fashioned Marie-Antoinette's jewellery. Beyond the Square du Vert Galant and the statue of Henri IV, the river slides silently past the tip of the island, caressing wistful willows. **Pont Neuf**, bisecting the island, is the oldest surviving bridge in Paris, where the first folk-singers of the capital congregated to lampoon the aristocracy. In 1985, the American artist Christo wrapped the bridge in brown paper and string.

Island next door: Far from the madding video-cameras, **Île Saint-Louis** is a privileged haven of peace and wealth under the shadow of its more boisterous neighbour. The island's elegance is 17th-century and its mansions are home to Paris' elite. At its eastern tip, **Hôtel Lambert**, built by an advisor to Louis XVIII, is the finest residence in the city,

A price for every purse.

now owned by the Rothschilds. Nearby, in **Hôtel de Lanzun**, Théophile Gautier and Baudelaire formed a hashish smoking society in 1845. Ironically the house is now the property of the City of Paris, reserved for official guests. On the main thoroughfare, **Rue St Louis-en-l'Île**, the church of the same name contains a plaque from the City of Saint Louis, Missouri, USA.

Île Saint-Louis' favourite attraction is edible: **Berthillon**, past the church, purveys 100 flavours of the most delicious ice cream. **Brasserie de l'Île Saint-Louis**, on Quai Bourbon, is an institution amongst institutions, serving the likes of singer Renaud and politician Roland Dumas. Grace Jones also likes a nibble here, while gazing up at the heights of Notre Dame.

Inland to Châtelet: Across the river on the right bank opposite the Conciergerie, **Quai de la Mégisserie** was once the city slaughterhouse. Now birds, cats, dogs and the odd monkey die a slower death in the dingy pet shops along the Seine. **Place du Châtelet**, flanked by its two theatres, is a fountain meeting-place for lovers above one of Paris' biggest Metro stations. In a small side-street, poet Gérard de Nerval hung himself one dawn, having left a message at his lodgings: "Don't wait for me, for the night will be black and white." Northeast of the square stands the **Tour Saint-Jacques**, seemingly dropped there by mistake. The tower was the belfry of a church on the pilgrimage route to Santiago de Compostela in Spain, but its chapel was destroyed during the Revolution. Pascal experimented with the weight of air from the tower's summit, which today is a weather station.

To the east, the wide esplanade of the **Hôtel de Ville** was the site of liberation celebrations in 1944. Robert Doisneau took his famous black and white picture of *The Kiss* here, under the archaic lamps. The building is 19th-century and flanked by bare-breasted maidens in characteristic French style.

If you leave the Île de la Cité via the

Hairstyling at Les Halles.

Pont Neuf, then you can hardly miss the edifice of **La Samaritaine** department store, one of the biggest and oldest in Paris, spread over five buildings joined by overhead walkways. On the roof of building number two, with its art-nouveau facade, the terrace restaurant provides one of the finest views of Paris, and one of the cheapest. Next door, **St Germain-L'Auxerrois** is another example of Gothic finery with an impressive collection of gargoyles and devils. At midnight on 24 August 1572 the church bells rang as the signal for the St Bartholomew's Day Massacre, when thousands of Protestant Huguenots, in Paris for the wedding of Henri of Navarre, were butchered on the orders of Catherine de Médicis, Charles X and the future Henri III. Beside it, the Mairie of the first *arrondissement* is almost a mirror reflection of the church.

Heading north, the narrow streets are heavy with history. **Rue St Honoré** was a major thoroughfare in the 12th-century. At the Croix-du-Trahoir Fountain, Frédégonde, Queen of Austria, was tied by her hair to a wild horse and dragged to death in 613. Rue de la Ferronnerie saw the assassination of Henri IV in 1610, when he was stabbed by Ravaillac next to a prophetic street sign – a crowned heart pierced by an arrow.

Pedestrian precincts: Just to the north, entering the pedestrian area around Les Halles, the **Fontaine des Innocents** is the sole Renaissance fountain in Paris. Tramps and tourists who inhabit this square are sitting on the site of the capital's infamous cemetery, Les Innocents. Filled with corpses since the 12th century, the graveyard had become a putrid metropolis by the 18th century, as the freshly dead were carried through vegetables and meat destined for the market at Les Halles. In 1780 the corpses were overflowing well above street level and it was decided to close the cemetery and move its inmates to the Catacombs south of the river, where their bones can still be visited.

Fortunately the living still flock the

SCOOPING THE POOP

Since 1977, when opinion polls revealed that the cleanliness of the streets came top among Parisian concerns, the newly-elected mayor, the proud and energetic Jacques Chirac, made it a priority to overhaul Paris's entire waste disposal and street-cleaning system. The city's distinctive green uniform and vehicles were introduced in 1980. An *école de la propreté* has been added to teach new recruits the finer elements of street cleaning, and today the green, gnashing wagons have become a symbol of the city.

Paris boasts one of the world's most efficient clean-up services, employing 4,525 men and four women to collect 3,500 tonnes of rubbish daily at an annual cost of 2 billion francs, about 10 percent of the city's annual budget. And the green gnashers have gone international: over 230 foreign delegations, including officials from Tokyo and New York, have travelled to Paris anxious to learn the secrets of efficient waste disposal.

The fact is that Paris faces a singularly challenging obstacle to maintaining the cleanliness of its streets: *déjections canines*, of which no less than 20 tonnes are vacuumed off the streets daily by M. Chirac's team of mobile pooper-scoopers. The annual bill amounts to 42 million francs; spread amongst the city's 200,000 dog population, that's 210 francs per dog.

Paris's unusually large canine population can perhaps be explained by the fact that the Parisian pooch is not merely man's best friend; he is also an essential fashion accessory. Just as residents of Los Angeles define themselves by their cars and Italians by their wardrobe, so Parisians tend to express their personalities through their dogs.

From the toy poodle prancing along the Faubourg Saint-Honoré in a tartan raincoat and matching hair ribbon, to the muzzled German shepherd dozing on the Metro after a hard night's guard duty, the capital's dogs are as diverse and eclectic a breed as the city's human inhabitants. In fact, the distinction between animal and human often seems blurred in a city where it is not uncommon to see dogs seated at café tables.

Indeed, far from being banned from shops and restaurants in France, almost every boutique or eating establishment worth its salt has its resident canine character, whose acquaintance it is advisable to make if you plan on becoming a regular customer.

Needless to say, this indulgence towards their pets does not translate well when it comes to teaching *Frou-Frou* the *toutou* (bow-wow) to use the gutter.

The discovery that the curious elongated sausage dogs with accompanying arrow which appear at regular intervals on the capital's pavements were not yielding satisfactory results inspired M. Chirac to introduce a system of hefty fines. The new law is enforced by an undercover 50-strong cleanliness squad, the plainclothes *agents de propreté*, who patrol the streets and are instructed to swoop on sight – presumably watching where they put their feet.

But despite their valiant efforts, Paris remains a city where canny pedestrians keep a wary eye on the pavement. An estimated two serious falls a day are the result of what the French call *le chocolat*. If, during an unguarded moment, you too find yourself thus inconvenienced, take comfort: Parisians believe it brings good fortune. ■

Praise for the pooper.

square, stopping to sip expressos at **Café Costes**, a palatial bar designed by Philippe Starck with requisite pastel, plastic and formica: try the post-modern toilets. In summer the café has 5,000 customers a day. Around the corner, Rue St Denis starts innocently enough but quickly develops into a torrid and vibrant red-light district.

Ignoring these baser attractions, crowds flock down the narrow streets, drawn as if by a magnet towards the cultural, architectural and fire-eating mecca of Paris – the **Centre Georges Pompidou** (known locally as Beaubourg). Recently usurped in popularity ratings by Euro Disney, Rogers and Piano's *enfant terrible* has an insolent charm worthy of any Walt Disney creation. The building, like an airport terminal with the skin stripped off, caused an uproar when it was finished in 1977, but has since attracted nearly eight million visitors a year (the most-visited cultural site in the world), who marvel at its pipes, tubes, scaffolds and external escalators. The pipes are not just for show: the blue convey air, the green transport water, the yellow contain electricity and the red conduct heating. The forecourt, slightly sunken, is a stage for egos from around the world: Peruvian pipers compete with Los Angeles rappers, whilst burly gypsies breathe fire and lie on beds of nails. A digital clock above marks mortality, counting the seconds to the year 2000. Feed the machine a coin and receive a postcard recording that very moment. Who said time stops for no one?

Nearby, the **Stravinsky Fountain** is home to a herd of spouting animals – weird fountains which suck and spit water, each named after a Stravinsky composition. **Le Café Beaubourg**, behind the aquatic monsters, offers a trendy tipple in avant-garde surroundings.

Inside, the Pompidou Centre is cavernous, since all the infrastructure is of course outer structure. The **Musée National de l'Art Moderne**, on the fourth floor, is the jewel in this crown of tubes.

The Pompidou Centre.

Far less frequented than the escalators leading to the pricey roof café, the museum's displays are addictively humorous, bright and airily presented; the colourful "fauves" are here – Dufy, Derain, Van Dongen and early Matisse, the cubism of Picasso and Braque, abstract childlike canvases of Kandinsky and Klee, and hallucinogenic surrealism of Miró and Dali. Here too are Warhol's "Boxes" and Lichtenstein's cartoon-like dot paintings. The outdoor terrace sweeps over the rooftops of Les Halles, displaying sculptures by Tinguely.

Elsewhere, the centre offers a free public library on the second floor, providing international newspapers, videos and language laboratories for those with the odd hour to brush up on their French. French children flock to the **Atelier des Enfants** on the ground floor where they paint, stick, and mould themselves into the artists of tomorrow. The cinema in the **Salle Garance** has a varied programme of films.

Dotted around the Beaubourg quarter are numerous modern art and photographic galleries, inspired by the ample shadow of the Pompidou Centre. Wander the side-streets, in particular Rue Beaubourg and Rue Quincampoix.

To the north, **Quartier de l'Horloge** is another pedestrianised area, with, as its centrepiece, a 3.5-metre (12-ft) Defender of Time clock made of brass and steel. On the hour a life-size soldier does battle with one of the three elements; the dragon of earth, the bird of the air and the crab of the sea. At six and 12 o'clock all three beasts attack together.

The market: West of Beaubourg, **Les Halles** (pronounced *Lay Hal*) has been a market area since 1183, when Philippe-Auguste erected permanent halls and ordered traders in the city to close two days a week, to encourage commerce at his own market. The huge food market was reorganised under Napoleon III, who demanded that his architect, Baltard, use "iron, nothing but iron!" The resulting 10 halls, resembling small railway stations, were fed by vast un-

Performance outside the Pompidou Centre.

derground storehouses, dark kingdoms of death and decay where cages of animals were piled amongst rotting fruits, ruled over by blind storekeepers. Above the surface, stall-holders, restaurant owners, pickpockets, artists, prostitutes and police crowded the market, shouting obscenities as colourful as the displays of food. An ancient edict stating that no hard objects could be thrown in the market (only mud and liquid detritus) was obeyed with gusto. Dairymaids accused of giving short measures were stood in the square and a slab of the offending butter placed on their heads.

The last night of the market, Thursday 27 February 1969, was a sad occasion for Parisians. The animated halls, so lovingly described by Zola in his novel *Le Ventre de Paris* ("The Belly of Paris"), were no longer suitable for 20th-century commerce, and trading was moved to Rungis, near Orly Airport. Vestiges of the past survive in the scattered 24-hour bistros of the area. Head to the Pied du Cochon for a white wine

Deliciously dressed.

at six in the morning, or La Poule au Pot, for tripe with film directors and singers.

The present-day **Forum des Halles** filled the large hole left after the razing of the market. This vast underground commercial centre, four floors beneath Paris, is a monument to impersonality. Above ground are glass and steel mushrooms housing the **Pavillon des Arts** and **Maison de la Poésie**, created to offset the commercial tone of the Forum. The central courtyard hosts the odd concert around a subtly pornographic Pygmalion statue by Julio Silva.

Four museums provide entertainment: **Musée Grévin**, a subsidiary of the larger Grévin museum in Montmartre has waxwork displays illustrating the *Belle Epoque* (1885–1900) with a talking Victor Hugo, Gustav Eiffel and others; **Les Martyrs de Paris**, showing waxworks in various acts of inhumanity, from the guillotine to the "iron maiden" torture chamber; **Musée du Rock**, with a waxy Elvis; and **Musée de l'Holographie** with miraculous holograms.

Park to the west: Away from the wax and glass, the area of Les Halles is now a pleasant park, a breath of fresh air for concrete-weary tourists. In the northeast corner a giant head and cupped hand, sculpted by Henri de Miller, attract children and pigeons to its benign seat, beneath the Gothic gaze of **Sainte-Eustache**. The 100- metre (330 ft) long church is one of Paris's most beautiful, resembling a pregnant Notre Dame. Berlioz and Liszt played premiers here, and music still swells in the huge dome.

To the left, glass pyramids recalling the new Louvre entrance reflect the stones of St Eustache. This is a new hothouse containing palms, papayas and banana trees. Metal walkways traverse the glasshouses to the **Bourse de Commerce**, a circular commercial exchange built in 1889 on the site of a luxurious brothel. Surrounding rose gardens and box hedges do their best to disguise the entrance to the vast underground parking complex of Les Halles. Sit, close your eyes and smell the roses.

THE MARAIS AND THE BASTILLE

On the Right Bank of the Seine, tucked behind the Hôtel de Ville and hiding away from the extravagance of the Grands Boulevards, nestle two *quartiers* which are steeped in royal and revolutionary history. The Marais and the area of the city around the Bastille are both proudly independent districts, possessing an intimate, animated charm that sets them apart from the more grandiose expanses to the west. These are villages within the great metropolis, small communities with their own traditions, folklore and heroes.

A former swamp: The Marais (literally "the swamp") was notable in the 13th-century for the mosquitoes and frogs that infested the bogs on either side of Rue St Antoine, the old Roman eastern highway. With the arrival of monks and monasteries, the marshes were drained and Charles V constructed a new wall around Paris, bringing the Marais into the city.

In 1605 Henri IV decided to build a sumptuous nest for his court at the present-day Place des Vosges, shifting the political and financial focus from the Louvre. As a result, the finest architects and stonemasons in Europe descended on the Marais, building countless grand residences, or *hôtels*, for the nobility, each more impressive than the last. These classical walls sheltered *salons* – living-room intellectual societies – where the bright and beautiful of the day would pontificate, lounging on ornate divans.

The pendulum of fashion swung away from the Marais with the development of Versailles, and nobility moved westwards to the Faubourg St Honoré and the Boulevard St Germain. The Marais's graceful *hôtels* tumbled into disrepair, and the narrow streets became a den of iniquity. In the 19th and 20th centuries the area became a centre for small industries and crafts, and successive de-velopers dug up and widened its picturesque streets. In 1962, the Law Malraux sought to preserve the Marais, and widescale renovation began. Today, many of the *hôtels* are beautifully restored, and whilst the area maintains a rougher edge which can add to its charm, its former elegance is returning.

The Marais is contained by **Rue Beaubourg** to the west and **Boulevard Beaumarchais** to the east, covering much of the 3rd and 4th *arrondissements*. It is historic home of the Jewish community in Paris, and now houses the capital's largest homosexual community; local cafés and bars are animated day and night. Modern art galleries pepper the side-streets, enticing the curious. At night the ancient lamps flicker along quiet streets, and this becomes one of the most romantic hideaways in the capital.

A guided tour: Behind the Hôtel de Ville stands the **Church of St Gervais-St Protais**, with its Italianate steps and evil-looking gargoyles. Famous for sa-

cred music, the church possesses an 18th-century organ played by eight generations of the Couperin family. Its twin saints, Gervase and Protase, Roman officers executed by Nero, failed to protect 51 worshippers killed when a rocket from Germany's "Big Bertha" landed on the church in 1918.

Rue François-Miron, at the northern crossroads, was nearly demolished in the 1940s. Now under restoration, many of its residences are creeping back to their former glory. At the corner of Rue Cloche Perce is a half-timbered medieval house; at No 68, the **Hôtel de Beauvais** was built by Catherine Beauvais in 1654, with money and land from King Louis XIV.

"One-eyed Kate", as she was known, was 40 years old when she "educated" 16-year-old Louis in the ways of the world under the benign gaze of his mother, Anne of Austria. Louis' marriage procession passed under these windows, from which Kate winked at the bridegroom. She is later said to have

entertained archbishops. More innocently, the composer Mozart stayed here at the age of seven – before he too became considerably more profligate – on his first visit to Paris.

Neighbouring Rue de Jouy contains **Hôtel d'Aumont**, designed by Versailles architect Le Vau, and now the administrative court of the Seine region. Along the river, the **Cité Internationale des Arts** is resolutely modern in the midst of antiquated refinement; the building provides lodging and studios for artists from around the world. In stark contrast stand the château-like turrets of one of Paris' few medieval residences, the **Hôtel de Sens** which now houses the city's historical and fine arts library, the Bibliothèque Forney.

Built at the end of the 15th century for the Archbishop of Sens, a soldier and cleric, the building is military in style, with simple but immaculate gardens. In the 18th century it was the departure point for the Paris-Lyon stagecoach run – a route deemed so unsafe that passen-

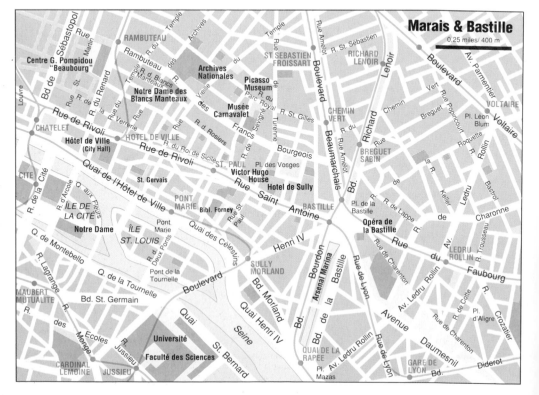

gers were encouraged to make a will before setting out.

Many of the old residences in this area have been converted into apartments; on **Rue Charlemagne** wooden walkways between the buildings have been restored as they were in the Middle Ages. Along the street, the remnants of the Philippe-Auguste wall rise solemnly – two towers and ramparts shadow the games of local children. At the end of the road stretches the **Village St Paul**, a series of small courtyards and fountains, sheltering bustling antique shops and second-hand stalls. The area is romantically tranquil by night, beneath the halo of street-lamps.

The adjacent **Church of St Paul-St Louis**, on Rue St Antoine, was constructed by Jesuits in 1627. Here, the hearts of Louis XIII and Louis XIV were embalmed, only to be removed during the Revolution and sold to an artist who crushed Louis XIV's heart to make red paint for one of his pictures. Later he sold back the body of Louis

XIII to the newly-installed King Louis XVIII, in return for a golden snuff-box.

If it is nearing lunchtime, continue towards the Place de la Bastille to Rue de la Cerisaie, where 1,000 cherry trees used to grow, and **Le Temps des Cerises**. This is the Parisian bistro as it was and should be; a blackboard menu of fresh market produce, served by jokingly disarming waiters. Elsewhere, **Le Beautreillis** on Rue Beautreillis is the restaurant where Jim Morrison, deity of the Doors pop group, drank his last bottle of wine with his girlfriend Pamela Courson. He was found dead in her apartment across the street on 3 July 1971, officially the victim of a heart attack in the bath. Unofficially...

Rue St Antoine is the ancient jugular of the Marais. Built wide and straight in good old Roman fashion, the road became a site of jousting tournaments from the 14th century until, in 1574, Henri II was knocked off his horse by Captain of the Guard, Montgomery. The blow to the eye wounded the king, who was

taken to his physician, Ambroise Paré. The latter ordered the immediate decapitation of every prisoner on death-row, and their heads were rushed to the surgery for experiments to save the king. Henri died ten days later and the unfortunate Captain Montgomery was executed on the spot.

Hôtel de Sully at 62 Rue St Antoine, is one of the finest in the Marais. Under the courtyard's grumpy statues, Voltaire was beaten with clubs by followers of the Count of Rohan following a slanging match between the two at the Comédie Française. Through the courtyard temporary art exhibitions are housed in what is now known as the **Caisse Nationale des Monuments Historiques**, the place to inquire about walking tours of Paris. Behind, the intimate garden is an unexpected surprise with clipped privet hedges *à l'anglaise*. A small door in the corner leads to the **Place des Vosges**.

This enchanting 17th-century square, with its garden surrounded by arcaded residences, was constructed by Henri IV as a showcase for his court. Here courtiers paraded, preened and pranced. After the Revolution, when the statue of Louis XIII was melted down then reforged, the square was christened after the department of France which paid its taxes most promptly in 1800 – the Vosges. Today this is the most beautiful square in Paris, and one of the capital's most sought-after addresses. The arcades house chic cafés, as well as Issey Miyake's European headquarters and boutique. In the south-east corner is **Victor Hugo's House**. The romantic writer penned his greatest works here including *Les Misérables*. The house is a museum containing manuscripts and pieces of furniture knocked together by Victor in moments of boredom.

On Sunday the gardens are a playground of children and lovers, whilst ducks happily waddle in the dancing fountains. Louis XIII points down over them all, his moustache finely waxed. In summer, the arcades host open-air **Place des Vosges.**

classical recitals – not a new thing; it was here that Mozart gave his first recital in 1763. If you are hungry, and not poor, **L'Ambroisie** at 9 Place des Vosges is one of Paris's Michelin three-star restaurants. To be sure of a table, you should either book a long time in advance or become a famous politician.

The Jewish quarter: Turning left from the square, Rue des Francs-Bourgeois leads along sculptured walls to **The Hôtel Carnavalet**, once home to woman of letters, Mme de Sévigné. Transformed into the **Museum of Paris**, the mansion contains well-displayed exhibits tracing the history of the capital in painting, sculpture and costume. From the *hôtel* organised walking tours of the Marais visit those parts other guides do not reach – see the notice on the gates for further details.

Turning left down Rue Pavée, pass the **Hôtel de Lamoignan**, where 60 people were murdered during the massacres of 2 September 1792 (including the Princess of Lamballe, whose head was presented to the Queen on a spike), to the Jewish Quarter. In the 13th century King Philippe-Auguste moved the Jewish community living by Notre Dame to the Marais, which was then outside the city walls, and the area has been vigorous ever since. **Rue des Rosiers** is the heart of the district: a narrow extravaganza of kosher delis, falafel stands, old men on motorbikes selling watermelon and tiny shops packed with religious artifacts.

Yet the past is not forgotten; shop signs are partly effaced, victims of fascists during World War II. Here, on 16 July 1942, French police arrested every man, woman and child in the district, and sent many of them to concentration camps. More recently, at 7 Rue des Rosiers, the world-renowned **Goldenberg's Restaurant** suffered a bomb attack in 1982.

For less expensive fare and a bustling ambience, turn the corner to **Chez Marianne** (2 Rue des Hospitalières-Saint-Gervais), where the owner André

Hôtel Carnavalet, home to the Museum of Paris.

Jornot writes his saying-of-the-week on the restaurant window. André's gems include: "Man is a dung-heap where the Lord seeks to grow a rose" (collected works available in paperback). Next door, small children kick footballs on a small square – the site of a primary school whose pupils were all sent to Buchenwald camp. To the south, on Rue Geoffrey l'Asnier stands the **Memorial to the Unknown Jew**, whose eternal flame in an underground crypt is a poignant reminder of the not-so-distant Holocaust.

Pawn and Picasso: Back on the western end of Rue des Francs-Bourgeois, **Le Domarais** (53 bis) offers spectacular decor and unique dinner entertainment; its circular 17th-century dining room is overlooked by a balcony where musicians perform Chopin and Mozart. Next door is the austere facade of the **Crédit Municipal**, the state pawnbroker. Nicknamed "My Aunt", the lending facility was opened in 1777, and today you can still obtain cash on the

value of objects surrendered to its charge. Items remaining unclaimed by their owners are auctioned off to the public – an unforgettable place to browse away a rainy afternoon.

Opposite the house of the poor stand the houses of the rich. Palais de Soubise contains the **Museum of French History**. Here too are the **National Archives**; over six million official documents on 290 km (180 miles) of shelving, demonstrating the nation's love-affair with the rubber stamp.

Rue des Archives leads to Paris's finest collection of stuffed animals in the **Museum of Hunting and Nature**, Hôtel Guénégaud, which bears witness to the French aphorism: "if it moves, shoot it." To the east, **Hôtel de Rohan** is stunningly restored, but unfortunately only accessible when housing temporary exhibitions. If closed, the courtyard is worth a look in itself.

The northeast of the Marais contains a huddle of museums, including **Musée Cognacq-Jay** on Rue Elzévir, set in the

Picasso Museum, Hôtel Salé.

exquisite Hôtel Donon. The mansion houses the art collection of Ernest Cognacq, founder of the Samaritaine department store, and includes works by Rembrandt and Canaletto. Each room evokes a facet of 18th-century life, with lavish furnishing and decoration. On the corner with Rue de la Perle, Hôtel Libéral-Bruand accommodates a **Lock and Key Museum**, of interest to house owners and breakers alike, whilst Rue de Thorigny leads to the **Picasso Museum** in the Hôtel Salé.

Following his death in 1973, Picasso's family was faced with an enormous bill from the French government in the form of inheritance tax. In lieu of payment, they donated a large collection of his works. The pictures are not his most famous, but the setting is superb, and the museum layout provides a conclusive tour around the genius of the small man from Barcelona whose motto was, "I do not seek, I find". Giacometti's ironwork completes the artistic décor. In summer, amongst statues in the gar-den, a small outdoor café serves tea to weary art-lovers.

Mysteries: To the north of the Marais **Le Quartier du Temple** was once a town within a town, the headquarters of the Knights Templar, where 4,000 people lived in a safe haven out of bounds to the authorities. A 13th-century secret society of soldiers originally formed to protect pilgrims in the Holy Land, the Knights Templar owned much of France, and were in charge of the royal treasury until Philippe the Handsome burnt their leaders at the stake on an island in the Seine, and the society was forced to go underground.

With the Revolution, the Temple Tower (no longer standing) became the most famous prison in France. Here, the royal family was imprisoned, at first in luxurious apartments, and later in the dungeons. In 1793 Louis XVI was taken from here to the guillotine. His son stayed on, and mysteriously disappeared in 1795, when a body was spirited from the Temple and buried in a common

Children's hour in the museum.

grave at Ste Marguerite beyond the Bastille. The grave digger exhumed the corpse that night, and placed it in a foundation wall of the church. Presumed to be the Dauphin himself, this body was dug up in the last century, and proved to be that of an 18-year-old. The Dauphin was 10 years old when he disappeared.

The Temple Prison was razed by a superstitious Napoleon, and Haussmann replaced it with a wrought iron covered market, the **Carreau du Temple**, which still sells inexpensive clothes and cloth by the metre. The adjacent Rue Dupetit-Thouars is the place to purchase a leather jacket. Along the tree-lined Rue Perrée lies the sole remnant of the Temple fortress, the **Square du Temple** garden. Today ducks live in its confines and the pleasant park resounds to the sound of ping pong balls on two outdoor tables. Table-tennis is the number one sport in this area, which is predominantly Chinese and Vietnamese. In 1914, the French government brought in 100,000 Chinese subjects to replace workers enlisted in the army, among them an unknown boy called Deng Xiao Ping.

From the Temple district, Rue Réaumur leads to the France's most prestigious technical college, the **Conservatoire National des Arts et Métiers**. The college also houses the **National Technical Museum**, immortalised by Umberto Eco's finale to his novel *Foucault's Pendulum*, in which 20th-century Knights Templar hold bizarre ceremonies under the pendulum. The museum includes such innovations as Volta's battery, Pascal's adding machine and Blériot's airplane.

To end a visit to the Marais, head down Rue du Temple past the jewellery boutiques to 41, and its courtyard. This was the "Aigle d'Or", the last stagecoach company in Paris. Today it is a seductively bustling place: **Le Café de la Gare** puts on alternative theatre and music, whilst **Le Studio** is one of the better, and most fun, Tex-Mex restaurants in Paris. As the tables in the court-

Scenic history at the Metro.

yard fill and the margaritas flow, you can hear the dancers in neighbouring studios striving for fame.

Infamous area: To the east of the Marais squats the **Bastille** district. Once a fearsome bastion of royal strength, the quarter fell into disrepair and disrepute after the destruction of the Bastille during the French Revolution. On 14 July 1789 crowds stormed the prison, and freed the inmates – all seven of them. Louis XVI was unimpressed, recording in his diary: "Today – nothing". Following the dismantling of the Bastille, an enterprising workman made sculptures of the prison from the rubble, and sold them to local councils, who were denounced as anti-republican if they refused the high price demanded.

The ancient Bastille covered the present day **Place de la Bastille** and the **Arsenal complex**. The modern square is a wide, busy thoroughfare with the usual tall column in its midst, erected to victims of the revolution of 1830, who are buried underneath. Rumour has it

that along with the revolutionaries who lay in state at the Louvre came two ancient Egyptian pharaohs, who were surplus to the museum's requirements, and whose badly decomposing bodies were hidden by the curator with the revolutionaries and subsequently received full military honours.

Dominating the square, the huge modern **L'Opéra de la Bastille** has been the victim of much polemic from politicians, art critics and public alike. Although its appearance (half a goldfish bowl attached to a black triumphal arch) has shocked traditionalists, the opera house is gradually creeping into Parisian hearts. Opened on 14 July 1989, when President Mitterrand inaugurated his "Opera for the People", the house's recent seasons included works by Wagner, Verdi and Puccini.

The Bastille is one of Paris's most rapidly changing quarters. Old crumbling streets are being gentrified, and the old crumbling inhabitants moving out. Some of the rebellious charm re-

mains in streets such as Rue de Lappe and Rue de Charonne, yet the influx of the upwardly mobile has led to an epidemic of dimly lit bistro-bars which are full of serious souls dressed in black. Numerous modern art galleries have sprouted particularly on Rue Keller, and Rue de Lappe.

At night Rue de la Roquette becomes a buzzing mecca for the fashion gurus of Paris as Harley Davidsons roar up and down, oblivious to the past when this street echoed to the cries of prisoners being beheaded at the corner of Rue de la Croix-Faubin (five stones from the guillotine block remain).

Le Balajo (9 Rue de Lappe) is a hot, trendy Latin dance-hall, but be prepared to stand in line to get in. The **Théâtre de la Bastille** on Rue de la Roquette (nothing to do with the Opéra – as the tatty decor proves) currently offers Paris' most challenging dance works. At 17 Rue de la Roquette, **La Rotonde** is a young and chic bar – a far cry from its past life as a brothel whose owner was

shot dead by a blind accordion player.

The area is still lively during the day and addictive for anyone who likes people-watching. Off Rue du Faubourg St Antoine, you can wander through numerous passages of small workshops manufacturing furniture, rugs and jewellery as they have for centuries. Passage du Cheval Blanc leads off from the Bastille, with courtyards named after the months of the year. Passage de la Main d'Or is equally charming.

Less claustrophobic is the walk from Place de la Bastille north along the newly redesigned park of Boulevard Richard Lenoir. This walk continues for several kilometres along canals as far as **La Villette**. Alternatively you can do the same journey by boat from Arsenal Marina, with two departures every day in each direction.

Rest places: The elegant **Restaurant Bofinger** (7 Rue de la Bastille) claims to be Paris' oldest brasserie, magnificently decorated. Get here early for a seat under the glass cupola. Wine lovers

Père-Lachaise styles of remembrance: Jim Morrison…

should not miss **Bistrot Jacques Mélac** (42 Rue Léon-Frot), to the east. The vine that sprouts proudly from the bar sets the tone, and two signs on the wall state categorically: "Here, water is for cooking potatoes", and "Do not drink water, fish make love in it." M. Mélac produces 40 litres of wine annually, most of which he seems to consume himself. It is here that The Wine Growers of Paris meet. Recently, they have produced an average of around 600 litres (1,300 pints) a year, and the association is growing.

End your day as thousands of Parisians have ended theirs – in the **Père-Lachaise Cemetery**, some distance out to the east. When it was built in 1803, the dead were reluctant to be buried here as it was far from the city centre and far from fashionable. Napoleon promptly dug up Molière and La Fontaine, and buried them with pomp at Père-Lachaise, with the result that today the guest list is endless. A wander amongst the ornate graves is a unique experience, if only to watch the living who frequent this municipality of the dead. Wild cats play on the tombs whilst lovers, tramps, transvestites and young children do their thing in the shadowy alleys.

Probably the most visited grave is the stone marking Jim Morrison's resting place – graffiti ensures you will not miss it. Other graves are harder to find, and a map purchased at the entrance on Boulevard de Ménilmontant aids the confused pilgrim: here lie Chopin, Rossini, and Bizet; there Victor Hugo, Beaumarchais, Balzac, Marcel, Proust, Apollinaire and Oscar Wilde, the latter under a fittingly inscrutable Sphinx.

The cemetery was the site of the last battle of the Paris Commune in 1871, when remaining Communards were cornered and eventually shot against the southeast wall in the far corner by French troops. One hundred and forty-seven of them were buried in a ditch, christened the **Mur des Fédérés** and now a socialist shrine. Nearby are monuments to the world wars.

MONTMARTRE AND PIGALLE

The "village" of Montmartre occupies the highest point of Paris, nestling into a small hillside in the 18th *arrondissement*, north of the city centre. Extending from the seedy yet vibrant Place Pigalle in the south to the white cones of Sacré-Coeur, the village is an alluring huddle of small steep streets and hidden lovers' steps.

In parts, Montmartre resembles a country hamlet with its cobbled squares and gnarled inhabitants. Elsewhere, neon, fast-food, sex shows and tourist buses have tarnished the bohemian atmosphere. Follow the golf hats and Montmartre will seem predictably commercial. Follow a narrow side-street, a deserted flight of steps and you will be alone, wandering in Paris' least Parisian and most charismatic quarter. Away from the crowds and indifferent food on Place du Tertre, numerous inexpensive restaurants greet the hungry wanderer.

A tradition of rebellion: Montmartre has always liked to be different. Legend has it that, in AD 287, the Romans decapitated St Denis, the first Bishop of Paris, and two priests on the hill. St Denis calmly picked up his head and walked off with it to what is now the area of St Denis. The hill became known as "Mons Martyrium" (Martyrs' Mound). As local bar owners point out, people have been picking their heads out of the gutters of Montmartre ever since.

In the 12th century, a Benedictine convent settled on the hill, marking the spot of the St Denis martyrdom. Four hundred years later, Henri IV took over the convent when laying siege to Paris in 1589. His only conquest of the campaign, it appears, was the 17-year-old Abbesse of the time. The last Mother Superior here was guillotined during the Revolution, despite her deafness and blindness, at the age of 82.

Revolution has been the district's speciality ever since St Denis' rebellious behaviour, and in 1871 its inhabitants seized 170 cannon after the fall of Paris to the Prussians. The Thiers government sent in troops to recapture them but the generals were overwhelmed, lined up on the hill, and shot – so beginning the Paris Commune.

For much of the 19th century Montmartre was mined for gypsum and still retained a country charm with its vineyards, cornfields, flocks of sheep and 40 windmills. It was this charm and the lofty isolation of the hill that attracted artists and writers at the turn of the century. Painters and their models frolicked on Place Pigalle, and everyone flocked to the Moulin Rouge. Impressionism, Fauvism and Cubism were conceived in the lofts, bars and dancehalls of Montmartre.

When the bohemians migrated to Montparnasse, the district was left to sex-shop owners, pawnbrokers and cheap hotels and for many years Montmartre was synonymous with sleaze. Yet today the village is suddenly trendy

Preceding pages: caricaturist in Place du Tertre. **Left**, Sacré-Coeur. **Right**, school's out.

once more. Dingy strip bars are being transformed into chic rock clubs, peep shows are becoming American-style diners and the narrow streets roar with BMWs and Porsches.

The ideal way to see Montmartre is on foot, but the Montmartrobus and tourist train provide a less exhausting slice of the district (their route starts at Place Blanche). At Blanche, the **Moulin Rouge**, with its red neon windmill, provides a taste of tourist France to wealthy foreigners (the "French" dancers are selected from auditions in the US and the UK). The club's history is gloriously scandalous: Toulouse-Lautrec sat here, sketching the energetic can-can of Jane Avril. In 1896 the annual Paris Art School Ball at the Moulin Rouge was the scene of the first fully nude striptease, by one of the school's prettiest models. She was arrested, imprisoned and students went to the barricades in the Latin Quarter, proclaiming "The battle for artistic nudity" – two students died in subsequent scuffles with police.

The Folies-Bergère, further south on Rue Richer has much the same fare. Next door to the Moulin Rouge, modern hedonists gather at **La Locomotive**, a huge, train-shaped disco, ringing to rock, roll, and Europop.

Attractions: Along Boulevard de Clichy, the gateway to Montmartre is **Place Pigalle**. To the south, on Rue de la Rochefoucauld the **Gustave Moreau Museum** is a memorial to Matisse's teacher, containing 11,000 of Moreau's symbolist pictures. Less artistic attractions abound in Pigalle: "Pig Alley" (as it was known to American soldiers) has been the core of the Parisian sex trade for several decades. Along Boulevard Clichy, and the streets around Pigalle, tassled curtains provide glimpses into smoky interiors, slashed signs promote live sex shows and aggressive bouncers attempt to persuade tourists into "naked extravaganzas". Beware – prices quoted are much lower than you will pay once inside. Things are changing however. The advent of Aids has drastically re-

Best foot forward at the Moulin Rouge.

152

duced custom, and a hefty increase in value-added tax, from 18.6 percent to 33.3 percent, has been aimed deliberately at the sex trade.

The cabarets which once occupied half the houses along Rue des Martyrs in the 18th century are being taken over by hip clubs and trendy bars. **Café Pigalle** (99 Boulevard de Clichy) epitomises this metamorphosis – its recent renovation has restored the 1950s feel and the quality of the food, attracting a sharp and lively crowd. At 72 Boulevard Rochechouart, **L'Elysée-Montmartre** has come out of retirement to host up-and-coming rock groups. The old hall greeted Russian soldiers during the occupation of 1814. As they ordered their drinks (forbidden by the Russian military authorities) they shouted "bistro", or "quickly", thereby creating a Parisian institution. The *belle époque* facade alone is worth the visit. **Le Dépanneur** (27 Rue Fontaine) is the place to slam tequilas in an imitation American diner. Next door, **Le Moloko** (26 Rue Fontaine) is the hang-out of models, bad-boys and transvestites – the kitsch dance-floor, smoking room and cocktail bar are open from 2 pm to 6 am. Further south, **Le Palace**, 8 Rue du Faubourg-Montmartre greeted Prince and Tina Turner in their youth, but today holds up to 2,000 acolytes in a multi-floored grotto of groove.

Up the hill: From Pigalle, Rue Steinkerque leads to Square Willette at the foot of the hill, the "butte" of Montmartre. Here is the **Marché St Pierre** and its clothing and cloth stalls. The 1868 market hall designed by the architect of Les Halles, Baltard, is now a cultural centre.

On the summit of the hill stands the white bulk of **Sacré-Coeur**. The domed basilica was conceived by the Catholic church in 1873 to "atone for the sins of the Commune". The byzantine austerity of the church, added to its symbolic censure of a popular uprising, have rendered Sacré-Coeur one of the Parisians' least favourite monuments. Begun in

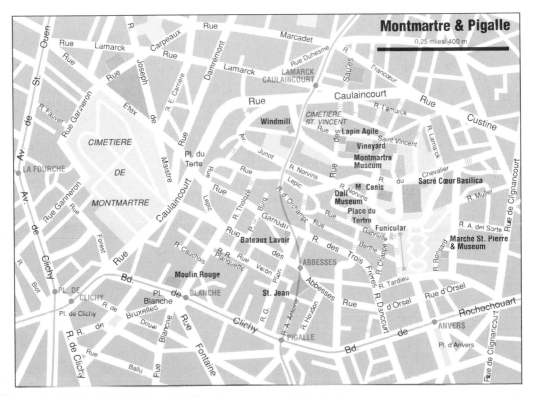

1875 but finished only in 1919, the dome offers a stunning view over Paris, up 237 narrow steps (this is the highest vantage point over the city). The bone-white colour of the building is due to its Chateau-Landon stone, which when it rains secretes calcite, bleaching the church. The interior is cavernous and little else. You'd do better to stay outside on the terrace where crowds gather at dusk to drink wine, strum guitars, watch the lights of Paris twinkle and forget the past.

Next to exotic Sacré-Coeur, the simple church of **St-Pierre de Montmartre** is second oldest in Paris (after St Germain-des-Prés), and the only remaining vestige of the Abbey of Montmartre. If you are here on 1 November, visit the small, romantic graveyard behind the church, because this is the only day in the year it is open.

Just to the west, **Place du Tertre** is the tourist honeypot of Montmartre with its "authentic" bistros, and even more "authentic" craft shops. The square was once the site of the village hall; today it is ruled by the mighty franc. The legions of mediocre artists on the square (two per metre, by law) are voluble and sometimes belligerent when selling their wares, yet despite this oppressive commercialisation the square retains an animated excitement under fairy-lights.

From the Place du Tertre quiet, winding Rue Poulbot leads to the **Espace Dali Montmartre**, with a select collection of Dali's sculptures and drawings, including his famous clocks representing "the fluidity of time". **Place du Calvaire**, the smallest square in Paris, offers a spectacular view and is the intimate home of kissers and drinkers.

Further north, Rue St Rustique is rustically ancient, leading away from the buzz of Place du Tertre past **La Bonne Franquette**, originally "Le Billard en bois", where Van Gogh and Renoir both painted, to Rue des Saules. Along this provincial street lies the famous **vineyard of Montmartre**, cultivated since the Middle Ages. At the

Place du Tertre.

154

beginning of October the grape harvest attracts hundreds of volunteers to pluck the purple fruit, and the surrounding streets host processions and parties. Three hundred litres (650 pints) are bottled and sold at auction, proceeds going to the pensioners of Montmartre.

Bordering the vineyard, **Musée du Vieux Montmartre** (12 Rue Cortot) chronicles the life and times of the "butte", in an old rural residence which housed Renoir, Dufy and Utrillo. The museum is an evocation of past simplicity, gaiety and bohemian living, with pictures by Van Dongen and Dufy, yellowing photographs and a view over the vineyard and roofs of Montmartre. At 6 Rue Cortot lived composer Erik Satie. His house is now a small museum, and seven-person concert hall.

Continuing along Rue des Saules, **Le Lapin Agile** stands opposite the vineyard at No 22. This was home to the bright and beautiful at the turn of the century: a restaurant-cabaret, where Renoir and Verlaine laid tables, and

Apollinaire sang songs with Max Jacob. Picasso paid for a day's meals at the Lapin with one of his "Harlequin" paintings – today worth several million pounds. The name of this small hut on the hill came from artist André Gill's 1880 wall picture of a rabbit jumping over a cooking pot. It later became known as the "Lapin à Gill". Today the rabbit is still going with its smoked-stained walls, original paintings by Léger and Gill, and the old wooden tables. Get here by 9pm, and imbibe, sitting in the corner once inhabited by Picasso or Verlaine. The cabaret performers come off the street at about 9.30pm when a seemingly impromptu talent contest ensues with audience participation.

Passing the St Vincent Cemetery where Utrillo lies in peace, Rue des Saules leads to the **Musée d'Art Juif**, a collection of Jewish art, which contains works by Soutine, Pissarro and a Bible illustrated by Chagall.

Quiet streets: Far from the helter-skelter animation of Pigalle, the west of

Montmartre bar.

Montmartre is a puzzle of small old streets and tumbledown houses. Take the steps from Place Constantin-Pecqueur to **Square Suzanne-Buisson**, one of the most romantic corners of Montmartre with its terrace and antiquated lamps. The square occupies the former garden of the **Château des Brouillards**, an 18th-century folly occupied by Renoir and poet Gérard de Nerval and later turned into a dance-hall. During the 19th-century, the "château" could only be seen when the thick fogs (*brouillards*) of Montmartre lifted, hence the name. In the middle of the square, a statue of St Denis washes the blood off his head whilst watching the old men playing *boules*.

From the square, **Avenue Junot** is one of the widest and most expensive streets in Montmartre. Constructed in 1910, the avenue cut through the ancient *maquis* scrubland which covered the hillside, where windmills turned their graceful sails and goats scampered amongst the trees. The street's 1920s art-deco elegance has attracted the cream of Montmartre society – the singer Claude Nougaro lives in the big ochre house. **Le Hameau des Artistes** (No 11) still houses artists' studios.

Below, on the corner of Rue Girardon and Rue Lepic, is the last of the great windmills of Montmartre, **Moulin de la Galette**. Built in 1604, the windmill became an illustrious dance-hall in the 19th-century. Emile Zola held a party here to celebrate the success of his novel *L'Assomoir*, set in the workers' hovels to the east of Montmartre. (The writer lived just below the village on Boulevard de Clichy). The party was riotous, and during the festivities Renoir began sketches for his famous painting *Le Moulin de la Galette*. Earlier, in 1814, the four Debray brothers had fought fiercely to save their windmill from the Russians – one of them was subsequently crucified on its sails. Today, the windmill is better protected; a notice proclaims "Residence under electronic, radar, and guard-dog surveillance".

Utrillo painted the Lapin Agile.

Picturesque Rue Lepic, leading from the windmill, descends to Place Blanche. The old quarry road housed Vincent Van Gogh and his brother Theo, at No 54. Vincent presented his paintings at Le Tambourin, a seedy cabaret on Boulevard de Clichy, until the owner demanded that he remove them, as they disturbed her customers.

Au Vrai Lepic (61 Rue Lepic) is an ancient bar-restaurant which preserves the traditions of Montmartre – busy, inexpensive and animated by local singers and poets. Further down the hill, where the lively Lepic food market is held each morning, stop at **Le Lux** (12 Rue Lepic) for a white wine or hot chocolate below the beautiful 1909 facade. **Le Restaurant** on Rue Verron, just off Rue Lepic, provides food as stylishly simplistic as its name, and is much loved by the young and beautiful of the district.

Montmartre Cemetery to the west reflects the artistic bias of the area. The tombs are elegantly sculpted, and their inmates appropriately famous: here lie Stendhal, Offenbach, Dumas, Théophile Gautier, Degas, the dancer Nijinsky, Berlioz, and Zola's bust (his body was moved to the Panthéon). Film director François Truffaut was buried here in 1984 in accordance with his dying wish.

Eastwards: Below the Espace Montmartre, **Place Emile-Goudeau** is particularly attractive. At No 13 modern studios have replaced the wooden ramshackle buildings that were Le Bateau-Lavoir. This artists' den housed Picasso and fellow Cubists Braque and Van Dongen in its narrow ship-like corridors. Picasso painted *Les Desmoiselles d'Avignon* here in his chaotic studio, recalling the prostitutes of Barcelona. Poets Apollinaire and Max Jacob liberated verse-form in the rooms alongside. Unfortunately the original building was burnt down in 1970 just as it was about to be renovated.

From the square, Rue Ravignan leads to **Place des Abesses**, and its remarkable art-nouveau Metro station, designed by Guimard. At No 9 Rue Yvonne-Le-Duc Ignatius Loyola and François Xavier founded the Society of Jesus, the Jesuits, in 1534, on the site of St Denis' decapitation.

To the east of Montmartre is the little visited district of **La Goutte-d'Or**. This close-knit quarter is undergoing rapid renovation, and the old workers' hovels are being razed for new developments. Visit this small area while the antiquated charm of its workshops and apartment blocks, vividly described by Zola in *L'Assomoir*, survives. The present-day conglomeration of Islamic butchers, African grocers, West-Indian bakers, Jewish jewellers and Arab tailors is a never-ending spectacle of sight, sound and smell. More than 30 nationalities live side-by-side in the streets around Rue de la Goutte-d'Or, Rue de la Charbonnière, and Rue des Poissoniers.

This is the place to hunt for that artist's smock or 1970s disco dress: **Tati** on Boulevard Rochechouart is the king of cut-price clothes stores.

A cosy restaurant on the hill.

THE LEFT BANK

The **Latin Quarter** is the ancient heart of the Rive Gauche or Left Bank, an intimate puzzle of small streets and historic architecture covering the 5th and 6th *arrondissements*. Here, thanks to the concentration of academic institutions, Latin was virtually the mother tongue until the Revolution in 1789. The quarter spreads from the crossroads of Boulevard St Germain and Boulevard St Michel, stretching out to encompass the Jardin du Luxembourg to the south, and the Jardin des Plantes to the east. The elegant and chic hide in neighbouring St Germain-des-Prés and flirtatious Montparnasse.

Birthplace of Paris, cradle of philosophy and art since the middle ages, the Latin Quarter conjures up contradictions and delights in paradox. As student and poet of the Latin Quarter, François Villon wrote in 1456: "I laugh in tears." Villon debated with professors at the Sorbonne and drank with thieves in the brothels of St Michel.

His legacy of rebellion has survived. It was here in May 1968 that demonstrations against deteriorating conditions in the Nanterre faculty led to students tearing up the old cobblestones of Boulevard St Michel to hurl at riot police. Hundreds of students were arrested, the University of Paris was decentralised, and the ancient cobbles were eternally buried under concrete. More importantly at the time, however, the riots spread nationwide through a disenchanted population, and General Charles de Gaulle was forced to leave Paris and give up the presidency of France. Protests, albeit subdued, persist in the quarter today, and roads are sometimes blocked by squatting students, eager to relive the glorious past of their revolutionary predecessors.

The Latin Quarter is still a place of happy incongruity, where countless Greek *souvlaki* vendors stand amidst traditional cafés, and new wave cinemas front ancient academic facades. The area maintains a roguish charm in its beautiful tree-lined streets, manicured parks and imposing monuments, as well as an intellectual arrogance that manages to stay just the right side of pretentious. This is the place to stroll, imbibe and look cool. Sit in the shaded parks by day and scan the menus in the fairy-lit streets by night. Be warned, though: this is not the place to go looking for typical Parisian cuisine.

By the bridge: Across the river from the palaces of justice and salvation (the Préfecture de Police and Notre Dame), **Place St Michel** revels in recklessness. The fountain depicting St Michael and a surprised dragon often seems buried under scooters, lip-locked lovers and the ubiquitous tramps (*clochards*), sitting philosophically amidst youthful chaos. Extending south, the grand **Boulevard St Michel** ("Boul' Mich" to the initiated) will nourish the senses, the mind, and the stomach, with its array of

stalls, bookshops, alternative cinemas and fast food joints.

At the crossroads of Boul' Mich and Boulevard St Germain stands the 15th-century **Hôtel de Cluny**, now a museum. Within these Gothic walls is one of the world's finest collections of medieval artefacts, including exquisite tapestries. Here too are remains of the Roman baths, built by the guild of boatmen in AD 3. As elsewhere in their empire, the Romans decided to civilise a barbarian people with hot baths and mindless violence. To the east of the Cluny baths is the ancient gladiatorial arena, the **Arènes de Lutèce**, half-way to the Jardin de Plantes. These days the arena serves as a children's playground and echoes to the lazy clink of *pétanque* balls on shady afternoons.

Centres of learning: In a reversal of history, Greeks now seem to have overrun Romans in the streets leading from the Cluny baths, where Greek restaurants of dubious pedigree vie for custom with a ferociousness rarely seen outside Athens. Continue south down Boul' Mich to the eternal pulse of the Latin Quarter, **La Sorbonne**. Founded in 1253, the oldest university in France has been rebuilt many times since its inception as a dormitory for theologians. Here you can wander through galleries to the 17th-century **chapel**, soaking up wisdom. The chapel was commissioned by Sorbonne alumni Cardinal Richelieu, and houses his tomb. Above hangs the Cardinal's hat, which will fall, legend has it, when Richelieu is released from hell. The Sorbonne is no longer the omnipotent force it used to be and, following decentralisation, there are now 13 universities in the Paris region.

Next door on Rue St Jacques is the school where Jean-Paul Sartre taught, **Lycée Louis-le-Grand**. Baudelaire was expelled from here; other old boys include Molière, Victor Hugo and Georges Pompidou.

Two doors down, dominating the summit of Mt Ste-Geneviève, the **Panthéon** is the sort of domed monument famous

The rooftops of further education.

people would die to be buried in, completed following Louis XV's rash vow to build a church should he recover from illness in 1744. Money was short, however, and public lotteries were organised to raise funds. The building was finished just in time for the Revolution, and the church was designated the resting place of the "Founders of Liberty", a place to rival the Royal Mausoleum at St Denis. Thus Voltaire and Rousseau lie in the crypt, as do later additions, Victor Hugo, Emile Zola and Louis Braille, inventor of writing for the blind.

Across Place Ste Geneviève rises the richly ornate church of **Ste Etienne-du-Mont**. Writer Racine and the scientist Pascal are buried here, and a marble slab near the entrance marks the spot where the archbishop of Paris was stabbed to death by a priest in 1857. To the right of the chancel historically-minded Paris lovers would do well to give thanks at the shrine of Ste Geneviève for the salvation of Paris from the hordes of Attila the Hun in AD 451.

Next door, the prestigious **Ecole Polytechnique** was the scene of poet François Villon's most famous heist, when on Christmas Eve 1457 he broke in to his own university and lifted 500 gold coins (he was found out five years later and imprisoned at Le Châtelet).

Northeast of the Sorbonne is the equally bohemian district of **Maubert and St Séverin**. Cross Rue des Ecoles to **Musée de la Police**, an intriguing jumble of macabre objects, weapons and documents, including a menu proposing "rat stew à la Robert". Cinema aficionados should pop into Action Ecoles or Action Rive Gauche (23 and 5 Rue des Ecoles) for quirky film classics, both American and French.

Latin lanes: At this point **Boulevard St Germain** mixes extravagant shop windows with restaurants and sumptuous patisseries. **La Quincaillerie** at No 4, offers high-tech, and therefore expensive, home utensils from Paris's top design stars, such as Mario Botta. From Place Maubert you should stroll north-

The Panthéon.

wards down the small medieval streets to the Seine, where jumbled boutiques reveal their shadowy interiors to the curious. **Shakespeare and Company** on Rue de la Bûcherie is Paris's most famous English bookshop, containing a menagerie of literature from the Bard to Beatniks. Founded by Sylvia Beach, the original *librairie* was home to a motley collection of American writers in the 1920s, from Gertrude Stein to Ernest Hemingway. The shop closes at midnight, too soon for the addicted.

From here insomniacs should head for **Le Petit Pont**, and the lights of the Seine. Here the Quais St Michel and Montebello combine picture-book views of the Île de la Cité with a ramshackle riverside charm. By day ancient bookstalls line the riverbanks, offering overpriced, antique volumes. Cine-addicts gather at **Studio Galande** on Rue Galande, which offers nightly showings of *The Rocky Horror Picture Show*, complete with transvestites and rice-throwing. For more historical inspira-

tion, take Rue du Fouarre, named after the bales of hay which served as seats for students during open-air lectures in the Middle Ages. Dante sat here in 1304. Further on, trial by revolutionary council has been replaced with trial by jazz at **Caveau de la Huchette** (5 Rue de la Huchette). Danton and Robespierre selected guillotine victims in the cellars where Maxim Saury now executes dixie stomps to great acclaim. Five doors down, at No 10, a young Napoleon dreamed of world domination.

Refuge from *souvlaki* and Vespa fumes is to be found in the church of **St Julien-le-Pauvre** on the tiny square Viviani, overshadowed by Notre Dame. Pass quickly through the intimate interior to sit under the second oldest tree in Paris, and contemplate those who have done the same over the past 300 years. The neighbouring **Eglise de St Séverin** is famous for its mighty organ loft. The church has been a place of pageantry since the Fourth Crusade set out from St Séverin to conquer the Holy Land in

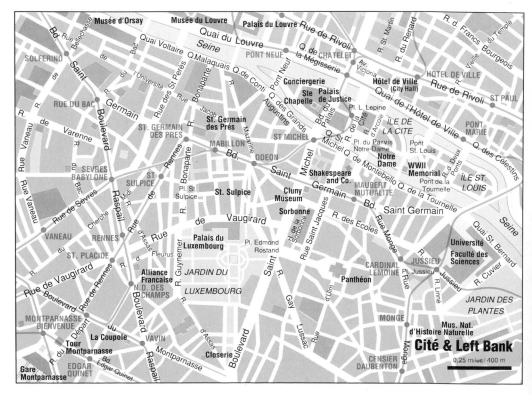

1204. The adjacent cemetery witnessed the world's first gallstone operation, carried out on a death-row criminal in 1744, who was pardoned following the operation's success.

South of the Sorbonne: The area around **Rue Mouffetard** is one of the most ancient and colourful in France. To the right of the Panthéon Rue de l'Estrapade leads to **Place de la Contrescarpe**, a beautifully restored square. In the corner house (No 1) Rabelais composed risqué rhymes in the tradition of his predecessor, François Villon.

Just off the square, Ernest Hemingway moved into his first Parisian residence at 74 Rue du Cardinal Lemoine. He idealised La Contrescarpe as a place of danger and excitement, yet with gentrification the district has lost some of its edge, and gained a refined charm.

Rue Mouffetard itself is an intriguing blend of ethnic fast-food and medieval passages; a place to discover. Walk down its cobbles in the early morning to the most enjoyable street market in Paris, a lively riot of bright vegetables and North African dialects. On your stroll note the ancient shop fronts – the carved oak at No 69, where a dance hall of ill-repute flourished in the 19th century – and narrow passages, at Nos 101 and 104. At No 122, towards the bottom of the hill, the well carved onto the facade dates from Henri IV (1590).

The cemetery of the small **Eglise St Médard** next door was the scene of cult hysterics in the 18th century. Parisians flocked to the tomb of a young priest whose ghost was said to cure all ailments. Things got out of hand, and the graveyard was closed by Louis XV, with a perfunctory notice: "On the King's orders, it is forbidden for God to perform miracles in this place."

Greenery: Terrestrial miracles abound in the **Jardin des Plantes**, the Parisian botanical gardens. To the east of Rue Mouffetard, this large park is a verdant retreat from the bustle of the city. Opened in 1650, the gardens were originally conceived as a farm for plants which were to be used to cure the King, and every explorer or missionary returning to Paris would present a seed or two to earn royal favour.

The wild and wonderful collection that resulted includes a Lebanese cedar planted in 1734 (legend states that the botanist Bernard de Jussieu brought it from Syria, keeping it alive in his hat with daily water rations), and a 2,000-year-old American sequoia trunk. The Alpine garden and winter garden hothouse attract the amateur and specialist alike, whilst the box hedge maze, life-size dinosaurs and small dishevelled zoo are children's favourites. The reptile and insect vivarium are not for the squeamish, and if the assorted llamas, bears, dromedaries and porcupines look sad, it might be in mourning for their ancestors, devoured by starving Parisians during the Prussian siege of 1870. More ancient remains are found in the palaeontology and zoological galleries; the latter has been recently renovated.

For a riverside stroll, take the Quai St

Rue Mouffetard market.

Bernard, and the Jardin des Sculptures en Plein Air, a lively park-cum-modern sculpture exhibition.

Just outside the southern gates of the Jardin de Plantes the green and white elegance of the **Paris Mosque** is a subtle reminder of Parisian ties with the Arab world. Built in 1922 by three French architects, the Mosque commemorates North African participation in World War I. The carvings and tiles, interior courtyard and arcades are delicately impressive. In addition to the thickly-carpeted Mosque, there is a library (where the Aga Khan married Rita Hayworth), a restaurant and a *salon de thé*. Next door, do not miss luxuriating in the **Hamman** (Turkish bath), followed by mint tea while reclining alongside the small courtyard fountain; an imperative for walk-weary limbs.

To venture further into the Orient, head northwest to the **Institut du Monde Arabe**, at the west end of Quai St Bernard. One of President Mitterrand's numerous *grands projets*, the nine-sto-rey palace of glass, aluminium and concrete was built by France and 20 Arab countries. Egypt did not participate until 1989, due to French ties with Israel, but the institute has subsequently entertained Yasser Arafat and has agreed to receive a future Palestinian state into its membership. Politics aside, the museum is a fascinating voyage around the Muslim world. Finish your visit on the 9th-floor roof, where the restaurant's breathtaking view over the city is accompanied by strangely non-Arab, Gallic dishes.

For more traditional fare, at a traditionally exorbitant price, pop in next door to **La Tour d'Argent** (15 Quai de la Tournelle) for Michelin three-star cuisine, five-star service, and 10-star bills. The young Henri IV ate here when it was opened in 1582 – but then, as Mel Brooks once remarked, "It's good to be the king."

Westwards: Across Boul' Mich from the Sorbonne, the **Odéon district** nestles halfway between the boisterous

The Paris Mosque.

Quartier Latin and the refined elegance of St Germain-des-Prés. The antiquated charm of its streets belies the area's bustling nightlife, which is as inspired and dedicated as any in the city. **Place de l'Odéon** is one of the livelier squares in Paris, especially at two o'clock in the morning. Here the **Odéon Théâtre de l'Europe** has large-scale productions of foreign language theatre (Ibsen, Miller etc), whilst the smaller **Petit Odéon** features avant-garde works. In 1968 the theatre was occupied by students who donned Roman helmets from the props department to protect themselves during battles with the police.

Revolution is the district's speciality; revolutionary leader Danton's statue at the **Carrefour de l'Odéon** on the Boulevard St Germain marks his old house, and Camille Desmoulins lived at No 2 before storming the Bastille. The rest of the revolutionaries of 1789 plotted in neighbouring streets to the north, which now host some of the more bourgeois boutiques and apartments in Paris.

Just south of the square at 26 Rue de Condé, Beaumarchais wrote *The Barber of Seville* in 1773, a play whose theme of man usurping the nobility prefigured the rebellion of the man in the street. Just north of Odéon Metro, the symbol of the revolution – the guillotine – was invented at **No 9 Cour du Commerce St André**. It was intended as "a philanthropic decapitating machine" and theoretically destined to facilitate the death of animals in slaughterhouses.

The charm of the surrounding streets belies its bloody past. Pass along Rue St André-des-Arts, Rue Gît-le-Coeur, Rue Suger and Cour de Rohan, with its 16th-century facades. At 1 Place de l'Odéon **Café Voltaire** was the watering-hole of the man himself, as well as Diderot. The tormented poets Verlaine and Mallarmé were also regulars, as were (somewhat later) the lost Americans, Hemingway and F. Scott Fitzgerald, who extolled its "sudden provincial quality." Fitzgerald finished *The Great Gatsby* a few blocks to the south at 58 Rue de Vaugirard, on

Islamic Parisians.

the doorstep of the world's most romantic gardens.

A Parisian favourite: No statistics exist relating exactly how many people have fallen in love in the **Jardin du Luxembourg**, but if poets as miserable as Baudelaire and Verlaine had a good time here, the garden's magic is evidently potent. Breathless lovers meet under the plane trees by the Fontaine de Médicis and stroll to the central pool to watch children push model sailing ships across the carp-filled water. Queens of France gaze benignly down from the terrace, whilst the thwack of tennis balls disturbs the reverie of Chanel-dressed nannies pushing designer babies in designer prams. On Wednesday and weekends the famous Guignol puppet show takes place in the **Théâtre des Marionettes**. More serious entertainment is located at the corner with Rue de Vaugirard, where bearded old men take on earnest students at outdoor chess tables amidst the fragrance of orange trees. There are 200 varieties of apples and pears in the gardens, and the beehives produce several hundred kilos of honey a year. Here, in the midst of Paris, you can take lessons in bee-keeping.

The **Palais du Luxembourg** was built on the site of the legendary haunt of Vauvert, a 13th-century bandit who terrorised the quarter until he was kicked out by Carthusian monks in 1257. It was the monks who founded the tree nursery at the south of the gardens. The palace itself was built by Marie de Médicis on the site of a mansion belonging to Duke François of Luxembourg (hence the name), in the style of the Pitti Palace in Florence. During the Revolution it was the final prison for those awaiting the guillotine, and in World War II the Germans made it their headquarters for the Occupation. Now lucky French Senators enjoy its Restoration interior and luxurious views of the gardens, for it is the seat of the Sénat (the Upper House of Parliament, as chosen by an electoral college of politicians). The even luckier President of the Senate gets to live next

The Jardin des Plantes.

door, at the **Petit Luxembourg**. Ernest Hemingway, by his own admission, adored the Jardin de Luxembourg. His three principal residences during the 1920s neatly circumscribe the park, where he would saunter each afternoon. As he wrote later; "It was sad when the park was closed, and I was sad walking around it instead of through it."

Hemingway haunts: To the south and west of the gardens, the district of **Montparnasse** was the hub of Hemingway's Paris, known simply as **The Quarter**. You did not actually have to live here to belong in The Quarter, as Jake Barnes explains in *The Sun Also Rises*; "Perfectly good Quarterites live outside the actual boundaries of Montparnasse. They can live anywhere, as long as they come to the Quarter to think." Hemingway's first novel was written at the **Closerie des Lilas**, one of the many fashionable bars along Boulevard Montparnasse. The tables are inscribed with the names of its illustrious clients: Lenin, Modigliani and André Breton. Fittingly, Hemingway's plaque rests on the bar.

Other 1920s haunts include **Le Dôme**, a favourite of Sartre, **La Coupole** (art deco restored, 450 tables and late-night dancing) and **La Rotonde**, where the 19th-century poet Gérard de Nerval used to walk his pet lobster on a lead. At Metro Vavin, Rodin's dramatic **Statue de Balzac**, once despised, is now adored.

The district around the Montparnasse tower was christened Mount Parnassus (after the classical home of Apollo and his muses) by a local Dead Poets' Society in the 18th century, which gathered on quarry mounds to recite verse. In 1900, when the "bohemians" decamped from Montmartre, Modigliani, Chagall and Léger set up ateliers here, followed by Picasso. Magnificent studios still exist along Boulevard Raspail (peek in at Studio Raspail at No 216), Rue Froidevaux opposite the cemetery, and Boulevard Montparnasse (pass through to the second courtyard at No 126).

The world was here in the 1920s –

The Jardin du Luxembourg.

Lenin, Trotsky, Stravinsky, Man Ray, Cocteau, and the Americans (Stein, Miller, Fitzgerald, Hemingway) – as well as thousands of mere mortals, in particular Bretons, fleeing rural poverty and famine in Brittany. Consequently, Montparnasse is *the* place for crêpes, cider and wild bagpipe dances.

The district is now dominated by the **Tour Montparnasse**, 59 storeys of skyscraper inaugurated in 1973, a monument to high aspirations and low taste. The tower has one asset; from its top floor you cannot see the Tour Montparnasse. Two hundred metres (660 ft) below, the old railway station has been redeveloped, and a Japanese firm has concreted over the tracks for yet more office blocks, doubtless causing locals to turn in their graves in the densely populated, star-studded **Montparnasse Cemetery**, off Boulevard Raspail. Beer bottles and grass mark many tombs here, but the top 10 are still worth homage – Baudelaire, Beckett, Maupassant, Saint-Saëns, Sartre and de Beauvoir (together,

as always), 2CV king André Citroën, the artists Man Ray and Soutine, and a young newcomer, the singer Serge Gainsbourg.

Rattle them bones: Older bones overflow from Paris's most macabre attraction, the **Catacombs** (2 Place Denfert-Rochereau). Roman quarries became ossuaries in 1785, when millions of dead Parisians were relocated from cemeteries to make way for fresh corpses. The skeletons are stacked in miles of underground passages – a canine Nirvana. Take a torch, and preferably someone to hold your hand, but you have been warned – the inscription on the ossuary door reads: "Stop. Here begins the empire of the dead."

Escape from mortality to the east of Montparnasse cemetery, where, in **Rue de la Gaîté**, 19th-century merriment has been overrun by the fast-food and sex-shop industries. Bars and boutiques here are still vivacious – stop for a drink at Le Café d'Edgar, a family-fun, old style café-theatre. Fashion enthusiasts **La Procope.**

who've come this far should head a considerable distance south to **Rue d'Alésia** for designer outlet shops – cheaper than your average chic.

War in Spain, and then in the world, curtailed the gay Paris of Montparnasse. Art gave way to philosophy, and the intelligentsia moved north to the historical centre of literary Paris, **St Germain-des-Prés**. Here, elegant streets house elegant boutiques.

The **Place St Sulpice** and its Visconti fountain are dominated by the huge bastide front of the **Eglise de St Sulpice**. Apart from a fine organ, and Delacroix's *Saul and the Angel* (modelled on the painter's own struggle with Art), the great cavern of a church has little to offer. Outside, Catherine Deneuve (when she's in town) gazes down from her windows at the drunks in the square and the Roman Catholic tea shops on Rue du Vieux Colombier.

Heading north to the Boulevard St Germain, stop at the covered **Marché St Germain**, Rue Mabillon, for chromatic vegetables and colourful characters. Open-air stalls can be found across the Boulevard on Rue de Buci.

Coffee and existentialism: St Germain-des-Prés introduced coffee and existentialism to Paris, proving that there is meaning to life, if only in a morning espresso. At **La Procope** (13 Rue de l'Ancienne-Comédie), coffee made its Parisian debut in 1686. By World War II, writers of any repute would spend hours each day at their favourite table. **Les Deux Magots** (6 Place St Germain-des-Prés) diversified, and now serves the best hot chocolate in Paris. Verlaine and Rimbaud composed verse here, but it was left to Jean-Paul Sartre (Jean Saul-Partre to his friends) and Simone de Beauvoir to consolidate the highbrow reputation of the establishment. They smoked three ashtrays a day whilst chewing over existence. The waiters have less time to contemplate philosophy – according to scientific study they cover 12 km (7½ miles) a day.

Still popular with Left Bank *penseurs*

St Sulpice.

and posers is the **Café de Flore** next door, another Sartrean favourite. Politicians congregate at Paris's most famous brasserie across the road, **Lipp.**

The heart of St Germain-des-Prés is its **church**, the oldest in Paris, dating from 990. Ransacked and rebuilt over centuries, the resulting building is a none-too-subtle blend of simple Romanesque and pretentious baroque. In the small square alongside, Picasso's **Homage to Apollinaire** stands under the steeple. From the square take Rue Fürstenburg past the Delacroix museum (No 6), where the painter lived, worked and died. This is one of the most romantic corners of Paris, especially following the removal of the benches much loved by tramps. The white globed lamps and horse chestnuts inspire poetry and black and white photographs.

The elegant style pervades the whole district, and in the side-streets are some of the most fashionable boutiques this side of the river. Try Issey Miyake's **Plantation** (17 Boulevard Raspail) for

the maestro's cheaper range, look in on **Kashiyama** (147 Boulevard St Germain), or alternatively just follow the supermodel lookalikes laden with designer bags. On the way north to the Seine, pass along **Rue Visconti**, first populated in 1540. Racine died at No 24, Balzac set up a print-shop at No 17.

Language minders: A dictionary's throw from the river squats the majestic **Institut de France**, incorporating the **Académie Française**. The illustrious academy, created by Richelieu in 1635, safeguards the French language, compiling *the* French Dictionary (no "jogging", "camping", or "marketing" in sight, despite the common useage in France). It is almost more famous for those luminaries refused admission to its ranks – Descartes, Pascal, Molière, Rousseau, Diderot, Balzac, Proust and Zola, amongst others. The Academy has only ever selected four women to its ranks, proving that *fraternité* comes before *égalité*.

Next door is the **Hôtel des Monnaies**, the former royal mint. The architect Antoine so liked his creation that he lived in the building until his death in 1801. It is now a museum of money, and not for the easily bored.

Along the Seine the **Quai des Grands Augustins** is the oldest on the river, a facade of ancient bookshops and antique dealers. Picasso lived for 20 years on corresponding Rue des Grands Augustins. To the west, Quai Malaquais is home to Paris's finest art school, **l'Ecole des Beaux-Arts**, which holds public exhibitions of student work. Predictably, numerous galleries adorn this, Picasso's old stamping ground. **Galerie Adrien Maeght**, originated by Pablo's old friend of the same name, is still the most famous (42-46 Rue du Bac), although **Isy Brachot** (35 Rue Guénégaud) is decidedly more trendy.

End your day on the left bank on the **Pont des Arts**, which leads from the Institut de France to the Louvre. The iron bridge is pedestrian-only. Stop, look, and breathe in Paris at twilight.

Wise youth on the Pont des Arts.

L'ACADÉMIE FRANÇAISE

Traditionally seated at dinner parties above government ministers and just below cardinals and princes of royal blood are the 40 members of the Académie Française, popularly known as the "Immortals". They are the watchdogs of the French language, protecting it from the insidious onslaught of English, and to be admitted to their salubrious ranks is the ultimate honour to which all *hommes de lettres* aspire.

The Académie is a symbol of the importance the French attach to their language. Yet, paradoxically, it is an institution almost impossible to define. Simply put, it is uncertain what its members actually do. Apart from interminably tinkering with a dictionary designed to uphold the purity of the French language, the Académie serves no visible purpose, except perhaps to fulfil a deep-seated desire for grandeur. Even the Immortals themselves are confused about their role. Poet Paul Valbey summed it up: "We are what we believe we are, and what others believe we are, and neither we nor anyone else can say exactly what that is."

The Académie was founded in 1635 by Louis XIII at the prompting of Cardinal Richelieu. Its members were set the task of composing a dictionary and charged "to work with all possible care and diligence to give strict rules to our language and to make it pure, eloquent and capable of dealing with the arts and sciences." Louis XIV generously donated 660 volumes from his personal library, 40 goose quills and a lesson in equality. When one of the members, a cardinal, protested that his rank entitled him to a more comfortable seat than the straight-backed chairs used by the other academicians, Louis sent 40 of the now famous *fauteuils* (armchairs).

The Académie hit a rocky patch during the Revolution when, in 1793, it was accused of being infected with "the incurable gangrene of aristocracy". Three members were guillotined in the Place de la Concorde, two committed suicide and three died in prison. Restored by Napoleon in 1803, the Académie was ensconced in Cardinal Mazarin's former palace and urged to get on with the job of sprucing up the language.

A vacancy on the Académie occurs only after an Academician's death. While eligibility is simple (candidates must be of French nationality), getting elected is difficult. Voltaire was so desperate, he was driven to write obsequious verses praising Louis XV and he even denied authorship of his free-thinking *Lettres Philosophiques*. He made it on his third try. Victor Hugo's campaign lasted seven years until he was accepted on his fourth attempt in 1841.

Émile Zola was unsuccessful 24 times. The conservative Immortals disliked the realism of his novels and were wary of his courage in the Dreyfus Affair. Others who failed were the literary giants Molière, Balzac and Baudelaire. Women have been admitted only since 1980, with French-American author Marguerite Yourcenar the first. In its new spirit of non-chauvinism, the Académie now boasts four women members.

Not all are geniuses — one member is the author of a history of women's undergarments. As minor 19th-century novelist and Immortal Ludovic Halévy said: "Some Academicians are talented, others aren't. The latter are especially worthy of respect because they made it without talent." ∎

Immortal, in stone.

THE EIFFEL TOWER AND THE INVALIDES

Crossing Rue des Saints-Pères from the 6th to the 7th *arrondissement* is like stepping into a dream. Along polished boulevards stand ornate palaces, golden domed churches and iron towers. Immaculately-dressed people slip in and out of hushed courtyards, through immense wooden doors, behind high stone walls. No existential torment here, just the continuation of history. This is the way it was, is and always will be.

The 7th *arrondissement* is one of the most spectacular – and one of the quietest – in Paris. When Parisian nobility moved out of the Marais in the 18th century, and Versailles tumbled, the rich and famous built new town houses across the river from the Tuileries. The Boulevard St-Germain was the place to be and be seen. Unscathed by Haussmann's hand in the 19th century, the sumptuous *hôtels* (mansions) remain excessively beautiful. Now dedicated to embassies and government ministries, the secret courtyards of Laclos's *Liaisons Dangereuses* are still home to the nobility of Paris. Glimpses through the shuttered security are rare, but occasional open doorways reveal fountains and tropical plants, statues and soaring stairways. Rue de Grenelle and Rue de Varenne still retain an accessible charm.

Although graced by some of the world's most famous monuments, the district is surprisingly barren after dark and at weekends. When the civil servants and politicians go home the avenues are empty, and only the riverside walk, adorned with lights, welcomes the wandering visitor.

Symbol of Paris: Commanding the 7th *arrondissement*, and most of the city, with its presence, the **Eiffel Tower** symbolises Paris. Used in James Bond and Superman films, among many others, the Tower is a world superstar. Whereas many monuments prove disappointing, the Eiffel continues to impress, even

though it has been long, long overtaken as the world's tallest building. Like some prehistoric behemoth stopping to drink at the riverside, it is the most impassive inhabitant of Paris, impervious to the daily chaos at its feet. When Eiffel's icon of iron bars was chosen as centrepiece to the World Fair of 1889, agitation overwhelmed the artistic community of the time. The Opéra architect Charles Garnier and the writer Guy de Maupassant were the most vocal opponents, Maupassant organising a protest picnic under the tower's four legs – "the only place out of sight of the wretched construction."

But the public (always a better judge) loved it. Surviving a proposal for its dismantlement in 1909, when the placing of a radio transmitter at the top saved the day, the tower is now swarmed by 4 million visitors a year. Climb the first two floors on foot, and then elevate to the top (queues are as impressive as the tower – arrive early). The view, especially at dusk, is miraculous. At night

Preceding pages and **left**, new angles on the symbol of Paris. **Right**, in Les Invalides.

Paris appears as a horizontal Christmas tree of dancing illuminations stretching to the horizon, and the tower is transformed into a skeletal x-ray, lit by arc lights.

At its birth, the Eiffel Tower was the tallest building in the world. A masterpiece of engineering, its 9.1 million kg (10,000 tons) of iron exerts a pressure at the base of 4 kg (9lbs) per cm, the equivalent of the weight of a man sitting on a chair. On hot days the Tower grows, even as much as 15cm (6 inches).

For the best pictures of the Tower, cross the **Pont d'Iéna** up to the Palais de Chaillot and a quick step into the 16th *arrondissement* (the richest in Paris). From here, looking back over the cascading fountains and gold statues of **Trocadéro**, the Eiffel Tower is at its most magnificent.

Palace of museums: Trocadéro was baptised in 1827, following the re-enactment on this spot of a French victory at Fort Trocadéro in Southern Spain. Earlier, Napoleon had started work here on a palace for his son, but the Battle of Waterloo intervened. Today, against the backdrop of the Palais de Chaillot, the terraces and grassy banks welcome the capital's most flamboyant skateboarders and roller-bladers. In summer, when the giant hosepipe fountains are on, the large pond descending to the river becomes an impromptu (and illegal) swimming pool.

Away from African street merchants selling "authentic" Senegalese and Camerooni plastic necklaces, elephants and walking sticks, the **Palais de Chaillot** stands firmly and neo-classically on the hill. Jacques Carlu's design for the 1937 World Fair, the curved winged edifice contains four museums and a 1,000-seat theatre. The **Naval Museum** is for boat lovers, and includes the windsurf board that crossed the Atlantic (in 38 days) in 1985; the **Museum of Mankind** has mummies, shrunken heads, exquisite crystal skulls and 400 musical instruments from around the world; the **Museum of**

The École Militaire seen from Eiffel.

French Monuments, with its reproductions from around France, means you can sight-see the country without leaving the capital; and for cinema addicts, the **Museum of Cinema** traces celluloid history and the **Cinemathèque** shows four films daily.

To the east, at Place d'Iéna, the small **Musée Guimet** is one of the world's finest oriental museums, for lovers of silk, porcelain and jade. Next door, in the Palais de Tokyo, the much underrated **Musée d'Art Moderne de Paris** contains celebrity attractions, such as Picasso, Matisse, Modigliani and Soutine, and the world's largest painting, Dufy's *Fée de l'Eléctricité* (Fairy of Electricity), a celebration of energy.

Head quarters: Back across the river on the Rive Gauche, the **Champ de Mars** leads from the Eiffel Tower to the **Ecole Militaire**, still the centre of French military know-how. The ex-parade ground, where Napoleon stamped his stuff in 1784, having been admitted to the school on the recommendation that he would make a good sailor, is now a haven of peace, love and picnics. This is a place to get a suntan, kiss, or kick a football amongst pristine rose bushes, while the whistle-piping park attendants fight a losing battle for order and decorum. At the far end, the French military academy is an imposing 18th-century building where Napoleon graduated to Lieutenant, with the mention that he might go far, if circumstances allowed.

Behind this university of war is the foundation for reconciliation and understanding, the **UNESCO** headquarters. The graceful Y-shape of the building was designed by American, French and Italian architects. Inside, 142 countries cooperate in educational, scientific and cultural projects. Its decoration is equally cosmopolitan, including Miró ceramics, Moore sculptures, a Calder mobile, a Picasso painting, a Japanese garden and a spine-shivering relic from our nuclear age – a stone angel discovered after the atomic bomb blast at Nagasaki.

Along the Seine, the **Esplanade des**

The Palais de Chaillot frames the Tower.

Invalides is another stretch of grass much loved by strollers and sports fanatics. Here, suited businessmen kick footballs during their lunch break, whilst civil servants flick frisbees. The west side of the park is dedicated to matters more serious than politics; a series of *boules* courts.

Les Invalides, rising from its Esplanade, is dramatic yet delicate, as befits a one-time pensioners' retreat and mausoleum. Built by war-loving Louis XIV as a retirement home for his soldiers in 1676, the buildings once housed 4,000 men. It was here that revolutionaries seized 28,000 guns for the storming of the Bastille in 1789. The great courtyard, with its imposing arcades and array of captured cannons now hosts the odd military parade as well as society wedding ceremonies.

Inside, the **Musée de l'Armée** offers an extensive glimpse of man's inhumanity, and skill at warfare – terrifying selections of weapons, armour and poignant reminders of the two world wars, including the original copy of Adolf Hitler's *Mein Kampf.*

At the heart of the Invalides lies the heart of an empire. The beautiful **Dome Church**, the masterpiece of Louis XIV's reign, contains the body of Napoleon. Returned to France in 1840, following much wrangling with the British, the little emperor was given a state funeral during which a snowstorm enveloped the city. His coffin was opened for two minutes, in the presence of select guests. It was noted that, although dead for 19 years, the body was in a perfect condition, although the emperor's toe-nails had grown, tearing his socks.

Napoleon, never one to underplay things, lies in six coffins, one inside the other like a Russian doll – white iron, mahogany, two in lead, then ebony and then oak, on a base of green Vosges granite. The interior of the Emperor's resting place is predictably over-the-top, with 12 damsels, symbolising his 12 military campaigns, guarding the coffin. Hitler fell in love with the decor

Les Invalides.

on his visit here in 1940. High above the tomb, the dome is the most breathtaking in Paris, if not the world, thanks in part to its new coat of gold leaf, regilded for bicentennial celebrations in 1989.

Tea and deputies: If pomp and circumstance get too much, refuge is to be found nearby at **La Pagode**, Paris's most interesting cinema and tea house. An incongruous jewel on Rue de Babylone, the pagoda was built by a Japanese devotee as a society ball room in 1896. Almost bought by the Chinese as an embassy (until they found pictures of Japanese soldiers killing Chinese on the walls), it was saved from ruin with money from the film director Louis Malle. The tea is strong, the gardens tropical, and the films up-to-date.

Boulevard St Germain, which begins up by the river at Boulevard des Invalides, is the seat of French government. On the river itself, the colonnaded **Assemblée Nationale**, **Palais Bourbon**, is the French House of Parliament. The extravagant columns were grafted onto an 18th-century facade by Napoleon to complement his Madeleine project across the river, and are now home to heavily-armed police, protecting the 491 *députés* (members of Parliament).

Outside, the view from **Pont de la Concorde** is predictably stunning. To the south, on Rue de Varenne (Road of the Rabbit Warren), stands the residence of the French Prime Minister, **Hôtel Matignon**. It was here that the socialist leader Pierre Bérégovoy lived before defeat in elections in April 1993, and his subsequent suicide following May Day celebrations.

Numerous other residences adorn the streets, mostly behind heavily secured gates, since only French ministries and foreign governments can afford the rent (along with the odd Greek arms dealer). On Boulevard Raspail (No 45) stands **Hôtel Lutétia**, its extravagant statued facade fronting a deluxe four-star hotel where Charles de Gaulle enjoyed his first night of married life. When the hotel was requisitioned by the Gestapo

The Rodin Museum in Hôtel Biron.

in 1940, the owner bricked up the vintage wine cellar and, even though the hotel staff were interrogated to reveal the whereabouts of the finest wine collection in the capital, no one talked.

Northwards, the **Rue de Grenelle** is bursting with beautiful buildings, including the Swiss and Dutch embassies, the Ministry of Education and the National Geographic Institute. Poet Alfred de Musset lived at No 59 before embarking on an oriental voyage of discovery with Georges Sand.

At the east end of the street, the grandiose **Fontaine des Quatre Saisons** was a monumental response to a local complaint about lack of water. At the opposite end is situated one of the few *hôtels* open to the public: the **Hôtel Biron** now houses the unmissable **Musée Rodin**, which contains the best of the sculptor's work.

Huge talent: One of the world's smallest artists (at 1.65 metres/5 ft 4 inches), Rodin was born in the Latin Quarter, and grew up wandering the markets of Rue Mouffetard. Rejected by the École des Beaux-Arts, he trained himself, visiting the zoo at the Jardin des Plantes, and horse markets on the Boulevard St Michel for inspiration. Further stimulus came from his incessant love affairs, which were interrupted only momentarily when the sculptor took holy orders, following the death of his sister in a convent after she had been rejected in love by one of Rodin's close friends. Chastity did not suit him, however, and he returned a year later to art.

Rodin's first work of critical acclaim was *The Age of Bronze* in 1877, a naked youth caressing his hair, modelled by a Belgian soldier. The establishment was shocked, maintaining that the statue was too lifelike to be regarded as art. A card stuck to the work at the Salon read "Beware – moulded from the body of the model". Eventually the French government bought the statue, and Rodin's reputation was made. He came to live in the Hôtel Biron (ironically a former convent) in 1904. As rent, he donated

The Musée d'Orsay.

his best works to the state, and the museum overflows with excellence.

Here are *The Kiss* (removed from the Chicago World Fair of 1893 for being too shocking), *The Thinker* (reputedly Dante contemplating the Inferno), *The Burghers of Calais*, and lesser works; the excruciating *La Douleur* (Suffering), *Le Cri* (Scream) and *La Pleureuse* (the Weeper).

Set in beautiful gardens, recently restored to their white marble finish, the statues ripple with life, and small children often approach *The Thinker* to ask him what the matter is. Also included in the exhibition are works by Camille Claudel, most famous of Rodin's countless mistresses.

Consumer corner: Along **Rue du Bac** (named after the ferry which transported stone to build the Tuileries) are numerous fashion-conscious boutiques and food shops. At the corner with Rue de Sèvres stands Paris's first department store, the metal-wrought **Au Bon Marché**. It was here that M. Boucicaut

invented price tags, refund or exchange, and the trappings of modern consumerism. At 26 Rue du Bac, **Christian Constant** seduces with chocolates and cakes that lead to purgatory. Nearby **Jean-Luc Poujauran** runs the most mouth-watering bakery in the capital (20 Rue Jean-Nicot).

Art station: No visit to Paris is complete without a pilgrimage to the **Musée d'Orsay**. Considered by many as the most easy-to-use museum in the world, the former railway station is spaciously arranged and sumptuously stuffed full of the most beautiful art from the late 19th century (which, by coincidence, is 95 percent French). The building, finished in two years from 1898 to 1900, was almost torn down to make way for an immense hotel in 1970. Prompted by public outcry, government ministers fulfilled the prophesy of painter Edouard Detaille at opening ceremonies in 1900, that the station would make a better museum. Its glass and iron construction was a triumph of modernity at the time,

Sumptuous decor in the upper rooms.

rivalling Eiffel's steeple, whilst the facade mimicked the Palais du Louvre just across the river. In the vast cavern of the interior, Orson Welles set his film of Kafka's *The Trial*.

It is difficult to get lost in the museum. Designed by an Italian, Gae Aulenti, the exhibitions are arranged on five levels, the central hall surrounded by terraces. As airy as the Louvre isn't, the museum's lay-out is deceptively approachable. How many have launched into an inclusive tour of its riches, only to be exhausted before even reaching the Impressionists? Choose carefully; the d'Orsay is a place to come back to.

The ground floor is dominated by the academic school, and its regimented style. In contrast, Manet's shameless nude – *Olympia*, the first "modern" painting, stares insolently at her staid predecessors (the work was pronounced pornographic at the 1865 Salon des Artistes). On the top floor is the museum's treasure trove. The Impressionists are bathed in soft light from the station's

glass-vaulted roof, a setting they were painted for. Pass through rooms and rooms of Monet, Manet, Renoir, Pissarro, Degas, Cézanne and Van Gogh. The galleries end in a small cafe under a large clock, from where an outside terrace runs high above the Seine, offering appetising views over Paris.

Elsewhere, the central aisle is the place for sculpture (David, Rodin, Maillol *et al*), whilst art nouveau overflows from the middle floor, including the two towers at the east end, which present a bird's-eye view over the museum. For further information on favourite works, visit the documentation room upstairs, where computers give details on all exhibits, along with remarkable video reproductions.

Anyone interested in medals and military decorations should visit the next-door museum, **Musée de la Légion d'Honneur**, tracing the history of France's most celebrated award. The interior colonnaded courtyard is shelter for those who are less enamoured with bits of metal.

For the antidote to an excess of museums, walk down onto Quai Anatole-France, at the bottom of the Musée d'Orsay, and peer over at the **Piscine Déligny**. Much more than a mere swimming pool, this is Paris's number one venue for the body beautiful; a place to tan, strut and strumpet. It's all been done before at the Déligny, but that does not stop them trying.

For a more sobering (yet surprisingly entertaining) experience, continue along the Seine to the Place de la Résistance, and descend into the bowels of the capital. The **Musée des Egouts de Paris** is less a museum and more an excursion into the city's infinite sewer system. Described by novelist Victor Hugo in *Les Misérables* as the "other Paris", this network of tunnels follows the well-known streets above surface; walk along the "other" Champs-Elysées, stroll down the "other" Boul' Mich. The visit is accompanied by a film, and relevant odours – *the* alternative tour of Paris.

In the Musée des Egouts de Paris.

LOCAL CAFÉS

The café is the Parisian's decompression chamber, easing the transition from "dodo-Métro-boulot" – sleeping, commuting and working. It is the welcome pause at the end of the daily grind, a pause in which to savour a *pet't noir* or an *apéritif*, to empty the mind of troublesome thoughts, to watch the people go by, to dream, to revel in the exquisite pleasure of doing absolutely nothing in particular.

"What we sell here is time," says the proprietor of the trendy Café Costes in Les Halles. The elegant interior (designed by Philippe Starck), the sunny *terrasse* and the ideal corner location make the Costes, like its sister-establishment, the Café Beaubourg, opened a year later in 1986, a sure-fire success. Other French cafés have not been so fortunate. The neighbourhood *zinc*, named after its metal counter, is in danger of extinction, and, with it, part of the fabric of French life.

The figures are alarming. Four thousand cafés disappear each year. Paris alone has lost 1,000 in five years. In 1910, France boasted 510,000 zincs. By 1960, they had dwindled to 200,000. By 1990, only 70,000 remained.

While the invasion of fast-food restaurants is partly to blame (a nearby "McDo" can slash a café's profits by 30 percent), changes in the French way of life are also culpable. When customers move out to spacious homes in the suburbs, they begin to "cocoon", staying indoors to watch television or videos, and the neighbourhood café is eventually forced to close.

Then there are the ageing proprietors to consider. The café is traditionally a family business, but today fewer sons and daughters are prepared to take on gruelling 16-hour days with sparse holidays in a job bringing little prestige.

Sadly, even the atmosphere of remaining zincs is not what it was. Now there is formica where once there was marble. Piped muzak and the electronic beep of video games have replaced the song of the passing accordionist and the furious volleys of the "baby-foot" players. Only the Gauloise-induced haze (attitudes to the 1992 smoking ban are casual) and the hazards of the lavatories are

the same. Turkish toilets (literally a hole in the ground) are the order of the day. As Yvon Le Vaillant remarked in *Le Nouvel Observateur*: "Seeing that, you can only imagine what the kitchen must be like."

Yet all is not lost. Authentic zincs are still to be found in Paris and many are thriving. Try the stylish Café de l'Industrie on Rue Saint Sabin, La Palette on Rue de Seine or the tiny but lovingly restored Le Cochon à l'Oreille on Rue Montorgueil.

For literary atmosphere, order a *verre* (glass of wine) at Les Deux Magots, 6 Place St Germain des Prés, which has been home to almost every Paris intellectual from Rimbaud to Breton. At the nearby Café de Flore, Sartre and Simone de Beauvoir wrote by the stove. ("My worst customer, Sartre," recalls the patron of the Flore: "he spent the entire day scribbling away over a single drink.")

But go soon. For, if you have never ducked into a French café to make a quick phone call, met your lover for an apéritif on the *terrasse* or negotiated the contortionist's crouch of the *toilettes*, you cannot claim truly to know Paris. ∎

Zinc-topped bars are increasingly rare.

185

LA DÉFENSE

Heading west, crossing the city boundary at Porte Maillot, the historic avenues of Paris suddenly vanish. There ahead rises a futuristic metropolis, a city of gigantic glass blocks marching to the gates of the capital. "America-on-the-Seine", as Parisians affectionately refer to **La Défense**, is the city's newest attraction, enticing a million visitors each year with its glass, concrete and steel. This is "Europe's premier business centre", the capital of French industry and finance, and one of the world's most avant-garde architectural sites.

Once a desolate commuter-land of office-blocks, La Défense is rapidly becoming a bustling 21st-century community with the mandatory enormous shopping complex, high-tech entertainment centres and, as its focus, La Grande Arche, crowning glory of President Mitterrand's "progressive vision for the 1980s" ("megalomania" is another description offered by right-wing publications). La Grande Arche has given La Défense the symbol it needed, and finally connects this modern upstart to the ancient heart of Paris, via the Triumphal Way which runs east through the Arc de Triomphe to the Louvre and even as far as Bastille.

Like an onion: Since 80 percent of Paris is protected by preservation orders, new developments move outwards adding successive layers to the core. When in 1958 it was decided that Paris needed a business centre, a small hill overlooking the Seine was selected for development; La Défense, so-called because it was where citizens defended the capital against the Prussian siege of 1870–71. The first phase of building by EPAD (Etablissement Public pour l'Aménagement de la Défense) was completed in the late 1960s; a huddle of office towers, not exceeding 100 metres (330 ft), above a pedestrian zone (roads passed underneath the complex). The RER line was extended, placing the city centre five minutes away. Then recession hit and the planning corporation teetered on the brink of bankruptcy.

It was not until the recovery of the 1980s that La Défense finally took permanent root, towers soared to twice the height and the business world moved in. La Défense seems to have overcome its economic teething troubles. Today, the continuous construction, thousands of serious-faced business people, and almost as many tourists, make the district one of the fastest growing and most adventurous in Paris. Academic articles are talking about a "new spirituality" in Paris's newest quarter.

To cap it all, Jean-Michel Jarre gave a computerised concert extravaganza here on 14 July 1990 which was seen by 2 million people worldwide. La Défense is properly on the map.

Facts and figures: It is not difficult to get to La Défense. Metro Line 1 cuts straight through the centre of Paris to end up beneath the Grande Arche, and

Preceding pages: Vision of the future, La Défense. Left, eyecatching stuff. Right, many French companies have head offices here.

the RER A line winds all the way from Euro Disney to the same place (a journey of only 40 minutes). In addition, 20 bus routes converge here, making this small district, barely the size of an *arrondissement*, the most accessible in France. Such accessibility allows 70 percent of the 110,000 workers to commute by public transport, 80 percent of whom spend less than an hour a day travelling. Half the employees here are executives. La Défense, being a futuristic baby, loves statistics. There are 350,000 journeys to the district each work-day, 66,000 parking spaces, 1,300 companies achieving an annual sales volume equivalent to France's national budget.

Twelve of the top 20 French companies have headquarters at La Défense, such as Elf, Total and EDF: 13 of the world's top 50 companies are tenants – IBM, Apple, Hitachi, Unilever. In the residential sector, 30,000 people live in the great apartment complexes to the west. In a bid to render the residential district less artificial, cylindrical stacks are painted to resemble clouds against soft pastel backgrounds – a notion that doesn't quite achieve the desired effect.

Since 1981 the **Quatre Temps** shopping centre has provided a social focus for the complex, as well as a place to buy everything the time-squeezed businessperson of today needs – it contains three hypermarkets, 260 shops, 26 restaurants and nine cinemas, greeting 50,000 customers a day. Rumour has it that this is the biggest shopping centre in Europe: at La Défense, superlatives have become a way of life. Building has started on what will be Europe's tallest skyscraper, the controversial Tour Sans Fin (tower without an end), planned to exceed 400 metres (1,420 ft).

Symbol of success: On 14 July 1989, leaders of the seven richest nations on earth paid a visit to La Défense for the inauguration of **La Grande Arche**. Previously La Défense was a place to view from afar, with a certain traditionalist disdain. The spectacularly simple

Seen from afar, La Défense rises behind the Eiffel Tower.

Grande Arche changed that, seducing public and politicians alike, and today the view from its lofty summit is as famous as that from the Eiffel Tower, offering a unique vista back to Paris along the historic Triumphal Way. Now, it is La Défense that looks down with disdain. The magician behind this dramatic transformation was unknown Danish architect Otto von Spreckelsen; it was his idea which most impressed President Mitterrand amongst the 424 proposals for a building at the "head of the Défense". Spreckelsen died two years before his *"arche de force"* opened, but the project was completed by a colleague, who remarked on taking over that the architect "had seen God" when envisaging the edifice.

Artist Takis created the 49 spiral rods in this pool. They sway in the wind and light up in the evening.

La Grande Arche is the grandest of Mitterrand's *grand projets*. Entitled "The Arch of Man's Triumph", von Spreckelsen's design completes the Triumphal Way without enclosing it: the arch provides a window framing the new developments of the western sub-

urbs. As the architect himself said: "This is an open cube, a window on the world. The Arch will see far, in all directions."

Certainly, the view from the top is vast. Two glass bubbles whisk lines of visitors up to the roof at vertiginous speeds, through the symbolic "cloud", a canvas net suspended between the twin towers designed to cut down wind resistance. Here the Fraternity Arch Foundation has its headquarters, and is funded by profits from rooftop tourists. The foundation is a human rights organisation formed in 1989, and holds exhibitions and conferences in the arch. On the roof, Raynaud's Carte de Ciel (Map of the Sky) resembles an enormous sundial. Gaze across the Seine, down the Champs-Elysées and realise why the arch deserves its adjective.

Also housed in the huge flanks of the building is the Ministry of Transport and Public Works, a conference centre and numerous offices.

View from below: From the **Esplanade de la Défense** the great white arch seems

two-dimensional; when viewed from the sides, the third dimension mysteriously appears, an illusion created by the arch's alignment 6° off the axis of the Triumphal Way (a quirk shared by Peï's pyramid at the Louvre). Its size is symbolic: measuring 100 metres by 100 metres (give or take a few), the arch has the same dimensions as the Cour Carrée at the Louvre to the east. Spreckelsen's monumental vision also respects the historic pattern of Parisian arches; L'Arc de Triomphe du Carrousel is 25 metres high, L'Arc de Triomphe is 50 metres high, so La Grande Arche is 100 metres high. At weekends, its majestic sweep of steps is dotted with families, children and tour groups, enjoying one of Paris's most modern picnic spots.

Below the arch the **Information Centre** of La Défense provides free information packages and houses an interesting scale model outlining the district's development, past and planned. The adjacent shop is rife with arch souvenirs and T-shirts.

To the north of the wide Parvis at the foot of the Grande Arche is the district's oldest resident, recently given a facelift; the **CNIT** business centre. This curvaceous structure was built in 1958 as the focus of La Défense but now seems a bit dated. Its lofty concave dome is supported by just three pillars, the roof seemingly hanging in mid-air. Inside, recent refurbishment has created a high-tech bowl of glass offices tapering outwards from the roof to the floor, interspersed with hanging gardens of small trees and shrubs.

Within this deluxe greenhouse, the **World Trade Centre** is the heart of the Parisian business machine, where market dealers, business service consultants and researchers plug into the network of 237 trade centres around the world. Here too are three conference amphitheatres, 21 committee rooms, 14 restaurants, shops and a four-star hotel.

Opposite the CNIT centre, **La Colline de l'Automobile** is the district's most recent tourist attraction, created to cream

On the steps of the Grande Arche.

192

off some of the coach-loads of visitors who swarm the Grande Arche. From the southern corner of the arch, wide steps lead past orange, blue and green cubes, designed by Piatr Kowalski to stimulate a "mental geometry".

Once inside the "colline", things become less intellectually demanding: to the left, the **Musée de l'Automobile** is a sparkling new display of the history of the car, exhibiting vehicles from prehistory to 1972, including the box-like hippomobile (horse-drawn), and the fantastical Rolls-Royce Phantom III.

Immaculate reconstructions portray cars in their original settings: an elegant Renault 8 is parked next to a chic 1930s bistro, while an old truck lies, disembowelled, in a 1940s garage. The museum is surprisingly entertaining, even for automobile agnostics. Alongside the memories of yesterday, more up-to-date models are displayed in the **Espace Marques**, a unique car showroom allowing prospective buyers or the simply curious to view and test-drive the latest offerings from top car manufacturers.

There are shops here too.

Dominating the "colline" is the immense silver globe of **Dôme IMAX**, the world's largest hemispheric cinema. Designed by the IMAX corporation of Canada, the dome is 1,200 metres (13,000 sq ft), and shows pictures 10 times the size of a normal cinema image. The programme includes voyages into Outer Space, Antarctic life amongst penguins, the oil fires of Kuwait, and, most alarming of all, a giant close-up of Mick Jagger and the Rolling Stones in concert. Reservations are recommended, although the dome is less crowded than its rival La Géode at Parc de la Villette.

La Défense is not just a one-arch story. On either side of the Esplanade, rising from the marble plateau, stand forests of towers, including some of the most adventurous architecture in Europe. The monolithic black block of the Fiat Tower stretches 46 storeys of tinted glass above the CNIT centre. The windows of the district's tallest building are wider at the top, to prevent it seeming

narrower as it rises. At the entrance to La Défense, dominating the Seine, the Russell-Hoescht Tower was the first skyscraper to sprout; a mere 34 storeys built in 1967. Just behind, Willerval's PFA Tower is a triangular temple of sleek glass pointing towards Paris.

The newest developments in the district are concentrated behind the Grande Arche, and are beginning to make the central buildings look prehistoric in comparison. Here, the Japanese architect Kurokawa has conceived an oriental response to the classical rigidity of Spreckelsen; the Pacific Tower is gracefully curved, set on a convex arch. Elsewhere, the Société Générale headquarters is formed of two semi-circular edifices, both of which are seemingly on the verge of rotating.

The attractions of space: The large open spaces of La Défense, in particular the **Esplanade de la Défense**, are becoming Paris' newest strolling arena. Sixty-seven hectares (7,200 acres) are pedestrianised, including a 25-hectare (2,700 acre) **Parc André Malraux** with rolling lawns, lake, botanical gardens, adventure sand-pit and the Dance School of the Opera of Paris. The Esplanade itself stretches from the arch to the Seine, providing a high-tech soccer pitch for local children, whilst the major roads pass underneath, unseen and unheard.

La Défense is also a cradle of art. The area takes its name from the statue to the defenders of Paris in 1870, which was sculpted by Barrias following submissions by 100 artists, including Rodin; the *Defence of Paris* stands at the heart of the district, and represents a young guardsman and girl symbolising the valour of the innocent civilian population confronting the Prussians. Above it, the quarter's most amusing attraction spurts forth its erratic water: the Esplanade Fountain, designed by Yaacov Agam, is a series of 66 fountains, each shooting up at different levels and at different times, cascading over a multi-coloured mosaic. The fountains are sometimes accompanied by computer- **Miró's Two Figures.**

ised music, when they seem to dance and wriggle in time to the tune. Head to the small white building to the left of the fountains: mysteriously christened **Art 4**, this is the office of the artistic wing of La Défense, and provides a free guide to works of art on the site. Take the brochure, and sip a glass at **Le Bistro de Vins**, with a ringside view of Agam's fountains as you decide what to see.

Sculpture park: With more than 50 modern sculptures, La Défense is one of Europe's most interesting open-air art museums: the works are consistently interactive, complementing and contrasting surrounding buildings, demanding the participation of even the most preoccupied passer-by. You should start at Miyawaki's *Utshori* sculpture, commissioned by Spreckelsen himself to sit alongside the Grande Arche; a series of pillars, from which spring nests of silver wires (the spectator is required to admire the space between the wires, according to Miyawaki).

At the entrance to the RER station, Rieti's 60-metre (200-ft) mural offers a teasing choice between a painted kiss, a flock of birds, or a running woman, depending on the perspective of the onlooker. Nearby, Miró's *Two Figures* loom above the square, marking the entrance to the shopping centre. These surreal beasts leer happily at the rigid angles of surrounding buildings, and are a favourite site for photographs with the prosaically white arch behind. Facing Miró's anarchic couple across the square, *The Spider* by Alexander Calder is one of the American artist's "stabiles" – huge steel structures, painted red-orange. Inside the shopping complex, Beatrice Casadesus has brought *Charlie Chaplin* and *Brigitte Bardot* to La Défense, in the form of her bas reliefs.

Outside once more, in the shadow of the EDF Tower, Derbre's *The Earth* is a beautiful bronze whose two figures suggest the rotation of the globe. More dramatically, Guy-Rachel Grataloup has decorated the chimney at the foot of the Total Tower with a 850-sq metre (9,000

sq ft) ceramic of tree-like branches swirling sky-wards into mists of colour.

Further to the east along the Esplanade, the Terrasse de l'Iris houses the happiest sculpture in La Défense; Claude Torricini's *The frog who became as big as an ox*. This corpulent frog is a favourite with children, most of whom want to take it home with them. Stroke the frog's head and drink water from his mouth. In the centre of Place de l'Iris, De Miller's *Sleepwalker* is contrastingly graceful; a slender figure with arms outstretched, standing on a smooth sphere.

End a visit to La Défense at sunset by the huge pool which overlooks the Seine to the east. This mirror of water is inhabited by 49 spiralling, swaying rods, designed by the Greek artist Takis. Each rod is crowned by a coloured light which blinks lazily as twilight gathers and the Arc de Triomphe in the distance turns soft pink. Here, at the gateway to one of the most modern developments in the world, the future somehow doesn't feel all that bad.

A third figure.

PARKS ON THE PÉRIPHÉRIQUE

"We must cultivate our garden", declared Voltaire in 1759, and Paris has not looked back since. Here is a city where parks and gardens are a matter of philosophy, a touchstone for the state of mind and health of the capital, a reflection of the sinuous course of the city's history. A recent article in *Le Monde* asserted that "when we argue in favour of our gardens, we are arguing for the whole city".

Now, more than ever, Parisians are looking to their green spaces as an escape from the increasing congestion of urban living. The 1980s were the decade of the *grand projet*, the monumental building; the 1990s are the decade of the park and garden. Derelict industrial sites are flowering, blossoming into suburban parks, with a fervour not seen since Haussmann's day. Never before has Paris been so green.

The woods: Past the necklace of the *périphérique* (circular motorway) to the west of Paris, the **Bois de Boulogne** is one of the reasons that the 16th *arrondissement* is preferred by the wealthy: Avenue Foch, perhaps the most expensive residential street in the capital, leads to its gates. Embraced by the elbow of the Seine, this 863-hectare (2,150-acre) expanse of woods and gardens has been the Sunday afternoon playground for generations of Parisian families. It was not until 1852 that Napoleon III had the surrounding wall of the royal hunting ground demolished and the hand of Haussmann swept through, modelling the park on Napoleon's cherished Hyde Park in London.

From the Metro stop at Porte Dauphine head to the **Pavillon Royal**. Near here, bicycles can be rented – the best way to visit the park, and ideal for museum-jangled nerves (every day, May

Preceding pages: in the Espace Albert Kahn.
Left, lakeside, Bois de Boulogne.

to September; the rest of the year only at weekends). To the west, **Parc de Bagatelle** surrounds a small chateau constructed by the Count of Artois, who bet Marie-Antoinette he could build a house in three months. The bet was won at great cost, hence the ironic name – "bagatelle". The gardens are magnificent: 8,000 roses bloom in June, a walled iris garden flowers in May. Notices announce which plants are in bloom.

In the centre of the Bois, the **Pré Catalan** is the most romantic spot in western Paris. In spring, narcissus, tulips and daffodils carpet the manicured lawns, bathing the foot of the colossal copper beach, well over 200 years old, whose branches stretch over half a kilometre. Le Pré Catalan Restaurant, in the gardens, offers Roland Durand's *auvergnat* cuisine, including carrot and cumin soup, and fruit tart with hot wine. Nearby, the intimate **Shakespeare Garden** is planted with flowers, trees and shrubs that star in Shakespeare's plays; Scottish Macbeth heather, Mediterranean Tempest herbs, Ophelia's stream. Romeo and Juliet would have approved. (The garden is mysteriously open only from 3pm to 3.30pm, and from 4.30p to 5pm). In summer, open-air productions are put on in the leafy theatre.

The **Jardin d'Acclimatation**, also in the Bois, is an amusement park for children, with a hall of mirrors, zoo, go-kart racing and a wooden fort. Here the **Musée en Herbe** organises art exhibits and workshops for future Picassos. Elsewhere, Longchamp and Auteuil are France's premier racecourses.

Avoid the Bois at night, when the innocent pleasures of the day give way to drug-dealers and the capital's most exotic transvestites.

On the eastern border of the park lies another secret of western Paris; the **Musée Marmottan**, containing 100 paintings by Monet, donated by his son. Once home to Paul Marmottan, art collector extraordinaire, the beautiful mansion contains Monet's *Impression – Sunrise*, which christened the Impressionist

The Shakespeare Garden.

movement. Pissarro, Renoir and Gauguin also appear. Not far away, **Balzac's House** (47 Rue Raynouard) contains a beautifully rural garden, complete with rustic blue chairs, overlooking the Eiffel Tower. The house is now an atmospheric museum to the novelist who wrote 16 hours a day to meet his debts. He lived here under a false name, and fled out of the back door if the password agreed with his friends, "I'm wearing Belgian lace", was not given.

New places: The far-flung southwest of Paris is the capital's most populated district, and home to two of its newest parks. **Parc George Brassens** on Rue des Morillons (Metro Convention) was opened in 1982. Incorporating the slaughterhouses which it replaced, the park is a child's paradise with playhouses, rock-piles, rivers and mini-lakes. The **Jardin des Odeurs** is designed for the blind: close your eyes, follow the trickling of fountains and sniff the fragrant foliage. Braille signs give relevant information on herbs and shrubs. Along

Rue des Morillons, 700 vines parade proudly, producing the annual *Clos des Morillons* wine (full-bodied, fine bouquet). At weekends, the ancient abattoirs house a giant book market.

Further west, dereliction became creation when the site of the Citroën car factory was turned into the **Parc André-Citroën**. Here too industrial buildings have become floral palaces; two huge glasshouses shine forth over the esplanade where children leap in and out of spurting fountains while impatient mothers wait with towels in six smaller glasshouses. Behind the glass lie two gardens; "black" and "white", side-by side in botanical harmony. A series of six more colourful gardens completes the park; gold, silver, red, orange, green, and blue – with appropriately chromatic plants. Each garden is linked to a metal, a planet, a day of the week, and a sense: thus gold is linked to the sun, Sunday, and the intangible sixth sense.

More traditional horticulture is found beyond the southern *périphérique*, at

The Jardin d'Acclimatation.

the **Espace Albert Kahn** (14 Rue du Port, Metro Boulogne-Pont de St Cloud). Here the legacy of financier Albert Kahn takes the form of an extraordinary park; Japanese, English and French gardens lie alongside an Alpine forest and North American prairie. The grass is cut at different levels, from "beatnik" style to "sailorboy". Wander beneath the blazing maples of the Japanese garden in autumn. In spring admire the camellias rioting against the lawns. At any time of the year, eat cream cakes in the palm house amidst perspiring tropical plants. Kahn called the gardens "the vegetal expression of my thoughts concerning a reconciled world", an idea complemented by 72,000 photographs of world landscapes, taken by his researchers and displayed on permanent rotation.

City of sciences: To the northeast of Paris, nestling against the *périphérique* on the edge of the 19th *arrondissement*, **Parc de la Villette** is France's third most visited site after Euro Disney and the Centre Pompidou. The park is built on the site of yet another huge abattoir, this one rendered obsolete by improved refrigeration techniques and poor design (the cows could not even get up the steps). Thirty-five hectares (86 acres) of futuristic gardens surround a colossal science museum – **La Cité des Sciences et de l'Industrie** – as well as **La Géode**, a giant silver golf ball housing a huge wrap-round cinema (reservations required for the 357 seats), described by President Mitterrand as "a rude protuberance, contrary to French good taste", and **Cinaxe**, a flight-simulator-cum-cinema, not for the queasy.

The Cité des Sciences et de l'Industrie was designed by architect Adrien Fainsilber, and built by the company that masterminded the moving of the temple of Abu Simbel in Egypt. This is not a museum for academics: all the exhibits are obligingly interactive, with buttons, levers, keyboards and screens to keep mind and body alert. Begin at L'Univers, to the west, with its spectacular planetarium, and explanation of **Parc André-Citroën.**

202

the inexplicable Big Bang. To the south, La Vie is an eclectic mix of medicine, agriculture and economics: a working meteorological station traces the day's weather, and a computer allows you to select the characteristics of a baby which is then born before your eyes. To the east, La Matière reproduces a nuclear explosion, and permits you to land an Airbus 320. Finally, the north wing contains La Communication with its displays of artificial intelligence, 3-D graphics and virtual reality.

Across the canal, the former cattle market now houses a cultural and conference centre in the immense 19th-century **Grande Halle**. Next door, the **Cité de la Musique** is an edifice of angles designed by Christian de Portzamparc, containing the National Music Conservatory and concert hall.

The gardens of the park are the biggest to be constructed in Paris since Haussmann. Designed by Bernard Tschumi and opened in 1993, they comprise several thematic areas such as "The garden of childhood fears" with a huge dragon, "The garden of mists" amongst sculptured streams and "The garden of winds" with its multicoloured bamboo. Abstraction continues in the form of Tschumi's *follies*: red, angular tree houses minus the trees, and a submarine on land – the *argonaut*, which served in the French Navy until 1982, a favourite with small children. Seventy percent of the park's visitors are under 16. The rest are just young at heart.

Older parks: To the south of La Villette, **Parc des Buttes-Chaumont** was built by Haussmann on the ruins of a gypsum mine. The uneven ground provides a perfect setting for a rocky terrain, crowned by an artificial mountain in the middle of an artificial lake. This 50-metre (150-ft) "mountain" is capped by a temple. From the mountain a waterfall falls 20 metres (60 ft), bordered by artificial stalactites. The puppet-show or "Guignol" in the open-air theatre has been going for 150 years.

King of Parisian parks, the **Bois de**

**La Géode,
Parc de la
Villette.**

Vincennes, on the edge of the 12th *arrondissement* to the southeast of Paris, is renowned for its chateau, its racecourse and its zoo. The forest, 12 km (7 miles) across, was Philippe-Auguste's hunting ground in 1200. In 1370 Charles V moved into his chateau here, which in turn became a prison housing, among others, Diderot and Mirabeau. Much embattled during Napoleon's capitulation and during the German occupation in 1944, the chateau is being renovated to its former glory. A video display in the dungeon relates the history of the fortress.

Next door, **La Cartoucherie de Vincennes**, once full of gunpowder, now resounds to the sound of some of France's most avant-garde theatre companies, including Soleil d'Ariane and Mnouchkine. Three theatre stages grace the ancient arsenal.

To the west of the park, the **Musée des Arts Africains et Oceaniens** is one of Paris' least known museums, containing a fascinating collection of Afri-

can and Australasian art. Picasso used to come here to wander the displays, seeking inspiration. Once the scene of much political argument, when the museum was accused of celebrating colonial oppression, the displays are now suitably politically correct; Nigerian death-masks, Algerian jewels and South Pacific fertility symbols. The star attraction is an impressive Tropical Aquarium, much favoured by children, who gasp in awe at baby sharks, turtles, cat-fish and the crocodile pit.

Next door, less aquatic wildlife roams the **Parc Zoologique**. This zoo was all the rage when it opened in 1934, because for the first time the animals roamed free. Each spacious cage is different, inspired by the animal's natural environment, although the Giant Panda, Okapi and company still look somewhat forlorn. A giant artificial mound houses monkeys, gazelles and goats.

On the other side of the lake, where rowboats and trout fishermen compete for space, rises the exotic **Buddhist Temple of Paris**, whose 180,000 roof tiles were carved from a single chestnut with a single axe. The enormous golden buddha sits serenely inside; meditations take place daily, at 9am, and 6.30pm. To the east of the park, the **Indochinese Temple and Tropical Garden** continue the oriental theme.

In the centre of the park, **Le Parc Floral** is a favourite with Parisian families who wander the "valley of flowers", "pine wood", the "water-plant garden" with its reeds and water-lilies and the "four season garden", permitting the smelling of flowers all year round.

To the west of Vincennes lies **Parc Montsouris**, the second of Haussmann's 19th-century parks; 16 hectares (40 acres) of gently undulating grass and trees, much loved by Cubist Georges Braque, who lived at what is now 6 Rue Georges-Braque, and Lenin, who lived on Rue Marie-Rose. On the day of the park's inauguration, the lake suddenly and inexplicably drained dry, and its engineer committed suicide.

Left, Parc Zoologique and right, lake in the Bois de Vincennes.

SHOPPING AREAS

Paris is a shopper's paradise. The capital of high fashion, gourmet foods and luxury products: everywhere you turn are colours, textures, shapes and scents. But don't fall into the trap of sticking only to familiar boulevards and established tourist routes. If you are willing to go a little off the beaten track, you can find beautiful and unusual items to suit any pocket. The secret lies in knowing where to look.

District by district: To help you find the best shopping, this chapter has divided Paris into five areas: **Les Halles**, **Bastille**, **Marais**, **Faubourg St Honoré** and the **Left Bank**. Each has its own distinctive character.

As a rough guide, the most luxurious and therefore expensive shopping is to be had around the Faubourg St Honoré where the glitterati of Paris fashion are to be found. For boutiques with young fashion, head for Les Halles, where many of the city's most innovative designers are also located. More avant-garde design can also be found in the Bastille, where, if you are willing to venture off the main shopping streets, it is still possible to buy direct from workshops at considerable discounts.

For more art galleries and many fine antique shops, head to the Left Bank, which also boasts a wide selection of designer shopping and some good discount stores. If your goal is to combine shopping with sightseeing, try the Marais, the oldest part of Paris, where the narrow streets are crammed with wonderful boutiques, imaginative gift shops and the most mouthwatering delis in the city.

For a nostalgic glimpse of hidden Paris, stroll through the old *galeries*, the elegant covered shopping arcades of the 19th century, most of which are to be found in the area around the Palais Royal.

Lastly, for a taste of gourmet Paris, don't miss the shopping experience of a lifetime: the city's street markets, where the whole boar hanging in the butcher's shop will vye for your attention with dripping honeycomb straight from the hive; where small round goat cheeses from the Auvergne are displayed alongside pyramids of amber nectarines, and where the fresh lobster tries to make his escape from the ice piled high at the fishmonger.

Les Halles: 1st and 2nd *arrondissements*. Where once the old fruit and vegetable market stood at the very heart of Paris there is now a giant underground shopping centre, the infamous Forum. This area is something of a paradox. It manages to be both seedy and trendy, although, unfortunately, many of the shops tend to the cheap and touristy. But if you look slightly to the north you will find some of the best shopping in the city.

Inside the apple-green exterior of Absinthe on **Rue Jean-Jacques Rousseau** are clothes by Costume National, Katharine Hamnett and Dries Van Noten. Tucked away in the courtyard at number 62 is one of the most beautiful shops in Paris: Sybilla, which stocks the exquisite clothes of the Spanish designer of that name.

On the corner of Rue Etienne Marcel, the mainly menswear branch of Kashiyama stocks an eclectic selection of designer gear, often at discount prices.

Art historian, painter and milliner Marie Mercié's witty hats are a delight. Stop by her narrow shop at 56 Rue Tiquetonne and then continue on into the wonderful market street of Rue Montorgueil. Pause here to savour the mouth-watering patisseries available in the many bakeries which line the street.

On **Rue Montmartre**, stop in at the Comptoir De La Gastronomie for a good selection of *foie gras* and at Tehen for Irina Grigori's figure-skimming outfits in fluid jersey. Further on, Mokuba has a vast collection of ribbons in silks, velvets and iridescent voiles.

Agnes B fans should head for the narrow **Rue du Jour** where they will also find her Lolita line for teenage sirens, as well as Enfant and further down Agnes B Homme. Upstairs in the main store you can also find the designer's line of beauty products.

Also on this street you can find young Parisian fashion at Claudie Pierlot, and cotton and silk knitwear at Pôles. For a selection of young designers, try Details at number 15. They also have kids' clothes. Next door Pompadi sells wonderful children's shoes in original designs, guaranteed to please the under fives. La Droguerie sells a rainbow selection of wools, buttons, chunky beads, feathers, ribbons, etc. Junior Gaultier stocks the less expensive line from Paris's bad boy of fashion.

Rue Etienne Marcel, which runs from the downmarket Boulevard de Sebastopol to the elegant 17th-century **Place des Victoires** is home to many of the capital's most exclusive designers.

For hip interiors, try En Attendant Les Barbares with eclectic furniture by 40 French designers. Go to Equipment's tiny shop for a wonderful selection of unisex shirts in rainbow silks. Ventilo's three-storey emporium at 27 bis Rue du Louvre has American country-style clothing for men, women and children. Best of all is the home furnishings department with its natural linens and the pleasant wicker furnished tea-room on the top floor.

Back on Rue Etienne Marcel are designers Comme Des Garçons and Dorothée Bis. Be sure to check out the exquisite jewellery-filled shelves of the tiny Gas. Jean Louis Imbert has great accessories and leather goods. The British chain Joseph is here with amazing sweaters and butter-soft leather and suedes by Maxwell Parrish.

At 44 Etienne Marcel, Yohji Yamamoto's statuesque assistants model the designer's deconstructivist black and white creations. Yohji Yamamoto Hommes is next door at 45 with more elegant clothes from the same minimalist palette.

Musée & Compagnie at 49 contains a

In the arcades of the Palais Royal.

small but distinctive collection of items inspired by the museums of Paris. A good place to find unusual and moderately priced gift items.

Romantic French classics can be found at Cacherel, 5 Place des Victoires. Next door, Kenzo stocks men's classics in jazzy colours. Upstairs you can find more of the same bright shades and jungle prints for women. Kenzo Enfants is tucked away in the courtyard of number 3 in a charmingly converted *atelier*. At number 6, Stephane Kelian, darling of the Paris style crowd, sells his mens', women's and children's shoes.

Would-be Vanessa Paradis lookalikes go next door to Aridza Bross for their 1970s gear. This is a good place for crochet dresses and waistcoats and canvas espadrilles.

Victoire at numbers 10-12 is a smaller version of London's Browns, stocking Jil Sander, Romeo Gigli, Max Mara and Dolce & Gabana, among others. American sportswear for both sexes is available from the Esprit shop on the corner of Rue Etienne Marcel.

On Rue Latinat, Spanish designer Adolfo Dominguez's seductively simple tailored clothes for men and women in ice cream shades are well worth a look, although prices tend to be high.

Fans of Timberland's rugged outdoor gear should head for their shop at 52 **Rue Croix des Petits Champs**. This is a good area for accessories: next door, Soca sell Spanish-inspired leather bags and belts. Across the street at number 45, the British company Mulberry stocks beautiful classic leather goods for the huntin', shootin' and fishin' set. Check out their wonderful alligator filofaxes. Next door Luann has attractive straw bags in a variety of colours.

Isabel Martin's romantic evening wear and wedding dresses are at number 40. Also look out for her unusual chairs in pastel velvets.

Around the corner on **Rue Herold**, be sure to check out SIC, a tiny boutique with an eclectic collection of handmade bags, jewellery and scarves. Leonidas,

with exquisite Belgian chocolates, is also on this street.

From here you should stroll through the graceful arcades of the **Palais Royal**, lined with curious shops and galleries. Don't miss Didier Ludot's collection of perfectly preserved designer clothes and accessories from a bygone age. This is the place to find a 1960s Chanel suit or a Givenchy gown worthy of Audrey Hepburn. L'Escalier D'Argent specialises in hand-embroidered waistcoats in silk moiré. Shiseido's hand-stencilled lavender and mauve boutique is the only place in the world to find their distinctive scents.

Arcades: Be sure to visit some of the elegant *galeries* (arcades), many of which were built in the first half of the 19th century. Forerunners of the modern shopping mall, they are centuries removed in atmosphere. Suffused with soft, hazy light which filters through the glass rooftops, they are ethereal, mysterious places, tinged with nostalgia.

The **Passage Verdeau** is the place to

Boutique on Place des Victoires.

find antiquarian booksellers and old prints. Librairie Roland Buret specialises in old *Tin-Tin* comic books and memorabilia. Cinema buffs should head for Cinedoc in the **Passage Jouffroy** with over 4,000 film posters, postcards and books. Under the sign of the moose head, M & G Segas stocks a diverse selection of antique walking sticks. Pain D'Epices is a charming toy shop with old-fashioned playing cards and paper dolls. Next door, their gift shop has something for everyone, from preserves to pot-pourri.

Jean-Paul Gaultier's boutique is just one of the chic stores in the recently restored **Galerie Vivienne**.

Bastille: 11th and 12th *arrondissements*. Originally a working-class area, in recent years the Bastille has gained a reputation for hot young design. Rising rents have forced out some of the more avant-garde boutiques, but it is still possible to find stylish clothes at good prices. Some of the best buys are in workshops which sell direct to the public.

Wonderful one-off hats are made in the back room of Cheri Bibi on 82 **Rue de Charonne**. They also make hats to order. Raffia bags and lampshades are sold here too, as well as a selection of handmade jewellery designed by young French artists.

Designer Nathalie Dumeix sells moderately priced clothes with quirky street flair direct from her workshop at 10 Rue Théophile-Roussel.

If you are willing to pick your way through discarded paper patterns and scraps of fabric you might find a bargain in the workshop of German designer Brent Carstenschulz at 1 **Rue Keller**. Magic Circle, 9 Boulevard Richard Lenoir stocks an eclectic mix of designer gear and *fripes* (secondhand clothes) in an atmosphere of 1960s and '70s kitsch.

Overlooking a charming courtyard, the cool black and white interior of L'Arbre A Lettres, 62 **Rue du Faubourg St Antoine**, provides the perfect backdrop for browsing through the good

Fresh flowers...

selection of art and design books. Five or six jewellery designers show their work in the tiny Duelle, 21 Rue Davale.

For period furniture items go to the Rue de Charonne, once at the heart of furniture-making in Paris. For art deco, try Pirouette (29) and for 1960s and 70s pieces go to Dolce Vita (25). La Grande Mademoiselle at 36 Rue Keller often has antiquities at reasonable prices.

Miroiderie St Bernard, 4 Passage Charles-Dallery, stocks a glittering array of Venetian mirrors engraved with flowers and birds and wonderful coloured glasswear and vases. Each piece is unique and signed by the artist.

The Marais: 3rd and 4th *arrondissements.* Originally built on marsh land, the Marais is the oldest surviving *quartier* in Paris and the most atmospheric in which to shop. The area is predominantly Jewish and, in the maze of narrow cobbled streets, wonderful delicatessens selling mouthwatering falafels and poppyseed cake jostle for space with high-fashion boutiques.

...and fine fish.

Rue des Francs-Bourgeois is the backbone of the *quartier*, parallel with the other main shopping drag the Rue des Rosiers around which many of the kosher restaurants and delis are clustered.

A La Bonne Renommée, at 26 **Rue Vieille du Temple**, is the home of patchwork like you've never seen it before. Catherine Legrand and Elisabeth Gratacap create exquisite cushions, bags, coats and evening wear using scraps of richly coloured velvet and silk. The results are spectacular.

Nicole Puech's boutique Croissant, 3 **Rue Saint Merri**, stocks her delightful and original designs, many of them handmade, for babies and children up to eight years. More attractive baby clothes can be found at Klodo, 18 **Rue Ferdinand Duval**. Across the street, a non-profitmaking French ecology association has opened Robin Des Bois, stocking recycled stationery, natural beauty products, knitwear and "vegetable ivory" from the nut of the palm tree.

L'Eclaireur, 3 **Rue des Rosiers**, is

one of the trendiest shops in Paris: customers have included Madonna, Sinead O'Connor and Roman Polanski. Even Arnold Schwarzenegger has bought a pair of shoes here. The aim, says owner Armand Hadida, was to create a forum where "fashion mixed with art." The shop is a pot-pourri of objets d'art – a velvet sofa by Garouste and Bonetti, the unique plates of Fornasetti and glass and silver objects by Borek Sipek – and are displayed cheek by jowl with the latest fashions by top designers. The exposed brickwork and hardwood floors provide the perfect foil for the rich colours and eccentric shapes of Costume National, Dolce & Gabana, Martin Margiela and Ann Demeulemeester.

Nor are men neglected; downstairs are collections from Issey Miyake, Dries Van Noten, Paul Smith and Comme des Garçons.

Chevignon Trading Post is worth mentioning for its location here in an ancient *Hammam* (Turkish bath), once a feature of the *quartier*. The dusky rose

and green exterior has been left untouched.

Another unusual shop front is Le Garage at 23 **Rue des Francs-Bourgeois**, located in an old *boulangerie* (bakery). Here are decorative, fun shirts for men and women. There is another branch at 3 bis Rue des Rosiers. Across the street, Faycal Armor's figure-hugging designs are in the baroque interior of Plein Sud.

A L'Image Du Grenier Sur L'Eau at 45 Rue des Francs-Bourgeois recaptures another era with more than 1 million old postcards, film and advertising posters. For knitting enthusiasts, Anny Blatt across the street has a rainbow selection of mohair in subtle shades.

Those with a sweet tooth should visit the charmingly old-fashioned sweet shop, La Maison Des Bonbons on Rue de Sevigné.

Hier Pour Demain, 4 Rue des Francs-Bourgeois, is the place to go for art deco furniture and ornaments. In his silver shop at 17, Jean-Pierre Castro sells bracelets made from old spoons and forks.

Art Du Bureau, 47 Rue des Francs-Bourgeois has the latest hi-tech office accessories and chunky fountain pens.

Autour Du Monde has several stores along this street, the best being their home shop which is crammed with country furnishings, American style. Some of the portable items include colourful patchwork, pot pourri and natural beeswax candles in the shape of hives.

For accessories, try Aicha at 19 Rue Pavée for unusual bags in leather, Anna Kaszer, 7 Rue Malher for hats and Didier Lavilla at 38 Rue de Sevigné for great bucket bags in soft suedes. The Marais boasts some great shoe shops, including Stephane Kelian, Rue de Sevigné, and Gelati, Rue des Francs-Bourgeois.

For many Parisians, the 1930s and '40s look of Jean Gabin and Arletty – all accordions, braces and floral dresses – is more than an attitude, it's a whole way of life. To find it, go to L'Apache, 45 Rue Vieille du Temple, a treasure trove of vintage clothes.

Somewhere expensive to sit.

One of the most interesting shop windows in Paris is at 6 Rue Pas de la Mule where Andre Bissonnet displays his collection of old musical instruments.

The graceful arcades of the 17th century **Place des Vosges** make for shady strolling on a hot day. Several top designers have their shops here including Issey Miyake and Poppy Moreni. It's also a good place to look for antiques and paintings.

The Left Bank: *5th, 6th* and *7th arrondissements*. Parisians often remark that the Left Bank has an entirely different *ésprit* from the Right Bank. While the bohemian lifestyle and innovative design it once stood for in the 1920s has largely moved to east Paris, the Left Bank still retains a unique atmosphere. Traditionally the intellectual heart of the city, the Rive Gauche is now packed with designer boutiques. Some residents claim never to cross the Seine. For the dedicated shopper or just the casual browser, there are certainly enough interesting shops to keep you entertained from morning to night. It is for you to decide which you prefer: Rive Droite or Rive Gauche.

Most of the best shopping action is to be found concentrated in the area north of Boulevard St Germain and around St Sulpice. Stroll along the narrow **Rue de Grenelle** for some of the capital's most chic boutiques. Montana is here, as is Kenzo and Sonia Rykiel Enfant and Inscription, brainchild of daughter Nathalie, whose styles tend to be more casual than her mother's. Princesse Tam Tam has pretty cotton lingerie in fruit and flower prints. Michel Perry's shoe designs are witty and up-to-the-minute.

On the nearby **Rue des Saints-Pères**, former Chanel muse, Inès de la Fressange has opened her candy-coloured boutique at number 81. The wonderfully named Elvis Pompillo at 62 bis is the place to go for unconventional headgear. Two of the best shoe shops in town are also on this street: Maud Frizon and Philippe Model.

For more shoes and accessories in

There are markets in most districts.

fine leather, continue down the **Rue du Cherche-Midi**: Robert Clergerie, Fausto Santini, Accessoire and Bottega Veneta are among the big names with shops on this street.

Even in August, the queue at Poilâne stretches through the front door. This famous bakery sells crusty country bread decorated with grapes and wheatsheafs, as beautiful to look at as it is delicious to eat. The loaves are enormous, so order "*un quart*" (a quarter). If your appetite is small, you can request a tiny loaf personalised with your name.

Nearby, the colourful Comtesse Du Barry specialises in *foie gras*. Gift baskets are also available, including other mouthwatering gourmet items like orange marmalade with whisky.

Behind the elegant curved window of Shu Uemura, 176 **Boulevard St Germain**, lies a treasure trove of make-up. Beloved of models and stylists, the reasonable prices, unbeatable colour range and beautiful brushes make this shop a must for any make-up enthusiast.

Kashiyama, 147 Boulevard St Germain, stocks a diverse range of big names including Romeo Gigli, Ann Demulemeester, Martin Margiela and Issey Miyake. The shop also has wonderful accessories and some very seductive lingerie downstairs.

The British Crabtree & Evelyn at No 177 are famous in Paris for their line of soaps and bath products.

Diptyque, 34 Boulevard St Germain is one of the most delightful shops in Paris. Founded by three English artists, it sells deliciously scented candles in an atmosphere of old world courtesy.

Traditional fabrics from Provence can be found at Souleiado, 3 **Rue Lobineau**. Next door, the vibrant colours of Africa and South America are at Textiles D'Ailleurs Et D'Ici. More Provençal prints are stocked by Les Olivades on Rue de Tournon.

La Chambre Claire, 14 **Rue St Sulpice**, has a great selection of beautiful coffee table books on photography.

For the latest in French design, check

All the scents under the sun.

out Avant Scène on Place de L'Odéon. Next door Virginia Mo has intriguing glass *objets d'art*, candlesticks and soap dishes in translucent colours.

At L'Heure Du Bijou, 70 **Rue Bonaparte**, costume jewellery from the 1920s sparkles among the lace camisoles and delicate period costumes.

Another good address for jewellery from the 1930s, 40s and 50s is Schmock Broc, 15 Rue Racine. A diverse collection of bakelite, art nouveau lamps and old fountain pens can also be found beneath the red velvet awning.

For fine wines visit the 16th century wine cellar of Jean Baptiste Besse, 48 Rue de la Montagne Sainte Geneviève. One of Paris's best known wine merchants, Mme Besse has 50 years' experience and will gladly offer you friendly and knowledgeable advice.

Leading off St Germain, the **Cour du Commerce St André** is one of the most charming passages in Paris. The narrow cobbled street is lined with restaurants and boutiques. Go to Via for the latest in French design, including Gaultier and Philippe Starck, Karawan for kilims and ethnic jewellery and Bonsai Lola for fascinating miniature Japanese trees.

At 19 **Rue Gregoire de Tours** is one of the best kept secrets in Paris: Le Mouton à Cinq Pattes has been selling discounted designer style to elegant Parisians for more than 30 years. This is the place to pick up a Gaultier suit or a Katherine Hamnett evening dress at a huge discount.

One of the most beautiful jewellery shops in Paris is Exactement Fauve, 5 Rue Princesse, where Christine Vallet sells her exquisite necklaces and earrings of handmade glass pearls from the turn of the century.

As you pass Beaute Divine, 40 Rue St Sulpice, take time to peer into the dimly-lit interior at the gleam of luxury bathroom fittings from a bygone age. Everything you need to make bathing a truly decadent experience can be found here, from Provençal bath oils to antique silver towel rails.

Displayed outside Les Trois Marches, 1 Rue Guisarde, are 1950s floral print dresses, old lace and handsmocked children's clothes.

A big hit with trendy Parisians, the recently opened Conran Shop on the corner of **Rue du Bac** and Rue Babylone is British style-guru Sir Terence Conran's temple to good design.

The cosy red interior of Diners En Ville, 27 Rue de Varenne, is a perfect backdrop for the shop's pretty and unusual china and glasswear.

Italian master of knitwear Missoni's trademark rainbow sweaters for both men and women can be found at 43 Rue du Bac.

The amusingly named Volt & Watt, 29 **Boulevard Raspail** stocks outrageous lamps: this is the place to go if you want a real talking point for your sitting room. At number 26, Japanese designer Matsuda has beautifully understated fashions in natural fabrics for men and women. At the tiny boutique L'Ibis Rouge you can find exquisite made-to-

This man has a bargain to tell you about.

measure wedding dresses and evening gowns in antique lace and pearls.

The big names: *8th* and *9th arrondissements*. These areas include the major shopping venues of the Faubourg St Honoré, Avenue Montaigne and Les Grands Magasins.

The ritziest shopping in Paris is to be found on the famous **Rue du Faubourg St Honoré**. The list of luxury boutiques concentrated between Avenue Matignon and Rue Royale is a roll-call of the top names in haute couture. Lanvin, Hermes, Givenchy, Balmain, St Laurent, Cardin, Lacroix and more have boutiques here. On Avenue Montaigne, the opulence continues with Dior, Louis Vuitton, Chanel, Ungaro and Valentino. Don't miss French greengrocer to the stars, Fauchon. The Parisian version of Fortnum and Mason, where food takes on the status of an art form, is at 26-28 **Place de la Madeleine**. The cream and gold interior of Annick Goutal, 14 Rue de Castiglione, is the perfect backdrop for her beautifully-packaged perfumes, produced in 14 natural flower essences.

The "**grands magasins**" Galeries Lafayette and Printemps on **Boulevard Haussmann** offer a tantalising array of fashion and accessories in an atmosphere of 19th century elegance. Fashion shows and make-up demonstrations are daily events. If you are short on time or just want to get an idea which designers will appeal to you, the department stores are a good way to get an overview of what is in the smaller boutiques.

Printemps' recently renovated cosmetics department in ice cream shades and art deco shapes is well worth a visit, as is Galeries Lafayette's amazing lingerie department with the widest selection in town. Both stores offer VIP fashion advice services free of charge. Call ahead for an appointment. Printemps: 42 82 64 23 and Galeries Lafayette: 48 74 50 13.

City centre markets: Integral to the life of each quartier, the markets are part of the flavour of Paris. Wonderful displays of flowers, seafood, fruits and cheeses assail the senses.

The most colourful food markets are to be found on **Rue de Buci, Rue Lepic** and, perhaps most atmospheric of all, on **Rue Mouffetard**. Josephine Baker and Ernest Hemingway used to shop in the latter market which began in 1350. At the year-round Marché Aux Fleurs on the Île de la Cité hot-house orchids mingle with spring daffodils, offering an explosion of colour and scent. On Sunday, exotic birds add their song.

Most birds in the animal market on the **Quai Mégisserie**, are destined for the cooking pot. Geese, ducks, rabbits and even the odd goat are sold here.

Collectors peering through magnifying glasses gather at the weekend at the Marché Aux Timbres on Avenue Gabriel in search of valuable stamps.

The daily Marché d'Aligre, Place d'Aligre, is known mainly for fruit and flowers, but also has a small, quaint flea market in the middle of the square. Look out also for the old covered market, only a few of which remain in Paris.

Market man.

FLEA MARKETS

Hugging the *périphérique*, located at the gateways to the city, the flea-markets of Paris defy both the imagination and the authorities. Recent attempts to control the thousands of individuals who sell their worldy wares from the backs of cars or ramshackle stalls have not disturbed the chaotic, seductive atmosphere of these Parisian institutions.

Gone, perhaps, are the days when a Picasso or Rembrandt lay amongst dusty furniture, or a Ming vase hid under flea-bitten matresses. Bargains can still be found, but half the enjoyment of market wandering is in the looking. Take your time, a pocketful of small change and be prepared to haggle. The *marché aux puces* are open Saturday, Sunday and Monday, 7am–7pm.

The biggest flea-market in the world takes place at the extremity of the 18th *arrondissement*, beyond the Metro station at Porte de Clignancourt. The Puces de Saint-Ouen dates from 1841 when a market of secondhand clothes, furniture and sundry objects gleaned from the dustbins of the rich was established here. Today, at weekends, the seven official markets welcome over 200,000 customers. The stalls open, officially, at 7.30am, although things get going under the soft dawn street-lamps at 5am, when dealers gather over Gauloises to do business before the tourists arrive.

Among the seven markets at Saint-Ouen, Marché Biron offers antiques, with authenticity vouched by a charter; Marché Paul-Bert was once reserved for those whose property was destroyed during the Occupation, and now offers traditional junk and porcelain; Marché Serpette is the youngest, and trendiest of the seven, with 1900–1930 items; Marché Vernaison is the place to wander, and where a stop in the Louisette Restaurant, with a drink, impromptu singing and accordions, revives the feet; Marché Malik is the most visited and least bargainful, with extravagant 1960s and '70s clothes.

In between, along the streets lapping the *périphérique*, are legions of unofficial stalls and an eternally intriguing glimpse of what some people think other people will be prepared to pay money for.

The hard sell. On the eastern outskirts of the city, the Montreuil flea-market, at the end of the 20th *arrondissement*, is smaller than its northern cousin, but more exotic; arab barbers shave pot-bellied truck drivers, crouching between their trucks. It opens at 6.30am, but the stalls here are less organised than at Saint-Ouen. Take the Métro to Porte de Montreuil and the stalls start on Avenue de la Porte de Montreuil. On Monday, Montreuil is the place for secondhand clothes, when scavengers plough through dunes of tattered garments for the odd spectacular bargain – a Gaultier jacket, a Chanel skirt. The clothes are sold by weight.

The smallest of the three main flea-markets lies south of the city centre, at Porte de Vanves. Open on Saturday and Sunday, from daybreak until 7pm, the market is a myriad of small vendors, selling the bric-à-brac of the capital. Take Avenue Marc-Sangnier from the Porte de Vanves Metro, and turn right on Avenue George-Lafenestre. Complaints from locals have led to a strong police presence, checking the illegal stallholders. Don't be dissuaded, they often offer the best bargains, anything from ancient wine bottles to the kitchen sink. ∎

EURO DISNEY RESORT

Located at Marne-la-Vallée, 32 km (20 miles) east of Paris on a 1,943-hectare (5,000-acre) site one-fifth the size of the city itself, Euro Disney is the most popular tourist attraction in France, with twice as many annual visitors as the Eiffel Tower or the Louvre. Evidently the land "where dreams come true", as Walt Disney put it, is more alluring than the harsh reality of stuffy old museums and iron flag-poles.

Nevertheless, this US-style formula of fun had a decidedly rocky start in Europe, and has fallen well short of its visitor targets. Talk of bankruptcy, of redundancies and of debt rescheduling filled the newspapers. In the short term, the happy result for the visitor has been shorter queues and lower prices.

Although hordes of school buses are the resort's staple diet, many of Euro Disney's attractions may also stimulate more sophisticated imaginations. The park is worth the detour from Paris, if only to glimpse France's most incongruous, yet enjoyable tourist mecca at the end of RER line A.

Following the success of Tokyo Disneyland, opened in 1983, Disney colonialists scoured Europe seeking a suitable site for another non-American venture. The Disney empire eventually chose the land of Napoleon (the UK was discounted, thanks to lack of land and inconvenient geography, as was Spain, thanks to infrastructural inadequacies and the all-eclipsing 1992 Barcelona Olympics). France was somewhat of a homecoming, suggest Disney officials, since Walt's family originated in Isigny-sur-Mer, on the Normandy coast (d'Isigny became Disney). Generous financial incentives from the French government might also have influenced the final decision.

Disney has enjoyed a love-hate relationship with its hosts since the opening of the park in April 1992. President Mitterrand turned down an official invitation to the inauguration, saying it was not his "cup of tea". Publications such as *Nouvel Observateur* and *Libération* tripped over each other in their race to condemn "*la folie Disney*". Yet 3½ million visitors in the park's first year of operation were French. The park's first language is French, some rides having uniquely French commentaries. Sixty percent of the 12,000 staff are Francophone, although most of them are bilingual French/English.

Whilst the whole site will not be fully developed, if present plans are maintained, until 2017 at the earliest – when there will be an MGM studio theme park, new golf course and 13,000 more hotel rooms – the present resort is impressive enough. Aside from the park itself, there is a complex of American theme bars, shops and restaurants (known as **Festival Disney**) and six hotels situated just outside the main turnstiles.

To the south lies a campsite, whilst to the east stretches the 27-hole golf course, with a putting green the shape of a certain mouse's ears.

On popular days, the Magic Kingdom receives in excess of 40,000 visitors. In higher season it is possible for the main road exit to be closed by 8.30am, along with the RER station (the park opens at 9am). If you have time and money, it is preferable to get a two-day pass, and spread out your visit. These passes do not have to be used on consecutive days, have no date limit and offer approximately 20 percent discounts. Combining a two-day pass with a night in one of the resort hotels is the least stressful way to see the park. During peak season hotel guests are granted access to the park one hour before the general public arrives (see information at the end of this chapter on the various hotels). In summer months, when the park closes at 11pm, the "Star Nights" pass allows entrance after 5pm at a reduced rate.

If you are restricted to a straightforward single day-out at Euro Disney, it is advisable to plan your visit. If possible buy a Disneyland "passport" before getting to the park, to avoid delays at turnstiles – the passport is available at FNAC and Virgin stores throughout France, and all major stations of the RER line A in Paris.

The park can be a daunting place, especially for mild-mannered Europeans unaccustomed to American-style fun. The best advice is to decide on priority attractions, and get to them early, as lines of restless pilgrims form at top rides from 10am. Heading round the park in an anti-clockwise direction avoids the bigger crowds, since the circular Euro Disney train chugs clockwise. Tuesday and Thursday are less busy, as is the low season (November to February, not including Christmas and New Year) when prices are reduced.

It does rain in Marne-La-Vallée, but since attractions are built under cover and sheltered walkways lead from area to area, the park is designed for all-year-round enjoyment. Even the paint used is brighter than elsewhere in the Disney

empire, to counter grey skies. Eternally optimistic, Disney points out that rain leads to a stunning array of vegetation in the park, unrivalled by its developments in Florida and California. Here are 150,000 trees, as many as in the whole of Paris; native North American varieties, such as Red Cedar, Honey Locust, and Giant Sequoia, as well as exotic Judas trees, Monkey Puzzle, cacti and palms. The park is visited regularly by gardening journalists, who are there (of course) to undertake serious horticultural studies.

The gardens are immaculate, as is the entire complex, with teams of roving cleaners ensuring nothing sullies the Disney brilliance. The code of cleanliness extends to Disney workers, who are not permitted facial hair, ear-rings, tattoos or short skirts, causing intermittent disputes with French trade unions.

Getting your bearings: Euro Disney theme park is divided into five main areas, or "lands"; a floor plan cloned from the other Disneylands in California, Florida and Tokyo. Designed by the Disney's "Imagineers", the artistic and mechanical wizards who spend their lives thinking up weird and wonderful attractions, this is Disney's most technologically advanced park yet, benefiting from state-of-the-art robotics – Disney's unique "Audio-Animatronics" where life-size, life-like figures speak, sing and dance with gusto.

Once through the Victorian turnstiles, already humming along to ubiquitous Disney music, you enter **Main Street USA**, the first of these five areas and an evocation of 19th-century small-town America. City Hall, on the left, is the central information centre, contact point for lost children and property. Here, too, is the Main Street Station, from where the train circles the park. The station is often crowded, and it is better to get on it at one of the other stations on route, such as Frontierland. The bandstand in Main Street square is the best place from which to view the daily parades which traverse the park; Mickey's **Riverboat ride in Frontierland.**

11.30am parade, the 4pm Grand Parade and the night-time Electrical Parade, with its illuminated floats lit by 700,000 light bulbs (weekends, and daily during the summer season).

The park takes on an even more mystical face at night, with thousands of miniature lights blinking like fireflies. The parades pass around the bandstand, and exit the park through the large green gates to the right, between Discovery Arcade and Ribbons and Bows Hat Shop. At weekends, and each summer night, this is also the place from which to view the five-minute Fantasia in the Sky firework display.

Many of the most popular attractions in the park are found in **Frontierland**, to the left of Main Street, so head here first. Frontierland evokes dreams of the Wild West, and its centrepiece, Big Thunder Mountain, is a towering triumph of red rock reminiscent of every Western movie you have seen. The surrounding small town of Thunder Mesa represents a pioneer settlement of the late 1800s, including Cavalry Fort, and Lucky Nugget Saloon, where Miss Lil entertains on a vaudeville stage. Get to Big Thunder Mountain Roller-coaster early to avoid a long wait, and enjoy a bird's-eye view of the park, and a spectacular hurtle around an old gold mine. Even the waiting area is consistent with this theme; the lines move through a mining shack, oil and grease in the air, past the foreman's office and water pumping station.

Meticulous detail plays a part in all Disney's evocations – researchers scour the United States for period pieces such as iron mine pulleys from Montana, and Minnesota light fittings. Such evocative detail helps ease the wait, and encourages "guests" to enter into the spirit of the attraction before they embark. Anticipation is heightened by glimpses of the ride as you shuffle along to take your turn. Phantom Manor, home to some of Disney's most spectacular Audio-Animatronics provides a high-tech rollicking ride through a haunted house.

A ride to the future.

If the house itself seems vaguely familiar, it may be because it is copied from Norman Bates's abode in Hitchcock's *Psycho*. The "dead" tree outside is not actually dead, but specially treated by Disney botanists so that it grows no leaves. Inside are singing cowboy skeletons and holographic ghosts.

The Rivers of the Far West, an artificial lake in the midst of Frontierland, can be enjoyed by Mississippi paddle-steamer, keelboat, or Indian canoe. The Indian canoe station, a quiet dead-end, verdant and full of birdsong (taped, but it fools the real birds) is a tranquil contrast to the roller-coaster ride.

From Frontierland, paths lead almost imperceptibly into **Adventureland**. Sparse scrub gives way to lush bamboo and flowers, the twang of Wild-West guitar fading into the beat of African drums. The palms are real, and survive the winter months insulated in foil painted to look like bamboo. Here is another top attraction, the unforgettable Pirates of the Caribbean (queues usu-ally move quickly). As you descend into the castle the air cools, water drips and the darkness is punctuated only by flickering firelight. The water ride, through tropical swamp to the open sea, is orchestrated by jovially barbaric Disney workers. The boats pass the Blue Lagoon Restaurant, serving Caribbean fare in the heart of the attraction, under a starlit sky. For the six-minute journey you remain spellbound by animated pirates invading a treasure-rich port – here, a singing donkey; there, an inebriated pig that taps its trotters in time to the music.

Rival to Big Thunder Mountain, the first-ever 360° looping roller-coaster created by Disney is Le Temple du Péril, near Explorers' Club Restaurant. Hold onto your stomach as the ore-carts plunge through rain forest, and turn upside down above a mock archaeological dig inspired by the *Indiana Jones* saga. As with other top rides, get here early. Elsewhere, Adventureland offers the ultimate tree-house, home of the

Main Street USA.

226

Swiss Family Robinson, a Treasure Island complete with rope bridge and Captain Hook's Pirate Ship.

The most popular land for younger children (and thus best visited later in the day, when they have worn themselves out) is **Fantasyland**, containing the centrepiece of the park, Disney's emblem – **Sleeping Beauty's Castle**, or Le Château de la Belle au Bois Dormant. Unlike Florida, California, or Tokyo, you can enter into Sleeping Beauty's fortress, where her tale is told through rich tapestries and stained-glass windows. Beneath, through Merlin's Workshop, lies the lair of the dragon, La Tanière du Dragon, a breathtaking 27-metre (88 ft) long creature which roars, curls its claws and hisses smoke. Next door, Snow White and the Seven Dwarfs lead children through the classic fairy tale, and terrifies them with a holographic floating witch's head.

Not even Disney executives can account for the popularity of Peter Pan's Flight, which is another site to visit early in the day, before the tour buses arrive. Take a pirate galleon into the skies above London, as far as Never-Never Land. Next door, Toad Hall Restaurant is Disney's impression of Ye Olde English Pub, which now even has beer, since Euro Disney relaxed its ban on alcohol in order to increase profitability. Nearby, the Fantasy Festival Stage puts on glittering musical revues featuring favourite Disney characters. Whimsical madness is found in Alice's Curious Labyrinth, another mecca for small children, and the crazily spinning Mad Hatter's Tea Cups. You control how quickly you feel sick by regulating the speed at which the cups spin.

More sedate amusement is found in the **It's a Small World** kingdom, where nationalistic stereotypes are realised in a cheerful puppet kingdom of singing children, first designed by Walt Disney for Pepsi's stand at the 1964 World Fair. This attraction is sponsored by France Telecom; the other big attractions are similarly paid for by multinational com-

The parade goes by.

panies, who receive advertising rights in exchange. It may be a small world – but it's certainly lucrative.

The final stage on the journey around Disney's kingdom is **Discoveryland**, with its futuristic rides. Undoubtedly, the top draw here is Star Tours, a trip into space with George Lucas's *Star Wars* characters. Walking past hard-working robots, which are complaining about the trials of life, any delays pass quickly – each robot has a 10-minute spiel to ensure customers do not get bored. Once at the ride itself, the five minutes spent in the air force-designed flight simulator are riveting as the spaceship crashes through meteors and engages in a laser battle with the enemy.

Next door's Cinémagique lets you sample Michael Jackson's feet in your face, with a 3-D motion picture of Captain EO and his merry band of dancers. For a voyage around the world in 10 minutes, join the robotic timekeeper at the Visionarium. A 360° screen provides a panoramic view of Europe, from the Swiss Alps to Gérard Depardieu's nose. The view of Paris 200 years from now is the most interesting and disturbing feature of the show.

Beyond the rides: The wider resort – **Festival Disney** and the hotels – make up a celebration of "Americana", a direct response to Disney's vision of how Europeans view America. Continuing the cinematic motif of the theme park, the six hotels are Hollywoodesque in design. **Hotel Cheyenne** is the most imaginative – a film-set western town, complete with saloon, sheriff's jail and wooden planked stores. At the other "moderately" priced hotel, **Santa Fe**, Clint Eastwood grimaces down from a mock drive-in movie screen above reception. Designed by Antoine Predock, the hotel is a series of blocks recalling Mexican villages. Water runs in irrigation channels through desert landscapes, past a 1956 Cadillac buried in the sand. The first-class hotels, **Sequoia Lodge** and **Newport Bay Club**, overlook Lake Buena Vista. One recalls Hitchcock's *North by North-West* in its pine surrounds, and the other is a New England mansion straight from *The Great Gatsby*. Across the lake, **Hotel New York** offers luxury rooms in a Manhattan-style skyscape designed by Michael Graves. Attached is the New York Coliseum Conference Centre, with capacity for 2,000 delegates.

But the jewel of the resort's hotels is, naturally, the **Disneyland Hotel**. Its Victorian style whispers of turn-of-the-century elegance. It is here that Michael Jackson stays when he jets in to enjoy the park after hours.

Five kilometres (3 miles) from the theme park is **Camp Davy Crockett**, served by a free shuttle bus, offering 181 camping places and 418 cabins in rustic logged style.

Festival Disney is the place to get a beer after a long day at the theme park. Open until 2am, the complex boasts flashing neon, country and western music and Cadillacs. The end nearest the lake is more sedate, and more expensive. The **LA Bar and Grill** offers a pizza terrace and Beach Boys music, whilst **Key West** provides seafood at the sign of the life-size shark, whose gaping mouth provides endless fun for children. Upstairs, you can sip a Cyclone Special under an alligator at the **Hurricane Disco** until 3am while experiencing Florida hurricanes on video.

The busier, more moderately priced restaurants further on fill up in the early evening with families. **Annette's Diner** is the most reasonable and most entertaining. A 1950s diner, recalling *Happy Days* and *Grease* (the latter playing non-stop on video screens), Annette's serves burgers and beer, brought to you by roller-skating waiters.

Across the strip, **Billy Bob's** presents chicken wings and bluegrass music in a two-tier Nashville saloon. **Rock 'n' Roll America** is a 1950s dance-hall. For more dramatic entertainment, **Buffalo Bill's Wild West Show** brings real Indian chiefs, buffalo and carousing cowboys to the suburbs of Paris.

Somewhere to lose the children.

DAY TRIPS

Any visitor to Paris will want to make an excursion out of town. Even the shortest trip to Paris should include a visit beyond the city limits. If your time is severely limited, then half a day in Versailles is the obvious choice, but you could make it a day's cycling in the Forêt de Lyons or a weekend in the Loire Valley. You may even decide to swap French culture for American fantasy for a day and venture to Euro Disney at Marne-la-Vallée.

The shortest hops: A subway ride to **Sèvres** takes you only the river's breadth away (cross the bridge) from the **Porcelaine de Sèvres** ceramics workshops, set in a wooded park along the Seine. Sèvres has been famous for its porcelain for 200 years. **Le Musée de la Céramique** is set at the foot of a hill that rises 11.5 km (7 miles) to the **Terrace de Meudon**. The chateau and

Preceding pages: Monet's garden in Giverny; Chartres Cathedral. **Left**, the Palace of Versailles.

terrace were built in the 17th century. Part of the surrounding forest is now occupied by the National Observatory.

Saint Denis Cathedral is less than 4 km (3 miles) outside Paris and the Metro takes you right there. The Cathedral is revered as an early masterpiece of Gothic architecture; it was also a favoured final resting place of France's kings and queens. The Renaissance and medieval sculptures which mark their tombs are some of the finest in France.

An RER line will bring you to **Saint-Germain-en-Laye**, for centuries a royal retreat and now a wealthy bourgeois surburb. The chateau, which still has a lovely Gothic chapel, was reconstructed under François I (his royal salamander and "F" can be seen in the courtyard) and again in the 19th century. Inside, you won't find any period furnishings or portraits, but rather a museum devoted to prehistoric and medieval times. The Gallo-Roman collection and the life-sized replica of the Lascaux cave drawings are favourite exhibits. The terrace gardens overlooking the Seine were designed by Le Nôtre and later inspired the impressionist painter Alfred Sisley.

Let them eat cake: Historians debate whether or not Marie Antoinette actually gave that advice to the starving population, clamouring for bread. But any visitor to **Versailles** will certainly be struck by the notion that so much splendour was once the exclusive domain of a monarch and his court. Louis XIV ordered the transformation of what was originally a simple chateau.

Inside, from the king's apartments (his bedroom is set in the exact centre of the symmetrical palace) to the long **Galerie des Glaces**, whose mirrors reflect the French windows open to the terrace and park, it is fabulously decorated.

In the form of a *fleur-de-lys* (symbol of royalty), the **Grand Canal** stretches out from the terrace steps, dividing the wooded park in two. Seen from the far end of the canal, the palace appears to

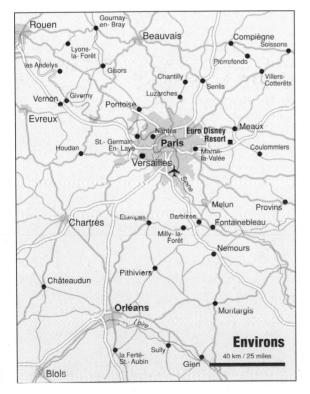

Environs
40 km / 25 miles

float on the breeze, buoyed up by the fluffy mass of trees on either side. Be warned before you set out along the canal, however. A trick of perspective makes it seem much shorter than it actually is – in all, it is nearly 5 km (3 miles) there and back.

The two sides of the park, with the fantastic chariot and horses rearing out of the waters of **Apollo's Pool** between them, are studded with groves, ponds, flowerbeds and shrubberies. The fountains are so many that only some of them are kept going all the time; however, on the first and third Sunday of the month between June and September, a glorious show begins at 4.30pm.

When the palace was too busy, or the constant problem of backed-up sewage made it too odorous, Louis headed off to one of the **Trianons** (either Grand or Petit), while Marie Antoinette played milkmaid at the **Hameau**, a make-believe farm.

On the banks of the Eure: The two spires of **Chartres Cathedral** soar above the surrounding fields. They were built over the course of 30 years at the turn of the 12th and 13th centuries. The famous **Rose Windows** fill the cathedral with changing colours. Traces of an ancient maze marking the floor are thought to be the vestiges of pre-Christian religious practices. Penitents and pilgrims followed its paths on their knees to reach the altar. Below is a 9th–11th century crypt (guided tours only) and from the towers above there is an exhilarating view over the plain.

The town of Chartres itself, easily reached by regular train services from Paris, provides an authentic glimpse of life "in the provinces". It isn't difficult to find a bakery which you will never forget or a cheese shop with more varieties than you can imagine. Along the river banks, a path passes typical countryside *lavoirs*, where you can hear the sound of laundresses washing linen.

Walk along the promenade which leads through quaint streets, past the **Eglise St-Pierre**, to the remains of the

Chateau at Fontainebleau.

old city wall, which for centuries protected the ruling aristocracy of Blois and Champagne.

Royal options: Another sumptuous palace within easy reach of Paris is **Chantilly**, which nestles in a grove in Chantilly forest. It is a real fairytale castle; white walls are topped by a blue-slate roof, and wild ducks bustle around its moat. Inside is the Conde Museum's collection of works by Botticelli, Raphael, Giotto and Holbein.

Near Melun is **Vaux-le-Vicomte**, the inspiration for Versailles, built by Louis XIV's Royal Treasurer, Nicolas Fouquet. A devoted patron of the arts, Fouquet built an impeccable house and garden *à la française*, but his own good taste defeated him. Jealous advisers whispered to the King that Fouquet had paid for it with treasury funds. Fouquet was imprisoned at Vincennes and Louis set out to build something even more splendid, using the very same architect and designers.

The chateau and its grounds and furnishings provide an interesting visit. One room traces the histories of its various owners, others are decorated in period style, with coffered, painted ceilings and Gobelins tapestries on the walls. The kitchen is equipped with a battery of shiny brass pots and pans and all manner of ingenious devices. For a wonderfully atmospheric visit, take the candlelight tour organised every Saturday evening, June to September.

Forestlands: All around Paris, thick forests help maintain the temperate, humid climate. To the northeast, the town of **Compiègne** sits between the Oise River and the **Forest**, one of the largest in France. The town's **Hôtel de Ville** has the oldest bell in France in its clock tower; little figures *(picantins)* strike the hour. The ruins of the **Saint Corneille Abbey** also merit a visit.

There are a number of things to see in the forest. On foot, head for **Les Beaux Monts** for a view over the chateau and the Oise. SNCF buses service the **Armistice Clearing**, where you can visit the railway carriage used for the signing of the 1918 Armistice between France and Germany. The museum is an eloquent record of the conflict, with fine archive photographs.

If you have a car, head for the village of **Vieux Moulin** and the **Etangs de St-Pierre**, where Napoleon's wife, the Empress Eugénie, used to go fishing. The couple also had an unusual hunting palace nearby, the **Château de Pierrefonds**. Entirely reconstructed in the 19th century, in idealised medieval style by Viollet-le-Duc, it is a remarkable architectural oddity.

The **Fontainebleau Forest**, once a royal hunting ground, is now the haunt of rock climbers and mushroom hunters. The chateau dominates the town, with its sprawling, eclectic buildings. Every king from the 12th century onwards seems to have added something to the palace: François I was responsible for the best of it, and Napoleon I had a throne-room built.

Visitors who want to see something

King of the forest.

off the ordinary tourist itinerary should head for the **Forêt de Lyons**. The centennial beech trees, thin and tall, make a walk in this forest a particular pleasure. There are fine views over Normandy-style villages of half-timbered houses set off by potted geraniums in the windows.

A poet and a painter: Another out-of-the-way spot is **Milly-La-Forêt**, not far from Fontainebleau. The massive covered **marketplace** dates from 1479 and is the village's centrepiece.

Just outside lies the **Chapelle Saint Blaise**, the only remains of a 12th-century leprosarium, redecorated by the artist Jean Cocteau in 1958. Medicinal herbs and flowers have been grown in this area for centuries and you won't want to leave without a packet of Menthe de Milly bonbons.

Along the Seine River west of Paris, **Giverny**, home of painter Claude Monet, is set on a hillside. His gardens are living works of art, from which he clearly drew inspiration. The bright contrasts of green foliage and luminous flowers, the Japanese bridge, the waterlilies, the willow and the pond – many of his favourite subjects are still growing. His house is also a riot of different colours. Across the road from Monet's house is a modern museum which celebrates the work of half a dozen American impressionists who worked in France.

All of the noble forests of the Île-de-France and surrounding regions are worth seeing. SNCF trains are generally quite convenient and, on arrival at the station, you will find the needs of visitors well catered for, with maps and information on tourist sights, hotels, restaurants and taxis. In Compiègne and Fontainebleau, tour buses are frequently scheduled for trips into town or through the countryside. From June to September, the SNCF runs a bike rental service at many of its stations. This is the best way to visit Monet's house or the Fôret de Lyons.

If you rent a car, take to the back

Lilies at Giverny.

roads, where your wanderings will lead to quaint old *auberges* serving hearty evening meals by the fire or lunch on a terrace overlooking a river.

A long weekend: Take a weekend away from the city and you may feel as though you have extended your trip by a week. Time seems to expand in the rolling countryside along the Loire River. **Gien** is only about 160 km (100 miles) from Paris, due south of Fontainebleau, but it is worlds apart in temperament. This pretty little town is the gateway to the **Loire Valley châteaux**. The bridge, castle, cloisters and church date from the 15th century. The town is also the home of the **Faïencerie de Gien** ceramics works. Its shop has worthwhile bargains on end-of-stock items.

The chateau, successfully restored in the regional style of patterned brickwork, now houses a hunting museum. In the summer, the streets are festooned with pennants and flags and the market is busy. On the hills bordering the Loire River, a few vineyards still produce the local Côtes de Gien wines. These little-known wines, though less sumptuous than their cousins from Pouilly-sur-Loire and Sancerre, are especially good with the regional cuisine and quite reasonably priced.

Just downstream, **Sully-sur-Loire Castle** is idyllic. It has two distinct parts: an early 14th-century defensive fortress and a 17th-century pleasure palace which was added by Sully, finance minister to Henry IV. In the older section, a high, keel-shaped timber roof made of huge chestnut tree-trunks is 600 years old. In the newer wing, beams are hidden by delicately painted coffered ceilings.

Nearby, **Orléans** is a busy little city with many interesting monuments and museums. Among them, the most significant are the **Cathedral** and the **Maison de Jeanne d'Arc**. It was here, where the Loire leaves its northward course to flow southwest, that the young Joan of Arc, the nation's most revered saint, drove the English from France. "I like the English," she is reported to have said, "in England."

Off the beaten track: The industrial city of **Rouen** was once the capital of Normandy and, despite the damage it suffered during World War I, it still has a number of Gothic churches and picturesque houses, as well as several fine museums. Joan was burned at the stake by a tribunal of clerics in cahoots with the English. They accused her of being a witch and relapsed heretic, although her real "crimes" were courage and patriotism.

Provins lies on the opposite side of Paris and it is the opposite of Rouen in many other ways as well. Forgotten by industry, spared by the wars, this medieval village seems to be under a spell. In ancient times it was a Roman outpost perched above the Voulzie River. In the 12th and 13th centuries, it was the powerful seat of the counts of Champagne, the third largest city in France and an important centre of trade.

Home with breakfast.

INSIGHT GUIDES
Travel Tips

So, you're getting away from it all.

Just make sure you can get back.

AT&T Access Numbers
Dial the number of the country you're in to reach AT&T.

*ANDORRA	19◇-0011	GERMANY**	0130-0010	*NETHERLANDS	06-022-9111
*AUSTRIA	022-903-011	*GREECE	00-800-1311	*NORWAY	050-12011
*BELGIUM	078-11-0010	*HUNGARY	00◇-800-01111	POLAND¹♦²	0◇010-480-0111
BULGARIA	00-1800-0010	*ICELAND	999-001	PORTUGAL¹	05017-1-288
CROATIA¹♦	99-38-0011	IRELAND	1-800-550-000	ROMANIA	01-800-4288
*CYPRUS	080-90010	ISRAEL	177-100-2727	*RUSSIA¹ (MOSCOW)	155-5042
CZECH REPUBLIC	00-420-00101	*ITALY	172-1011	SLOVAKIA	00-420-00101
*DENMARK	8001-0010	KENYA¹	0800-10	SPAIN	900-99-00-11
*EGYPT¹ (CAIRO)	510-0200	*LIECHTENSTEIN	155-00-11	*SWEDEN	020-795-611
*FINLAND	9800-100-10	LITHUANIA♦	8◇196	*SWITZERLAND	155-00-11
FRANCE	19◇-0011	LUXEMBOURG	0-800-0111	*TURKEY	9◇9-8001-2277
*GAMBIA	00111	*MALTA	0800-890-110	UK	0800-89-0011

Countries in bold face permit country-to-country calling in addition to calls to the U.S. *Public phones require deposit of coin or phone card. **Western portion. Includes Berlin and Leipzig. ◇Await second dial tone. ¹May not be available from every phone. ♦ Not available from public phones. ¹Dial "02" first, outside Cairo. ²Dial 010-480-0111 from major Warsaw hotels. © 1993 AT&T.

Here's a travel tip that will make it easy to call back to the States. Dial the access number for the country you're visiting and connect right to AT&T **USADirect**® Service. It's the quick way to get English-speaking operators and can minimize hotel surcharges.

If all the countries you're visiting aren't listed above, call **1 800 241-5555** before you leave for a free wallet card with all AT&T access numbers. International calling made easy—it's all part of **The i Plan**.℠

THE *i* PLAN™

AT&T

TRAVEL TIPS

GETTING THERE

BY AIR

Most major airlines have regular flights to Paris. Air France is the main agent for all flights to France from America and other European countries as well as its own services it also handles bookings for smaller operators such as Air Littoral, Air Vendée and Brit Air. For British travellers these smaller operators offer select flights from British cities to various provincial airports in France. The domestic carrier, Air Inter, has an extensive network and carries some 16 million passengers a year within France.

Travellers from America and other countries can get direct flights to Paris and other major destinations such as Nice and Lyon via Air France and most national airlines, although for long-haul passengers a charter flight to London, then onward to Paris from there may work out cheaper. In Paris itself Nouvelles Frontières and Forum offer competitive fares on both scheduled and charter flights.

Students and young people can normally obtain discounted charter fares through specialist travel agencies in their own countries; in the UK try Campus Travel, tel: 071-730 3402. Campus is part of the international group USIT, whose main US address is the New York Student Centre, William Sloane House YMCA, 356 West 34th Street, New York, NY 10001. Tel: 212-663 5435.

There are two international airports which serve Paris: Roissy/Charles de Gaulle, 23 km (15 miles) north of the city, tel: 48.62.12.12 and Orly (also for domestic flights), 14 km (9 miles) south of Paris, tel: 49.75.15.15.

FROM ROISSY/CHARLES DE GAULLE TO PARIS

Roissy rail: Take the free shuttle bus *navette* to the Roissy train station. From there take the RER to Métro station Gare du Nord or Chatelet. The RER runs every 15 minutes from 5am–11.59pm and costs 33 francs.
RATP Bus 350 (to Gare du Nord, Gare de l'Est) or bus 351 (to Nation) from terminals 2A and 2C gate 10; terminals 2B and 2D gate 12; or terminal 1, arrival level door 30. RATP buses run every 15 minutes from 6am–1pm.

Air France bus (to Métro Porte Maillot or Charles-de-Gaulle Etoile) leaves from terminals 2A and 2B; or terminal 1 arrival level gate 34. This bus runs every 15 minutes from 5.40am–11pm and costs 48 francs.
Taxi: This is by far the most expensive but unquestionably the easiest solution, especially for those laden with bags or children. The cost will be clearly indicated on the meter, although a supplement of five francs is charged for each large piece of luggage, pushchairs and pets. It is customary, although not required, to tip the driver 10 percent. Expect to be charged around 170 francs if going to the centre of Paris.

FROM ORLY TO PARIS

RER: Take the shuttle from gate H (Orly Sud) or from arrival level gate F (Orly Ouest) to the Orly train station. The RER stops at Austerlitz, Pont St Michel and the Quai D'Orsay. It runs every 15 minutes from 5.50am–10.50pm; costs 25 francs.
The Orlybus (to Place Denfert-Rochereau) leaves from Orly Sud gate F or Orly Ouest arrival level gate D. This bus runs every 13 minutes from 6.30am–11.30pm.
Orlyval: This is an automatic train which runs between Antony (the nearest RER to Orly) and Paris roughly every five minutes from 5.50am–11.48pm, but it isn't the quickest or easiest way of reaching Paris; cost 45 francs.
Air France bus (to Invalides and Gare Montparnasse) leaves from Orly Sud, gate J, or Orly Ouest, arrival level gate E. It runs every 12 minutes from 6am–11pm; cost 32 francs.
Taxi: Expect to pay around 130 francs to the centre of Paris.

In addition to the above, an Air France bus links Roissy and Orly leaving each airport every 20 minutes between 6am–11pm; cost 64 francs.

BY SEA

There are several ferry services operating from the UK, the Republic of Ireland and the Channel Islands to the northern ports of France. All of them carry cars as well as foot passengers. Hovercraft crossings are fast, but more dependent on good weather than the ferries. The new Sea Cat catamaran service offers the quickest crossing but, like the hovercraft, can only carry a limited number of cars. The ports of Boulogne, Calais and Le Havre offer direct access by motorway to Paris; there is an almost direct motorway link via Dunkerque and Caen.

There is a boat/train service to Paris from Victoria Station in London. From Victoria Coach Station there are frequent coach trips to Paris which use either the hovercraft or the Sea Cat and cost as little as £49 return.

BY RAIL

Other than the cross-Channel service mentioned above, Paris can be reached by train from all over continental Europe. In the city itself there are six railway stations, each serving a different region and different international destinations, and each on at least two Métro or RER lines. There are left-luggage facilities (*consigne*) and coin-operated lockers (*consigne automatique*) at every station.

SNCF's much publicised Train de Grand Vitesse (TGV) is developing all the time and offers a rapid and comfortable service from Paris to Bordeaux, Brest, La Rochelle, Lille/Calais, Lyon and Marseille. The TGV is not a particularly cheap method of travel and it pays to travel on off-peak days or to book one month to two months in advance and benefit from the Joker tariff which can offer up to a 50 percent reduction on 2nd class one way fares only. Other reductions can be found on 1st and 2nd class tickets if you ask about them (tariffs Vermeil, Carrissimo 50, Couple et Kiwi). You will have to ask: nobody will offer this information voluntarily!

Beware: before boarding any SNCF train you must have your ticket date stamped or *composté*. Failure to do so will be considered an offence and will render your ticket invalid. Before proceeding to your train insert your ticket into one of the bright orange *compositeur* machines at the entrance to each platform.

Any moment now (at the time of press) there will be a rail link between London's Waterloo station and the Gare du Nord which will use the Channel Tunnel. This journey is expected to take three hours.

Travel Essentials

VISAS & PASSPORTS

All visitors to France require a valid passport. No visa is currently required by visitors from any European Community (EC) country or from the US, Canada or Japan. Nationals of other countries do require a visa. If in any doubt check with the French Consulate in your home country, as the situation may change from time to time. If you intend to stay in France for more than 90 days at any one time, then a *carte de séjour* must be obtained (again from the French Consulate). This also applies to EC members until restrictions are relaxed.

MONEY MATTERS

The French franc is divided into 100 centimes. Coins come in 5, 10, 20 and 50 centimes and 1, 2, 5, 10 and 20 franc pieces. Notes come in 20, 50, 100, 200 and 500 francs. Certain credit cards are accepted, especially Visa known as Carte Bleue or CB. Larger shops and restaurants will accept American Express (Amex), Diner's Club (DC) or Access/Mastercharge but it is wiser to check before making a purchase. Most banks have an exchange counter *change* which is usually open from 9am–4.30pm (smaller branches close for lunch).

Airport Orly Sud Exchange is open seven days a week until 11pm and is situated on the departure level at gate H.

Airport Roissy Exchange is also open seven days a week until 11pm at terminals 2A, 2B and 2D. The *bureaux de change* at train stations vary their hours according to high or low season but generally they are open 5 days a week from 7am–7pm.

In case of emergencies note that Le Change de Paris at 2 Rue de l'Amiral de Coligny, 75001, is open every day from 10am–7pm. Remember always to bring your passport when you are cashing traveller's cheques.

HEALTH

There are no special health warnings for visitors to Paris. Visits to local doctors can cost anything between 100 and 350 francs with prescription costs on top of this, so do check your health cover before leaving on holiday.

CUSTOMS

In general, personal goods are admitted duty-free and without formality as long as it is obvious that they are for personal use and not for sale. Certain goods are strictly prohibited such as drugs, pirated books, guns, ammunition, counterfeit money or anything which does not conform to French legislation.

Nationals of an EC country (who also live in an EC country) can buy goods in France or any other Member State without limit, although some countries do prescribe advisory levels of alcohol and tobacco purchases. Exceeding these limits will raise suspicion of purchase for the purpose of resale, which is illegal.

Non-EC nationals are entitled to the following allowances: Tobacco: 200 cigarettes, 50 cigars, 250 grams of smoking tobacco (double these amounts if you live outside Europe); Alcohol: 2 litres of wine, 1 litre of over 38.8° proof or 2 litres of under 38.8° proof; Perfume: quarter litre of Eau de Toilette.

Non-EC nationals may not leave France with more than 12,000 francs in cash, but they can take out the same sum or more in a foreign currency if they fill in the Customs form on arrival declaring that they possess over 12,000 francs.

CLAIMING BACK VAT

On most purchases, the price includes TVA (VAT or value added tax). The base rate is currently 18.6 percent, but can be as high as 33 percent on luxury items. Foreign visitors can claim back TVA on purchases of 2,000 francs or more from any single shop which operates tax free sales. Some large stores and hypermarkets have information bureaux where you can obtain a refund form. This must be completed to show (with the goods purchased) to Customs officers on leaving the country (pack the items separately for ease of access and allow yourself extra time at the airport for all the paperwork to be completed). If you are leaving France by train the export documents will be stamped by a Customs official during the journey. French Customs will post the form back to the retailer who will refund the TVA in a month or two. Certain items purchased (e.g. antiques) may need special Customs clearance. There is no tax refund on foodstuffs, tobacco, medicines or alcohol. For more information contact:
Cashback France SA, 68 Rue de Paris, 93804 Epinay-sur-Seine Cedex. Tel: 48.27.24.54, fax: 48.27.23.46.

WHAT TO WEAR

Parisians are style-conscious and are not prepared to brave even the corner shop without displaying a fair amount of *élan*. To the Parisians style is a way of life; it is innate and as natural as breathing. But don't panic – visitors may slob. Parisians are used to bizarrely-dressed tourists and they won't turn a hair; but don't expect to catch a waiter's or shop assistant's eye quickly if you are dressed in standard tourist garb. If you want to eat in the more well-known and upmarket restaurants, you should dress up even if just to make the occasion more special. Bring warm clothes if visiting the capital in winter and be prepared for rain in spring and autumn. Comfortable walking shoes are essential.

GETTING ACQUAINTED

GOVERNMENT & ECONOMY

France has a population of 56.6 million or roughly the same as Britain, but has twice the land area to accommodate them (551,500 sq. km). The capital, Paris, is the country's largest city (population 8.7 million), followed by Lyon (1.2 million) and Marseille (1.1 million). The Ile de France region, which includes Paris, has a population density of 887 inhabitants per square kilometre.

Since 1977 Paris has had an elected mayor who works from the Hotel de Ville. He is seconded by the members of the Conseil Municipal and the mayors of the 20 *arrondissements*, all elected. Each *arrondissement* has its own town hall (*mairie*) and carries on the business of registering births, deaths and various legal documents, performing marriages (in France, the civil ceremony is required by law and the religious ceremony is optional) and, of course, hearing complaints.

France first became a Republic in 1792 after the abolition of the monarchy. Constitutional change resulted in the establishment of the Second, Third, Fourth and the current Fifth Republic, which was instituted when General Charles de Gaulle became Prime Minister in 1958. The President, who holds a powerful office, is elected for a term of seven years. He (to date it has always been a man), appoints the Prime Minister as head of government. Parliament is made up of two houses; the National Assembly and the Senate. The most important political parties are: the Partie Communiste Français (PCF), and the Partie Socialiste (PS), both belonging to the left. On the right there are two parties, Rassemblement pour la République (RPR) and the Union pour la Démocratié Française (UDF).

France has the fourth largest economy in the OECD (organisation of developed countries) and is the most visited country in the world. The Ile de France region, to which Paris belongs, contributes 40 percent of France's Gross Domestic Product from 18 percent of its population. The Paris stock exchange is the sixth most active in the world.

Paris is France's largest consumer market, and the focal point of all the country's communications systems. Most of its industries are located in the suburbs. The restraints on planning in the downtown area (the only building over nine floors in the central zone being the Tour Montparnasse) coupled

with the demand for high quality office accommodation has led to the recent completion of the huge La Défense project, to the west of Paris.

TIME ZONE

For most of the year, France is one hour ahead of Greenwich Mean Time, so if it is noon in Paris, it is 11am in London, 6am in New York and 9pm in Melbourne. The French use the 24-hour clock, therefore 1pm = 13.00hrs, 2pm = 14.00hrs, etc.

CLIMATE

The French climate is varied and seasonal, France being unique within Europe in that it is both a northern European and a Mediterranean country, and has an Atlantic coastline. In the north the climate is similar to that of southern England, while in the south summer temperatures can frequently rise to over 30°C (86°F). Springtime is often suggested as the best time to see Paris, and indeed the temperature then is ideal for sightseeing, but be prepared for showers. In the autumn, mornings can be quite sharp, but by midday the skies are usually clear and bright.

WEIGHTS & MEASURES

The metric system is used in France for all weights and measures, although you may encounter old-fashioned terms such as *livre* (roughly one pound in weight or 500 grams) still used by small shopkeepers. For quick and easy conversion remember that one inch is roughly 2.5 cms, one metre is roughly equivalent to a yard, 4oz is just over 100 grams and a kilogramme is just over 2lbs. As a kilometre is five-eighths of a mile, then 80 km=50 miles. Temperatures are always given in celsius (centigrade). To convert celsius into fahrenheit, multiply by 9, divide by 5 and then add 32.

Accurate conversions are given below:

Weight

100 grams	=	3.5oz
500 grams	=	1.1lbs
1 kg	=	2.2lbs

Length

1 centimetre	=	0.39 ins
1 metre	=	1.094 yards
1 kilometre	=	0.62 miles

Liquid

1 litre	=	2.113 pints
1 litre	=	0.22 Imp. gallon/ 0.26 US gallon
10 litres	=	2.2 Imp. gallons/ 2.6 US gallons

ELECTRICITY

The electric current is generally 220/230 volts, but still 110 in a few areas. If you intend to bring any electrical appliances don't forget to pack the appropriate transformer or adapter (two-pin plugs are in use in France).

HOLIDAYS

Banks and post offices are closed on:
1 January/*Jour de l'An*
Easter/*Pâques* (Monday but not Good Friday)
1 May/*Fête du Travail*
8 May/*Victoire 1945*
Ascension Day/*Ascension*
Pentecost/*Pentecôte*
14 July/*Fête Nationale* (Bastille Day)
15 August/*Assomption*
1 November/*Toussaint*
11 November/*Armistice 1914*
25 December/*Noël*

Make preparations for all these holidays. Particularly in Paris – where every opportunity is taken to get out of the city – everything does close bar the occasional *tabac* and restaurant. Details of public holidays are normally posted outside banks and post offices a few days beforehand. Furthermore, a holiday that falls on a Thursday or Tuesday is liable to cause a *pont* or bridge where the day before or after is also taken as holiday.

Many small shops and restaurants close for the entire month of August, when thousands of Parisians leave the city. If you can bear the heat, this is an excellent time to visit the capital as it is much quieter and calmer.

FESTIVALS

The **Festival du Marais** (dance, music and theatre) goes on throughout June and July, making up for the annual closure of many theatres and concert halls.

On the 21st June, the **Fête de la Musique** provides free concerts all over the city from dawn 'til dawn on this, the longest day of the year.

Bastille Day on the 14th July, celebrating the downfall of the monarchy and the beginning of the modern constitution, hardly needs any introduction. Celebrations normally start the evening before. It is a brave man (if not indeed mad) who takes a car into Paris on the 13th or 14th. There is a military parade starting at 10am on the Champs-Elysées which is quite splendid if you get there early enough to secure a good vantage point.

October is the wine month as Beaujolais Nouveau arrives. It's also the occasion of the **Montmartre Wine Harvest**.

In addition, key events in the Paris year are the fashion shows in January, the **Foire de Paris** in late

April, the **International Tennis tournament** in late May, the **Air Show** in June, the **Autumn Festival** from September all the way to December, the **Contemporary Art Fair** in October, and the **Boat Show** in December.

RELIGIOUS SERVICES

France is predominately Catholic and the many churches, including Notre Dame Cathedral, are open to the public and display the hours of Mass. For a complete list of all denominational churches, temples and synagogues buy a copy of the small book, *Plan de Paris par Arrondissement*, on sale in kiosks and bookshops or tel: 46.33.01.01 (International Centre for Religious Information). Suffice it to say that there are services in English around the capital, notably in the American church on the Quai d'Orsay.

COMMUNICATIONS

MEDIA

Newspapers: The main national dailies are *Le Monde* (a rather dry and leftish slant on politics and economic news) and the more conservative *Le Figaro*, which sell about 400,000 copies each. Representing the Communist Party is *L'Humanité* and not veering quite so heavily left is Jean-Paul Sartre's brainchild, *Libération*. *Le Point* (right) and *L'Express* (left) are the major weekly news publications, also selling around 3–500,000 copies. British, American and other European dailies are readily available at city centre kiosks and shops displaying the sign, *journaux* or *presse*. The *International Herald Tribune*, which is published in Paris, has some listings for the city.

To find out what is going on in the capital try *L'Officiel des Spectacles* or *Pariscope* (both out on Wednesdays) which give complete listings of museums, galleries, concerts, ballet, opera, theatre, cinema and nightlife in general.

Radio: France Inter is the main national radio station which offers a bit of everything (87.8 MHz). Radio Classique offers the listener uninterrupted lightweight classical music (101.1 MHz) but if you're looking for something a bit more demanding then try France Musique (91.7 and 92.1 MHz). RTL is currently the most popular station throughout France with the current charts, chat shows etc. (104.3 MHz).

Television: TF1, Antenne 2, FR3, M6 and Arte are the five television stations on offer – most of the larger hotels receive cable as well. CNN is sometimes available.

POSTAL SERVICES

The French post office is run by the PTT (Poste et Télécommunications). The main branches are open 8am–7pm and Saturday 8am–noon. The central post office at 52 Rue du Louvre, 75001 (Tel: 40.28.20.00) operates a 24 hour, 7–day service for international telegrams and telephone. Unless you arrive first thing in the morning or around 2.30–3.30pm be prepared for a long wait in all post offices.

Stamps are often available at tabacs and other shops selling postcards or greeting cards. Letters within France and most of the EC cost 2.80 francs for up to 20g; 4 francs for airmail to Ireland, the US and Canada and 4.40 francs for Australia.

Telephones, Telex, Minitel (directory enquiries), Fax and photocopying facilities are available in the larger post offices.

TELEPHONES

The French telephone system, once quirky, is now one of the most efficient in the world. That is not to say that you can be guaranteed to find telephone boxes that are always working. Remember that you get 50 percent more call-time for your money if you call on weekdays between 10.30pm and 8am, on weekends starting at 2pm.

There are two kinds of phone boxes in Paris from which you can make local and international calls: coin-operated booths which are extremely difficult to find as most have been replaced by modern card-operated ones. A *télécarte* can be bought from kiosks, tabacs and post offices. To use your card follow the instructions as they appear on the screen: *Décrochez* – pick up the receiver; *Introduire votre carte* – insert card; *Patientez* – wait; *Numérotez* – dial; *Raccrochez* – hang up.

You can also dial from all post offices, where they have both coin- and card-operated phones. Or if you wish to call long distance ask at one of the counters and you will be assigned a cabin – you pay when your call is over. Cafés and *tabacs* often have public phones, located next to the toilets which use either coins or *jetons*, coin-like discs which are bought at the bar.

You cannot reverse telephone call charges within France but you can to countries which will accept such calls. Go through the operator (12) and ask to make a PCV call.

Paris numbers should all be eight digits and begin with a 4 for the central area, 3 or 6 for the outskirts. If you're dialling from Paris to the provinces, dial 16, wait for the change in tone, then dial your number.

To call other countries first dial the international

THE WORLD IS FLAT

Its configuration may not be to Columbus' liking but to every other traveller the MCI Card is an easier, more convenient, more cost-efficient route to circle the globe.

The MCI Card offers two international services—MCI World Reach and MCI CALL USA—which let you call from country-to country as well as back to the States, all via an English-speaking operator.

There are no delays. No hassles with foreign languages and foreign currencies. No foreign exchange rates to figure out. And no outrageous hotel surcharges.

If you don't possess the MCI Card, please call the access number of the country you're in and ask for customer service.

The MCI Card. It makes a world of difference.

For the fastest weekend refunds anywhere in the world.

Ensure your holiday is worry free even if your travellers cheques are lost or stolen by buying American Express Travellers Cheques from;

Lloyds Bank	Leeds Permanent Building Society[*]
Royal Bank of Scotland	Woolwich Building Society[*]
Abbey National[*]	National & Provincial Building Society
Bank of Ireland	Britannia Building Society[*]
Halifax Building Society[*]	American Express Travel Offices.

As well as many regional building societies and travel agents.

[*]Investors only.

Not all travellers cheques are the same.

AMERICAN EXPRESS **Travellers Cheques**

access code 19, then the relevant country code: Australia 61; Germany 49; Italy 39, Netherlands 31; Spain 34; UK 44, US and Canada 1. If using a US credit phone card, call the company's access number below: AT&T, Tel: 078 11-0010; MCI, Tel: 078 11-0012; SPRINT, Tel: 078 11-0014.

EMERGENCIES

SECURITY & CRIME

Sensible precautions regarding personal possessions are all that should really be necessary when visiting Paris. The worst most tourists may be faced with is pickpockets (especially in the Métro), and this can easily be avoided by carrying your money safely. Areas which are obviously prostitution centres (Rue St Denis and parts of the Bois de Boulogne) are best avoided late at night.

Drivers are liable to heavy on-the-spot fines for driving offences such as speeding and drink driving.

LOSS

If you are victim of a theft, be it your personal documents, cash, belongings or traveller's cheques, you must first go to the Commissariat de Police nearest to where the theft occurred, and as soon as possible. This is necessary even before taking appropriate steps with the travel cheque service or your embassy or consulate. If you carry credit cards, note the telephone numbers for lost or stolen cards before you travel. Three key numbers are listed below:
American Express tel: 47.77.72.00.
Diner's Club tel: 47.62.75.00.
Visa/CB tel: 42.77.11.90.

MEDICAL SERVICES

A doctor will pay a house call in an emergency if you dial SOS médecins – tel: 47.07.77.77 – and explain your situation in French. This is a 24-hour service. You can reach English speaking health services at the American Hospital (Tel: 46.41.25.25) or at the British Hospital (Tel: 47.58.13.12). Please note neither of these hospitals have casualty departments. SAMU 24 hour ambulance service can be contacted by dialling 15. Otherwise call the fire brigade (pompiers) on 18 who are extremely professional in an emergency be it health, accident or fire.

If you need to see a doctor, expect to pay around

100 francs minimum for a consultation, with prescription charges on top. The doctor will provide a *feuille des soins* which you need to keep to claim back the majority of the cost (around 75 percent) under the EC agreement (if you live in an EC country). Check that the chemist has attached the *vignette* from any medecine prescribed to the *feuille des soins* so that you may claim for that too. When complete, the *feuille des soins* should be sent to the local *caisse primaire* (ask the doctor or chemist for the address) for your refund.

PHARMACIES

Most pharmacies, displaying flashing green, neon crosses, are open from 9am–noon and 2–7pm. At night, every pharmacy will post in the window or doorway the address of the nearest one that is open that night.
Pharmacie Dhéry, 84 Avenue des Champs-Elysées, Métro Georges V is open 24-hours – tel: 45.62.02.41.

HOSPITALS

All State hospitals within the capital have casualty departments. The following list includes some of the larger ones.
Boucicaut, 78 Rue Convention, 75015. Tel: 45.54.41.92.
Necker, (Children's hospital) 149 Rue de Sèvres, 75015. Tel: 42.73.80.00.
Bichat, 46 Rue Henri Huchard, 75018. Tel: 40.25.80.80.
Hôtel-Dieu, 1 Place du Parvis-Notre-Dame, 75004. Tel: 42.34.82.34.
Saint-Louis, 1 Avenue Claude Vellefaux, 75004. Tel: 42.49.49.49.

GETTING AROUND

METRO & RER

Run by the Régie Autonome des Transport Parisiens – RATP – the Paris Métro is one of the world's oldest subway systems and some of its stations are almost historic monuments. Despite that, it is quick and efficient. The Métro operates from 5.30–12.30am; its comprehensive map and signposting make it virtually impossible to get lost; the lines are identified by number and the names of their terminals e.g. M1–La Défense/Chateau de Vincennes. If you have to change lines, follow the orange signs which say *correspondence* when you get off the train. The Métro runs in conjunction with the RER (suburban regional express trains), which operate four main lines, identified as A–D.

Both the Métro and the bus system use the same tickets (6.50 francs for a single fare). A book or *carnet* of 10 offers a considerable saving at 39 francs. Buy them at bus or Métro stations and some *tabacs*.

Another option is the *Paris Visite* card, valid for three or five consecutive days on the Métro, bus and railway in the Paris/Ile de France region. The same card entitles you to a discount at several tourist sites and can be bought from main Métro, RER and SNCF stations. It is only available to tourists. Fares start at 90 francs for three zones over three days, up to 275 francs for five zones over five days.

For shorter stays, buy the *formule 1* card, which allows an unlimited number of trips on any one day on the Métro, bus, suburban SNCF, RER and the night buses (it extends as far as Euro Disney). It can be bought in all Métro stations. Fares start at 27 francs for 1–2 zones to 85 francs for 1–5 zones.

A *carte orange* for two zones allows unlimited travel on any public transport system for an entire month. Buy a *carte orange* or a *carte jaune* (unlimited travel for one week, from Monday to Monday) from any Métro or SNCF station but take along a passport photograph of yourself. You must sign your orange or yellow card and copy its number onto your ticket – if you are stopped by ticket inspectors and have not done this you will be fined.

For further information contact RATP, 53 Quai des Grands Augustins, 75006. Tel: 40.46.42.17. Open daily 6am–9pm. Or RATP, Place de la Madeleine, 75008. Tel: 40.06.71.45. Open daily 7.30am–7pm.

BUSES

Taking the bus is a pleasant way to see the city but can be much slower than the Métro because of traffic. Tickets can be bought from the driver or from Métro stations as the same tickets are used – always remember to punch your ticket (but NOT your travel card) in the *compositeur*.

Buses don't automatically stop at every station, so if you wish to get off, push one of the *arrêt* buttons. Each bus has a map of its route posted at the front and back, and also at every stop. Most buses run from 6.30am–8.30pm. Some routes do continue until 12.15am. There is a special night service that leaves Châtelet (Avenue Victoria or Rue Saint Martin) at 1.30, 2.30, 3.30, 4.30 and 5.30am which offers 10 different routes.

Also look out for the Balabus service at certain stops which visits the main tourist sites in Paris, every Sunday and on public holidays between 11th April and 26th September from 12.30–8pm. The visit lasts around 50 minutes.

TAXIS

Taxis are most readily available at airports and railway stations. In Paris there are almost 500 taxi ranks, but be careful in the capital to hail only a genuine taxi (with a light on the roof); other operators may charge exorbitant fares. Taxi drivers in Paris operate on three tariffs:

Tariff A 7am–7pm
Tariff B 7pm–7am
Tariff C at night in the suburbs and during the day in the outlying districts of Hauts-de-Seine, Seine Saint-Denis and Val de Marne, when the taxi has no client for the return journey.

A 10 percent tip is usual. Any complaints about Paris taxis should be addressed to: Services des Taxis, Préfecture de Police, 36 Rue des Morillons, 75015 Paris. Tel: 45.31.14.80.

BICYCLES

If you know Paris well, and have nerves of steel, a bicycle is an excellent way to explore the quieter areas of the city. You can rent a bicycle from:

Paris-Vélo, 2 Rue du Fer à Moulin, 75005 Paris. Tel: 43.37.59.22. Open 10am–12.30pm and 2–7pm, from Monday to Saturday. Hire by the day, weekend, week or month.
Paris Bicycle, 99, Rue de la Jonquière, 75017 Paris. Tel: 42.63.36.63. Hire by the half-day or the week.
Mountain Bike Trips, 6 Place Etienne Pernet, 75015 Paris. Tel: 48.42.57.87. Hire of mountain bikes by the day, weekend, week or month.

BREAK THE LANGUAGE BARRIER!

If you travel internationally, for business or pleasure - or if you are learning a foreign language - TI's electronic language -products can make communication a lot easier.

The **PS-5800** is a versatile 3-language dictionary with 30,000 entry words in each language. Available in English/German/French or English/Italian/French, It includes, travel sentences, business words, memory space to build and store your own vocabulary, currency and metric conversions, and more.

The **PS-5400** is a powerful 5-language translator fea-

turing up to 5,000 words and 1,000 structured sentences in English, German, French, Italian, and Spanish. Travel-related sentences, conveniently grouped by category, facilitate conversation in the language of your choice. To keep you on time and on top, there's also world time, alarm reminders, calculator, and metric conversions.

The **PS-5800** and **PS-5400**. Two pocket-sized ways to break the language barrier!

For more information, fax your request to:
Texas Instruments France, (33) 39 22 21 01

TEXAS
INSTRUMENTS

Cutter®
INSECT REPELLENT
Put on the Cutter®
...because it's a
jungle out there.
Unscented
BACKWOODS
Cutter
INSECT REPELLENT
Pump Spray
Unscented
BACKWOODS
Cutter
INSECT REPELLENT
Long Lasting
Protection
BACKWOODS
Cutter
INSECT REPELLENT
Cream
BACKWOODS
Cutter
INSECT REPELLENT
Stick
Cutter® Insect Repellent. Effective, long-lasting protection.
So no matter how delicious you look, mosquitoes will know
it's look, but don't touch. Protect yourself with Cutter®
...because it's a jungle out there.
© 1993 Miles Inc.

PRIVATE TRANSPORT

Driving in Paris requires equal measures of insanity and desperation to get where you are going, and an ability to allow for everyone else's madness.

Seat belts are obligatory in the front and back of the car and the speed limit in town is 50 km (30 miles) per hour. Do not drive in bus lanes at any time, and remember that priority should be given to vehicles approaching from the right. This also applies to some roundabouts, which means that those cars already on the roundabout have to stop for those coming onto it. If in doubt, be cautious. Helmets are compulsory for motorbikes.

Street parking is generally metered and the maximum allowed stay is two hours. Car parks, which are mainly underground, cost anywhere between 5 and 75 francs per hour.

Petrol in the city centre can be difficult to find, so if you're almost empty head for one of the *portes* at the entrance to the *périphérique* (the multi-lane circular road) which have 24-hour petrol stations.

CAR HIRE

Hiring a car is expensive, partly because it incurs the highest rate of TVA tax at 33 percent. Some fly/drive packages work out more cheaply if you are only going for a short visit. SNCF offer a good deal on their combined train/car hire bookings. Weekly rates often work out better than a daily rate and it may be cheaper to arrange hire in the UK or the US before leaving for France. The minimum age to hire a car is 23, or 21 if paying by credit card and the hirer must have held a full licence for at least a year. The central reservation offices of the major car hire companies are listed below. Car hire anywhere in France can be arranged through them or via their agencies abroad.

Autorent: 98 Rue de la Convention, 75015 Paris. Tel: 45.54.22.45, fax: 45.54.39.69.

Avis: Tour Franklin, 92042 Paris-La Défense Cedex 11. Tel: 49.06.68.68, fax: 47.78.98.98.

Budget/Milleville: 1 Rue des Hauts-Flouviers, 94517 Thiais. Tel: 46.86.65.65, fax: 46.86.14.13.

Citer: 125 bis Rue de Vaugirard, 75015 Paris. Tel: 44.38.60.00, fax: 40.56.08.08.

Eurodollar/Mattei: Place des Reflets, Z.I. Parc Nord II, 165 Avenue du Bois-de-la-Pie, B.P. 40002, 95911 Roissy Charles-de-Gaulle Cedex. Tel: 49.38.77.00, fax: 49.38.77.02.

Europcar/National/InterRent: 65 Rue Edouard-Vaillant, 92100 Boulogne. Tel: 49.10.55.55, fax: 46.20.47.81.

Eurorent: 42 Avenue de Saxe, 75007 Paris. Tel: 45.67.82.17, fax: 40.65.91.94.

Hertz: 4 Avenue du Vieil Etang, 78180 Montigny-le-Bretonneux. Tel: (1) 30.45.65.65, fax: (1) 30.58.46.21.

WHERE TO STAY

HOTELS

The capital is renowned for the diversity of its hotels, from the small, simple family run hotel to the luxurious palace.

It is advisable to reserve your room/rooms in advance, either directly with the hotel or via the Paris Tourist Office which will book your first night's accommodation if you apply in person.

Paris Tourist Office, 127 Avenue des Champs-Elysées, 75008. Tel: 49.52.53.54, fax 49.52.53.20. Open 9am–8pm every day except 1 January, 1 May and 25 December.

Subsidiary offices:

Gare du Nord, 18 Rue Dunkerque, 75010. Tel: 45.26.94.82. Open Monday–Saturday May–October 8am–9pm and November–April 8am–8pm.

Gare de l'Est, Hall d'Arrivée, 75010. Tel: 46.07.17.73.

Gare de Lyon, Sortie Grandes Lignes, 75012. Tel: 43.43.33.24.

Gare Montparnasse, 15 Boulevard de Vaugirard, 75015. **Arrivée Grandes Lignes**. Tel: 43.22.19.19.

All the above are open the same hours as Gare du Nord.

Gare d'Austerlitz, Arrivée Grandes Lignes, 75013. Tel: 45.84.91.70. Open Monday–Saturday 8am–3pm.

Eiffel Tower, Champ de Mars, 75007. Tel: 45.51.22.15. Open May–September daily 11am–6pm.

All the above addresses can supply you with a free booklet listing all hotels in Paris and the neighbouring suburbs which have been awarded a classification by the Direction de l'Industrie Touristique. Most of the hotels in the following shortlist are classified.

Hotel prices in Paris are not subject to any restrictions, and can be changed without prior notice so please check before booking. Also, the majority of hotels alter their prices according to the time of year. If you reserve by phone, state your arrival time, as the hotelier is not required to keep your room for you after 7pm.

The 1-star category offers rooms with a bed, a minimum of furniture and for 80 percent of the rooms, shared bathrooms. Many of these hotels are located in the Marais or the Latin Quarter, and can be pleasant if well-run and kept clean. As they are generally operated by families there is often a curfew, after which time the front door is locked.

A 2-star hotel is required to equip 40 percent of its rooms with private bathrooms (shower or bath), and provide breakfast and telephones.

Eighty percent of the rooms in a 3-star hotel must have private bathrooms, plus in all cases, telephone, TV and breakfast.

In 4-star hotels the reception staff is required to speak several languages. All rooms are equipped with private bathrooms, telephone and TV. Breakfast may be taken in the dining room or in the bedroom, and restaurant service must be available morning and evening. Four-star deluxe hotels have all conceivable amenities, top quality service and very spacious rooms and bathrooms.

The following list of recommended hotels is arranged into price categories, the price being the rate for the cheapest single room, first, then that for the most expensive double room.

175 to 300 Francs

Rouen, 42 Rue Croix-des-Petits-Champs, 75001. Tel: 42.61.38.21. 22 rooms. Small but excellent location close to the Louvre. Credit cards: Visa. 180–290 francs. ☆

Tiquetonne, 6 Rue Tiquetonne, 75002. Tel: 42.36.94.58. 47 rooms. In an old part of Paris close to Les Halles. No credit cards. 120–230 francs. ☆

Andrea, 3 Rue Saint Bon, 75003. Tel: 42.78.43.93. 26 rooms. Just off the Rue de Rivoli. No credit cards. 170–330 francs. ☆☆

Castex, 5 Rue Castex, 75004. Tel: 42.72.31.52, fax: 42.72.57.91. 26 rooms. Small well-run family hotel close to Bastille. Always busy – book well in advance. Credit cards: Visa. 170–380 francs. ☆☆

Des Argonautes, 12 Rue de la Huchette, 75005. Tel: 43.54.09.82, fax: 44.07.18.84. 25 rooms. Situated in a bustling part of town beside the famous Théâtre de la Huchette. Credit cards: Visa, American Express (Amex) and Diners Club (DC). 200–350 francs. ☆☆

Marignan, 13 Rue du Sommerard, 75005. Tel: 43.25.31.03. 30 rooms. In the Latin Quarter. 160–220 francs. ☆

Allies, 20 Rue Berthollet, 75005. Tel: 43.31.47.52, fax: 45.35.13.92. 42 rooms Ony a few rooms have a bath/shower. Credit cards: Visa. 120–290 francs. ☆

Palais Bourbon, 49 Rue Bourgogne, 75007. Tel: 47.05.29.26, fax: 45.55.20.21. 33 rooms. Modern hotel which is situated in a smart quiet part of town. Book well in advance for cheaper rooms. Credit cards: Visa. 200–445 francs. ☆☆

Regence, 3 Rue Laferrière, 75009. Tel: 48.78.29.96. 18 rooms. Small comfortable hotel which will accept dogs. Situated in a quiet road. Credit cards: Visa. 185–300 francs. ☆☆

Albouy, 4 Rue Lucien Sampaix, 75010. Tel: 42.08.20.09, fax 40.34.00.84. 34 rooms. Well equipped although a bit out from the city centre – close to Canal St Martin. Credit cards: Visa, Amex and DC. 180–300 francs. ☆☆

Royal Montmartre, 68 Boulevard de Clichy, 75018. Tel: 42.64.15.26, fax: 46.06.35.03. 48 rooms. All rooms have a WC. Dogs are accepted. Credit cards: Visa and Amex. 150–250 francs. ☆☆

Pacific, 77 Rue du Ruisseau, 75018. Tel: 42.62.53.00, fax: 46.06.09.82. 44 rooms. Reasonably comfortable hotel which is a couple of streets from the *périphérique*. Credit cards: Visa. 180–310 francs. ☆

300 to 500 Francs

Regyn's Montmartre, 18 Place des Abbesses, 75018. Tel: 42.54.45.21, fax: 42.54.45.21. 22 rooms. Simple and quiet. Credit cards: Visa. 360–435 francs. ☆☆

Timhôtel: this chain has several branches in the city, all fairly modern (every room has a bath). Call the central reservation office on tel: 42.96.28.28. Credit cards: Visa, Amex and DC. 350–490 francs. ☆☆

  Italie, 22, Rue Barrault, 75013.

  Tolbiac, 35, Rue du Tolbiac, 75013.

  Montmartre, 11 Place Emile Goudeau, 75018.

Victoria Chatelet, 17 Avenue Victoria, 75001. Tel: 40.26.90.17. 24 rooms. Small hotel in bustling part of town. Credit cards: Visa, Amex and DC. 300–400 francs. ☆☆☆

Vivienne, 40 Rue Vivienne, 75002. Tel: 42.33.13.26, fax: 40.41.98.19. 44 rooms. Close to the Bourse. Credit cards: Visa. 280–430 francs. ☆☆

Alexandre Montparnasse, 71 Boulevard de Vaugirard, 75015. Tel: 43.20.89.12, fax: 43.22.77.71. 31 rooms. Handy for antique shops of the Village Suisse and the Beaugrenelle quarter. Credit cards: Visa and Amex. 420–500 francs. ☆☆

Saint-Thomas-d'Aquin, 3 Rue Pré-aux-Clercs, 75007. Tel: 42.61.01.22, fax: 42.61.41.43. 21 rooms. Close to the Eiffel Tower and the Musée D'Orsay. Credit cards: Visa, Amex and DC. 440–520 francs. ☆☆

Glasgow, 3 Rue de la Félicité, 75017. Tel: 42.27.93.95, fax: 40.53.92.52. 38 rooms. Well equipped with facilities for the disabled plus private parking. Credit cards: Visa, Amex and DC. 375–490 francs. ☆☆☆

Grand Hotel de Lima, 46 Boulevard de Saint Germain, 75005. Tel: 46.34.02.12, fax: 43.25.47.73. 39 rooms. At the quieter end of St Germain. Credit cards: Visa and Amex. 280–500 francs. ☆☆

Place des Vosges, 12 Rue Birague, 75004. Tel: 42.72.60.46, fax: 42.72.02.64. 16 rooms. Small, comfortable rooms. Credit cards: Visa, Amex and DC. 290–415 francs. ☆☆

500 to 700 Francs

Aramis, 124 Rue de Rennes, 75006. Tel: 45.48.03.75, fax: 45.44.99.29. 42 rooms. Attractive rooms and well equipped bathrooms. Credit cards: Visa, Amex and DC. 500–750 francs.

Banville, 166 Boulevard Berthier, 75017. Tel: 42.67.70.16, fax: 44.40.42.77. 40 rooms. Marble bathrooms. Credit cards: Visa and Amex. 550–700 francs.

Berne, 37 Rue de Berne, 75008. Tel: 43.87.08.92, fax: 43.87.08.93. 136 rooms. Comfortable hotel in quiet street, particularly accommodating for young families. Credit cards: Visa, Amex and DC. 500–750 francs.

Brittanique, 20 Avenue Victoria, 75001. Tel: 42.33.74.59, fax: 42.33.82.65. 40 rooms. Comfortable hotel in central location. Credit cards: Visa, Amex and DC. 510–720 francs.

Louisiane, 60 Rue de Seine, 75006. Tel: 43.29.59.30, fax: 46.34.23.87. 80 rooms. Overlooks the bustling Buci market. Credit cards: Visa and DC. 350–600 francs.

Saint-Germain, 50 Rue du Four, 75006. Tel: 45.48.91.64, fax: 45.48.46.22. 30 rooms. Excellent location on the Left Bank; comfortable rooms. Credit cards: Visa, Amex and DC. 415–695 francs.

Saint-Louis-Marais, 1 Rue Charles V, 75004. Tel: 48.87.87.04, fax: 48.87.33.26. 16 rooms. Comfortable, rooms small. Credit cards: Visa. 480–720 francs.

Deux-Iles, 59 Rue Saint-Louis-en-l'Ile, 75004. Tel: 43.26.13.35, fax: 43.29.05.18. 17 rooms. Charming hotel in the heart of Ile-Saint-Louis. Credit cards: Visa. 670–770 francs.

700 to 1,000 Francs

Bradford, 10 Rue St-Philippe-du-Roule, 75008. Tel: 45.63.20.20, fax: 45.63.20.07. 48 rooms. Large, light rooms by the Champs-Elysées. 750–1,550 francs.

Angleterre, 44 Rue Jacob, 75006. Tel: 42.60.34.72, fax: 42.60.16.93. 29 rooms. In a smart corner of the Left Bank, very comfortable. Credit cards: Visa, Amex and DC. 750–1,200 francs.

Elysées Maubourg, 35 Boulevard de Latour-Maubourg, 75007. Tel: 45.56.10.78, fax: 47.05.65.08. 30 rooms. Modern, well-equipped with free sauna available. Credit cards: Visa, Amex and DC. 540–1,000 francs.

Bac Saint-Germain, 66 Rue du Bac, 75007. Tel: 42.22.20.03, fax: 45.48.52.30. 21 rooms. Pleasant hotel with glassed-in terrace on seventh floor. Credit cards: Visa, Amex and DC. 500–890 francs.

Buci Latin, 34 Rue de Buci, 75006. Tel: 43.29.07.20, fax: 43.29.67.44. 27 rooms. Redecorated in the style of Philippe Starck. Very fashionable area of St Germain. Credit cards: Visa, Amex and DC.

1,000 to 2,000 Francs

Château Frontenac, 54 Rue Pierre Charron, 75008. Tel: 47.23.55.85, fax: 47.23.03.32. 106 rooms. Modern and stylish but still intimate. Credit cards: Visa and DC. 880–1,550 francs.

Normandy, 7 Rue de l'Echelle, 75001. Tel: 42.60.30.21, fax: 42.60.45.81. 138 rooms. Only a stone's throw from the Louvre. Credit cards: Visa, Amex and DC. 1,195–1,815 francs.

Louvre, 1 Place André Malraux, 75001. Tel: 44.58.38.38, fax: 44.58.38.01. 200 rooms. A truly comfortable hotel in an excellent location – some rooms overlook a busy junction. Credit cards: Visa, Amex and DC. 1,300–2,000 francs.

Pavillon de Reine, 28 Place des Vosges, 75003. Tel: 42.77.96.40, fax: 42.77.63.06. 55 rooms. The smartest hotel in the Marais, in a very popular square. Credit cards: Visa, Amex and DC. 1,250–2,500 francs.

Ambassador, 16 Boulevard Haussmann, 75009. Tel: 42.46.92.63, fax: 40.22.08.74. 298 rooms. Pleasant hotel in the heart of the business area. Credit cards: Visa, Amex and DC. 1,300–2,000 francs.

Lutetia, 45 Boulevard Raspail, 75006. Tel: 49.54.46.46, fax: 49.54.46.00. 276 rooms. This early Art Deco hotel used to be frequented by writers Parker, Hemingway and Fitzgerald. Credit cards: Visa, Amex and DC. 1,100–2,260 francs.

2,000 Francs & Above

Bristol, 112 Rue du Faubourg St Honoré, 75008. Tel: 42.66.91.45, fax: 42.66.68.68. 195 rooms. Built in the 1920s with period furniture in all the rooms. Lovely gardens. Credit cards: Visa, Amex and DC. 2,450–4,150 francs.

Meurice, 228 Rue de Rivoli, 75001. Tel: 44.58.10.10, fax: 44.58.10.15. 179 rooms. Marvellous location, overlooking the Tuileries. Credit cards: Visa, Amex and DC. 2,200–2,950 francs.

Crillon, 10 Place de la Concorde, 75008. Tel: 44.71.15.00, fax: 44.71.15.02. 163 rooms. Beside the Tuileries. Credit cards: Visa, Amex and DC. 2,400–3,900 francs.

George V, 31 Avenue George V, 75008. Tel: 47.23.54.00, fax: 47.20.40.00. Renowned for its elegance. Credit cards: Visa, Amex and DC. 1,930–3,850 francs.

Hilton International, 18 Avenue de Suffren, 75015. Tel: 42.73.93.00, fax: 47.83.62.66. Good quiet location on the Left Bank with a view of the Eiffel Tower. Credit cards: Visa, Amex and DC. 1,800–2,300 francs.

Plaza-Athénée, 25 Avenue Montaigne, 75008. Tel: 47.23.78.33, fax: 47.20.20.70. More of a palace than a hotel. Credit cards: Visa, Amex and DC. 2,160–3,780 francs.

Ritz, 15 Place Vendôme, 75001. Tel: 42.60.38.30, fax: 42.60.23.71. Unashamed luxury in one of the most famous squares in the capital. Credit cards: Visa, Amex and DC. 2,300–3,900 francs.

Royal Monceau, 37 Avenue Hoche, 75008. Tel: 45.61.98.00, fax: 42.56.90.03. Very central but tends to cater more for business clientele. Credit cards: Visa, Amex and DC. 1,750–2,950 francs.

EURO DISNEY RESORT HOTELS

Local travel agents will often have better deals than Disney can offer direct from the park, especially for two- or three-day stays. **For all hotel reservations**: Paris Tel: 49.41.49.10. UK Tel: 071-753 2900.
Disneyland Hotel, Luxury Class 500 rooms. Expensive.
Hotel New York, Luxury Convention Class 574 rooms. Expensive.
Newport Bay Club, First Class 1,098 rooms. Moderately expensive.
Sequoia Lodge, First class 1,011 rooms. Moderately expensive.
Hotel Cheyenne, Moderate class 1,000 rooms. Moderate.
Hotel Santa Fe, Moderate class 1,000 rooms. Inexpensive.
Davy Crockett Campsite, 3 miles from the resort (free shuttle buses). 181 pitches, 414 cabins (4–6 people). Inexpensive.

FOOD DIGEST

The etiquette of eating out and selected restaurant venues *by Philip and Mary Hyman*. See chapter in Eating out, page 61.

Regardless of your budget, some basic rules apply to all French meals and respecting them will increase your pleasure and help you avoid awkward situations. The following advice should make you feel more at home in France – and the French more at ease with you.

Before any large meal one is offered an *apéritif*. In a French home this can be anything from scotch whisky to port but in restaurants a glass of Champagne, white wine, or a *kir* (white wine with blackcurrant liqueur), are preferred. Don't feel obliged to order an *apéritif* if you are on your own but if your French host offers you one, it can be taken as a (minor) insult to refuse.

Wine is, of course, the perfect accompaniment to French food. If you are adverse to wine then order mineral water, sparkling or not *(pétillant* or *plât*, respectively). Beer is drunk only with sandwiches, very simple meals like steak and French fries, as a thirst quencher or with Alsatian meals. Soft drinks, tea, or coffee are almost never served with a meal.

Even in extremely modest restaurants a meal is composed of three courses: starters/salads *(entrées/ hors d'oeuvres)*, a main course *(plat)* and dessert

(dessert). Americans used to referring to their main dish as an entree beware – an *entrée* (as its name implies) in France is a first course!

Though an *hors d'oeuvre* may be a salad, a green salad (lettuce with vinaigrette) is never an *hors d'oeuvre*. Grated carrots or boiled leeks with vinaigrette are typical *hors d'oeuvre* "salads". Unusually, in France green salad *(salade verte)* is served after the main course and before cheese. Though fewer and fewer restaurants offer green salads as a matter of course, most will be glad to prepare one and it makes a refreshing break mid-way through the meal.

Many French diners prefer to end a meal with cheese rather than something sweet, so it's extremely common for moderately priced restaurants to offer fixed-price menus that include a starter, a main dish and cheese or dessert. When ordering cheese in a restaurant, a cheese platter will be presented. Don't hesitate to try a small slice of several cheeses (in private homes three is the polite number to try) and keep in mind that a cheese platter is almost never offered a second time.

Bread is an indispensable part of every meal. It should be on the table virtually from the time you sit down until the moment dessert is to be served. Bread is almost never eaten with butter, though a little butter might be on the table in fancier restaurants to accommodate tourists; butter is, however, served almost automatically with radishes, country hams, sausages and Roquefort cheese.

Dogs are so loved in France that few restaurants refuse them entry. Don't be surprised, even in the finest establishments, to see them under tables or in laps sharing meals with their masters. This said, "doggy bags" are virtually unknown (there is no French name for them), so best forget their existence when visiting France.

Good value fixed-price menus are common in fine restaurants and in simple eating places alike, but better restaurants tend to offer them only at lunch. If you plan on ordering the menu in the evening, read it carefully to make sure the words *déjeuner seulement* (lunch only) do not appear.

Some better restaurants offer a *menu dégustation* (tasting menu) and usually everyone at the table must order it or no one can have it at all; it involves serving numerous courses and is difficult to orchestrate when some people at the table have ordered a simple three-course meal. Seven or eight different dishes will be placed before you in succession but, remember, this is a tasting menu so only half- to quarter-sized portions are served.

Coffee is never served with milk after a meal in France. *Café au lait* is considered hard to digest whereas black coffee is a stimulant that wakes you up. This said, decaffeinated coffee *(café décaféiné*, or *déca* for short) is available everywhere – it is made and served like expresso and can actually be good.

Lastly, a wide range of *digestifs* (after dinner drinks) is available in even the simplest of cafés. They range from the roughest of *marcs* (grappa) to the

K P M

KÖNIGLICHE
PORZELLAN
MANUFAKTUR
Berlin

BERLIN MASTERPIECES

ROCAILLE,
Breslauer Stadtschloß
The unusual reliefs and
opulent embellishments
of this rococo design
places extremely high
demands on the artistic
abilities of the craftsmen.

SCHINKEL Basket
Design: app. 1820
by Karl Friedrich Schinkel.

KURLAND, *pattern 73*
The first classicistic service
made by KPM was created
around 1790 by order of
the Duke of Kurland.

KPM BERLIN · Wegelystraße 1 · Kurfürstendamm 26a · Postal address: Postfach 12 21 07, D-10591 Berlin · Phone
(030) 390 09 - 226 · Fax (030) 390 09 - 279 · U. K. AGENCY · Exclusif Presentations, Ltd. · 20 Vancouver Road
Edgware, Middx. HA8 5DA · Phone (081) 952 46 79 · Fax (081) 951 09 39 · JAPAN AGENCY · Hayashitok Co., Ltd.
Nakano-Cho. Ogawa. Marutamachi · Nakagyo-Ku. Kyoto 604 · Phone (075) 222 02 31 / 231 22 22 · Fax (075) 256 45 54

Our history could fill this book, but we prefer to fill glasses.

When you make a great beer, you don't have to make a great fuss.

smoothest of Cognacs. Fruit brandies are particularly good. Pear (*poire*) and plum (*mirabelle*) are two favourites. Brandies are never mixed with anything else and always served at the end of a meal (scotch is the only strong drink served before a meal).

Voilà. You are now ready to confront your waiter and place your order. Speak slowly, listen attentively, relax and... *Bon appétit!*

RESTAURANTS

The following selection of restaurants covers the full range of dining possibilities in Paris. The price of fixed-price menus generally does not include the cost of wine and is followed by (menu) in this listing; *à la carte* prices are for a full meal with a reasonably priced bottle of wine. Those looking for a fuller list might purchase the red Michelin Guide to France. One should reserve in almost all the restaurants listed below and those listed under the heading *The Chefs* (restaurants with well-respected chefs) require reservations up to several months in advance. Most restaurants in Paris close in August and many are closed both Saturday and Sunday nights.

BRASSERIES, BISTROS & WINE BARS

Astier, 44 Rue Jean-Pierre Timbaud, 75011 (Métro Parmentier). Tel: 42.72.31.04. Closed: Saturday, Sunday, and public holidays, 24 April–9 May and 31 July–5 September. A modern bistro in the north of the city. Home cooking with an inventive touch and a few classics, all for a modest price. Best reserve. Credit Cards: Visa. 135 francs (menu only).

Au Sauvignon, 80 Rue des Saints-Pères, 75007 (Métro Sèvres-Babylone). Closed Sunday and public holidays; August and two weeks in February. A wine bar that does not serve hot food, but a glass of *Sancerre* and the goat cheese platter make an excellent lunch. Around 100 francs.

Benoit, 20 Rue Saint-Martin, 75004 (Métro Châtelet). Tel: 42.72.25.76. Closed Saturday, Sunday and August. The most expensive bistro in Paris but perhaps the best as well. The excellent *Boeuf Mode* (braised beef) merits every bit of applause it receives and the wine list rivals those of restaurants in much more prestigious surroundings. Around 400 francs.

Bofinger, 5 Rue Bastille, 75004 (Métro Bastille). Tel: 42.72.87.82. Open everyday. A classic *brasserie* that claims to be the oldest in the city. Excellent *fruits de mer* and one of the best Alsatian sauerkrauts (*choucroute*) in Paris. The more creative dishes can be disappointing. Credit Cards: Visa, Amex, DC. 166 francs (menu, including wine), *à la carte* 250 francs.

Chez Ribe, 15 Avenue Suffren, 75007 (Métro Bir-Hakeim). Tel: 45.66.53.79. Closed Saturday lunch and Sunday; 15–31 August. Near the Eiffel Tower and very good value. Traditional bistro fare as well as a sprinkling of southern dishes (fish soup, salt cod etc.). Credit Cards: Visa, Amex and DC. 168 francs (menu only).

L'Ange Vin, 24 Rue Richard-Lenoir, 75011 (Métro Voltaire). Tel: 43.48.20.20. Closed: Saturday, Sunday and July. Dinner served only on Tuesday and Thursdays (lunch everyday). On a back street north of the Bastille. This modest restaurant is open every day at lunch but only two nights a week for dinner. Don't expect a big choice of dishes (two main dishes at most) but the cooking is tasty, the cheeses superb and the wines good value. A noisy, young crowd will keep your waitress busy. Best reserve. Credit Cards: Visa. 130 francs.

L'Ecluse, 15 Place de la Madeleine, 75008 (Métro Madeleine). Tel: 42.65.34.69. Open every day. (Several other addresses in Paris: 64 Rue François 1er, 15 Quai des Grands-Augustins and 13 Rue de la Roquette). The choicest of wine bars, serving Bordeaux only, L'Ecluse is a mini-chain offering famous growths by the glass and a small collection of elegant dishes (smoked salmon and green bean salad, beef in red wine, *foie gras* etc.). Very busy at lunch. Open until one in the morning. Credit Cards: Visa. 200 francs.

La Regalade, 46 Avenue Jean-Moulin, 75014 (Métro Alésia). Closed Saturday lunch, Monday and August. A much-praised newcomer to the Parisian scene. Classic bistro fare re-interpreted by a former chef of one of the city's palatial hotel kitchens (Le Crillon). Very popular. Reservations a must. Credit Cards: Visa, Amex and DC. 150 francs (menu only).

Le Rubis, 10 Rue du Marché Saint-Honoré, 75001 (Métro Tuileries). Tel: 42.61.03.34. Closed Saturday dinner, Sunday, public holidays and two weeks in August. Wine bar/bistro. A favourite spot for a glass of Beaujolais and a slice of pâté; several *plats du jour* are served ranging from *boeuf bourguignon* to lentils with salt pork (*petit salé aux lentilles*). Very informal, crowded and very good. 150 francs.

Le Temps des Cerises, 31 Rue de la Cerisaie, 75004 (Métro Bastille). Tel: 42.72.08.63. Lunch only. Closed Saturday, Sunday and August. Extremely modest, family run restaurant in the Marais not far from the Bastille serving lunch only. Simple working man's food. Extremely good value. 100 francs.

REGIONAL SPECIALITIES

Campagne et Provence, 25 Quai de la Tournelle, 75005 (Métro Maubert-Mutualité). Tel: 43.54.05.17. Closed: Saturday lunch and Sunday. A contemporary view of Provençal cooking. Excellent *Salade niçoise* and a few specialities from the *campagne* (countryside) beyond Provence. Reservations a must. Credit Cards: Visa. 220 francs.

L'Oulette, 15 Place Lachambeaudie, 75012 (Métro Dugommier), Tel: 40.02.02.12. Closed: Saturday lunch, Sunday and 1–15 August. Marcel Baudis's restaurant is difficult to class. It could have been listed with *Les Chefs* since he is equally at home with creative dishes as with traditional fare. Dishes from his native Quercy in the southwest are exceptionally well done, the fixed-price menu (lunch and dinner) is particularly good value, and during the winter months the *grand menu* provides the best glimpse of Gascony cooking in the city today. Credit Cards: Visa and Amex. 50 francs (menu), 220 francs (menu), *à la carte* 300 francs.

Moissonier, 28 Rue Fossés St Bernard, 75005 (Métro Cardinal Lemoine). Tel: 43.29.87.65. Closed: Sunday dinner and Monday, 31 July–7 September. A Parisian institution serving a mixture of specialities from the Jura and the Rhone. A magnificent *saladier lyonnais* (a trolley full of salads to sample) and smoked beef (*brési*) from the Franche-Comté. Prefer simple meat and poultry dishes to fish. Credit Cards: Visa. 220 francs.

Pharamond, 24 Rue de la Grande-Truanderie, 75001 (Métro Les Halles). Tel: 42.33.06.72. Closed: Monday lunch and Sunday. Once famous for dishes from Normandy, Pharamond is now noted mainly for its magnificent turn-of-the-century decor. Its most celebrated speciality, *tripes à la mode de Caen* (tripe as cooked in Caen, the most famous tripe dish in France) – served on bed of red hot coals with a bottle of cider – is worth a detour. Credit Cards: Visa, Amex and DC. 250 francs.

THE CHEFS

Arpège, 84 Rue Varenne, 75007 (Métro Varenne). Tel: 45.51.47.33. Closed: Sunday lunch and Saturday. Alain Passard is one of the rising stars of French cuisine. His small restaurant is generally crowded and yet he still offers a fixed-price menu at lunch that is one of the best buys in town. A rare occasion to taste *haute cuisine* at a *bonne cuisine* price. Credit Cards: Visa, Amex, DC. 290 francs (menu, lunch only), *à la carte* 600 francs.

Jamin (Robuchon), 59 Avenue Poincaré, 75016 (Métro Trocadéro). Tel: 47.27.12.27. Closed: Saturday, Sunday and July. Robuchon is the most admired chef in France today. Modest and shy, he delights in juxtaposing ingredients to create unexpected and revealing taste combinations (like cauliflower and caviar) and turning humble dishes into culinary masterpieces (his mashed potatoes are as talked about as any *foie gras* dish). Reserve months in advance. Credit Cards: Visa. 900 francs.

La Cagouille, 10 Place Constantin Brancusi, 75014 (Métro Gaîté). Tel: 43.22.09.01. Closed: 1–10 May and 8–30 August. More a cook than a chef, Gérard Allemandou learned to love seafood on the Atlantic coast where he grew up. His restaurant could easily be transported to California and his cooking has much in common with that of chefs in that part of world. "The less you do to fish the better" is his creed. Grilled, roasted or fried, his seafood has an exquisite taste. Reservations a must. Don't leave without trying one of the superb Cognacs culled from cellars in his native Charente. Credit Cards: Visa and Amex. 150 francs (menu), 250 francs (menu, wine included) and *à la carte* 375 francs.

La Timonerie, 35 Quai de la Tournelle, 75005 (Métro Maubert-Mutualité). Tel: 43.25.44.24. Closed Sunday, Monday and 22–28 February. Chef De Givenchy is from Brittany and it shows. He loves fish but from his tiny kitchen he manages to serve an extraordinary variety of meat dishes as well. Despite his rising popularity, he still offers a very reasonable fixed-price menu at lunch. Credit Cards: Visa. 195 francs (menu, lunch only); *à la carte* 350 francs.

Le Bistro de L'Etoile, 19 Rue Lauriston, 75016 (Métro Etoile). Tel: 40.67.11.16. Closed Saturday lunch and Sunday. Not really a bistro but a full-fledged restaurant run by another of Paris's innovative chefs – Guy Savoy. Particularly good vegetables and fish. Reasonably-priced wines. Credit Cards: Amex. 250 francs.

Les Amongnes, 234 Rue Faubourg Saint-Antoine, 75011 (Métro Faidherbe-Chaligny). Tel: 43.72.73.05. Closed Sunday and Monday, 1–21 August. Once second to Alain Senderens (*see* Lucas Carton), Thierry Coué is slowly making a name for himself in this distant corner of the city. His fixed-price menu is exceptionally good value and helps make up for the somewhat gloomy decor. Credit Cards: Visa. 160 francs (menu), *à la carte* 250 francs.

Lucas Carton, 9 Place de la Madeleine, 75008 (Métro Madeleine). Tel: 42.65.22.90. Closed Saturday lunch and Sunday; 31 July–25 August and 23 December–2 January. Alain Senderens is one of the most creative and exciting chefs in France. Gastronomically speaking, sparks can fly in this magnificent turn-of-the-century decor. Be prepared for a jolting culinary experience (and a bill to match). Credit Cards: Visa. 375 francs (menu, lunch only), 780 francs (menu) and *à la carte* 900 francs.

OTHER RECOMMENDATIONS

Esther Street, 6 Rue de Jarente, 75004 (Métro Saint Paul). Tel: 40.29.03.03. Closed: Friday, Saturday lunch and August. *La Nouvelle cuisine Yiddish* not far from the picturesque Jewish neighbourhood on Rue des Rosiers, this young woman chef prides herself on serving lightened versions of traditional Jewish fare. Delicious Gefilte Fish and a variety of starters that can be turned into a meal (chopped liver, marinated herring etc.). Credit Cards: Visa. 200 francs.

Hawai, 87 Avenue d'Ivry, 75013 (Métro Tolbiac). Tel: 45.86.91.90. Closed Thursday. A Vietnamese soup kitchen on the edge of what Parisians call Chinatown. Inexpensive, authentic and very popular. Credit Cards: Visa. 100 francs.

Juvenile's, 47 Rue de Richelieu, 75001 (Métro Palais Royal). Tel: 42.97.46.49. Closed: Sunday. Certainly one of the oddest combinations in Paris. British owners, French wines and *tapas* of Spanish inspiration. Not to worry. Tim Johnston knows his wines (his selection of Rhone wines is exceptional) and the cooking can be quite good. Often crowded at lunch and dinner. The perfect post-cinema rendezvous. Credit Cards: Visa. 150 francs (menu), *à la carte* 180 francs.

Mansouria, 11 Rue Faidherbe, 75011 (Métro Faidherbe-Chaligny). Tel: 43.71.00.16. Closed Monday lunch and Sunday. A charming Moroccan restaurant that serves an excellent *couscous* (stewed meats, vegetables and semolina) and a collection of *tajines* (stews baked in a special utensil of the same name). A relaxed atmosphere, far removed from the hustle of most *couscous* restaurants in the centre of town. Credit Cards: Visa. 164 francs (menu); *à la carte* 280 francs.

Noura, 21 Avenue Marceau, 75016 (Métro Alma-Marceau). Tel: 47.20.33.33. Open every day. The finest Lebanese *mezze* in town, and reasonably priced. A take-out shop run by the same owner faces the restaurant and one can literally walk out with an entire feast in a plastic bag. Credit Cards: Visa, Amex and DC. 240 francs (*mezze* for 4 people); *à la carte* 220 francs (per person).

Au Pays du Sourire, 32 Rue de Bièvre, 75005 (Métro Maubert-Mutualité). Tel: 43.26.15.69. Closed: Monday. Not the best known Chinese restaurant in town but on Sunday and Thursday the chef makes pork dumplings (*raviolis pékinois*) just as they are served in Beijing. An excellent and inexpensive meal. 50 francs for 20 dumplings.

Wally Sahara, 16 Rue le Regrattier, 75004 (Métro Pont-Marie). Tel: 43.25.01.39. Closed Monday lunch and Sunday. Discreetly hidden away on Ile Saint-Louis, Wally's menu never changes. In fact, you are not offered a menu, simply a splendid meal. Soup, Moroccan meat-filled pastry, sardines, roast lamb, *couscous*, dessert and mint tea. All served in exotic surroundings with a smile. Credit Cards: Visa, and DC. 300 francs (menu, wine included).

THINGS TO DO

COACH TOURS

If you would like to see Paris with minimum effort then a coach trip is the ideal solution. Most companies provide cassette commentary in several languages. Tours pass the major sights such as the Eiffel Tower and Notre Dame but do not stop at each one. Costs around 120 francs for a two-hour trip.
Cityrama leaves from 4 Place des Pyramides, 75001. Tel: 42.60.30.14.
Paris Vision leaves from 214 Rue de Rivoli, 75001. Tel: 42.60.30.31.
Parisbus runs double-decker buses and allows you to break your journey at any of its pre-arranged stops (Trocadéro, Eiffel Tower, Louvre, Notre Dame, Musée D'Orsay, Opéra, Arc de Triomphe and the Grand Palais) which means you can hop off and get on a later bus. The trip takes two and a half hours, is in English and French, and costs 80 francs. Tel: 42.30.55.50.

BOAT TOURS

The following companies run cruises on the Seine which last approximately an hour with commentaries in several languages. During high season the boats leave every half hour from 10am–10pm.
Bateaux Mouches depart Pont de l'Alma. Tel: 42.25.96.10.
Bateaux Parisiens depart Pont d'Iéna. Tel: 44.11.33.44.
Vedettes de Paris depart Pont d'Iéna. Tel: 47.05.71.29.
Vedettes du Pont Neuf depart Pont Neuf. Tel: 46.33.98.38.

Leaving the Seine behind there is an interesting boat trip along the Canal St Martin which starts at the Port de l'Arsenal (Bastille) and continues almost to the *périphérique* at the north east of the city. This is a long trip, taking three hours, and you should take some warm jumpers as you spend a lot of time in shaded locks and under bridges. Cost 90 francs.
Canauxrama, 13 Quai de la Loire, 75019. Tel: 42.39.15.00. **Paris Canal**, 19/21 Quai de la Loire, 75019. Tel: 42.40.96.97.

Caisse Nationale des Monuments Historiques, 62 Rue Saint Antoine (in the Hôtel Sully), 75004. Tel: 44.61.21.50. Excellent guided tours of monuments and museums within any one *quartier*.

PARKS

Paris can, on a blistering, hot summer's day, seem depressingly short of parks compared to cities in Britain or Germany. The following are among the largest and most interesting.

Jardins des Tuileries, Métro Tuileries. Not a lot to recommend these famous but rather dusty, unimaginative gardens, at the moment, but by 1995 they will have been redesigned at great expense as part of the work linked with the Grand Louvre project. If you want more greenery, try the other side of the Place de la Concorde. Admission free.

Jardin du Luxembourg, RER Luxembourg. Traditionally Parisian in ambiance with a small café and pond for children's sailing boats. Always full of colourful flower-beds. Admission free.

Palais Royal, Métro Palais Royal. Elegant courtyard overlooked by the Ministry of Arts. Also home to the infamous painted columns of Daniel Buren. Admission free.

Jardin des Plantes, Métro Gare d'Austerlitz. Botanical gardens which are rather disappointing for plant lovers. Popular with children as there is a small zoo and large hot houses. The garden is also home to the National History Museum, open 10am–5pm Monday, Wednesday–Friday; 11am–6pm Saturday and Sunday. Admission free only to garden.

Parc de Monceau, Métro Monceau. Interesting plants in an elegant setting. Admission free.

Jardin d'Acclimatation, Métro Les Sablons. A park within the Bois de Boulogne for children, with lots of activities and a small zoo. Open 10am–6pm everyday. Admission 10 francs.

Jardin de Bagatelle, Métro Pont de Neuilly. Beautiful gardens and parkland with small chateau which has changing exhibitions. Expensive restaurant within grounds. Admission 6 francs.

Parc André Citroën, Métro Javel. Opened in 1992 on the site of the old Citroën factory and covers 14 hectares (35 acres) of land. There are several theme gardens within this large park with names such as The White Garden, The Black Garden and The Garden of Movement.

For a guided visit of the parks of Paris contact 3 Avenue de la Porte d'Auteuil. Tel: 46.04.52.80

SCHOOLS & COURSES

Paris is home to many schools, ranging from language and cookery to the famous Grandes Ecoles created by Napoleon with the sole purpose of training high-level technical specialists for the top posts in state administration. Today the Grandes Ecoles take in around 100,000 students who have to pass an examination after two years of intense preparation. Information sheets on any aspect of education in France can be bought for a nominal sum by writing to Le Centre d'Information et de Documentation Jeunesse (CIDJ), 101 Quai Branly, 75740 Paris Cedex15. Tel: 44.49.12.00.

The language and cookery schools listed here will send you information and may help you with travel and accommodation arrangements.

Le Cordon Bleu, 8 Rue Léon Delhomme, 75015 Paris. Tel: 48.56.06.06, fax: 48.56.03.96. Courses are conducted in French, English and Japanese.

Ritz Escoffier, 15 Place Vendôme, 75001 Paris. Tel: 42.60.38.30, fax: 40.15.07.65. Courses held in French or English.

Lenôtre, 40 Rue Pierre Curie, B.P. 6, 78373 Plaisir Cedex. Tel: (1) 30.81.46.34, fax: (1) 30.54.73.70. Courses held in French or English.

Cours de Civilisation Francaise à la Sorbonne, 47, Rue des Ecoles, 75005 Paris. Tel: 40.46.22.11. Run at several levels all year.

Ecole de Langue Francaise pour Etrangers (ELFE), 87 Rue Taitbout, 75009 Paris. Tel: 48.82.91.92. All levels in classes of 4–6 students.

Eurocentre, 13 Passage Dauphine, 75006 Paris. Tel: 42.25.81.40. Language and civilisation courses held at Paris, Amboise and La Rochelle.

France Langues, 2 Rue de Sfax, 75116 Paris. Tel: 45.00.40.15. Courses in language and civilisation.

Institut Parisien de Langue et de Civilisation Francaise, 87 Boulevard de Grenelle, 75015 Paris. Tel: 40.56.09.53, fax: 40.56.09.53.

Alliance Française,101 Boulevard Raspail, 75006 Paris. Tel: 45.44.38.28.

Union Nationale des Organisations de Sejours Linguistiques (UNOSEL), 293–295 Rue Vaugirard, 75015 Paris. Tel: 42.50.44.99, fax: 42.50.86.64. Organises language-learning stays in different regions of France.

EURO DISNEY

This European site for the Disney theme-park formula has had a troubled first few years, unlike the soaraway success of the US-based parks. As a result, prices may well drop for the accommodation and entry passes. The on-site hotels allow earlier access to the park. For the latest information call Euro Disney information on tel: (33.1) 64.74.30.00

However Euro Disney is also very accessible from downtown Paris. Situated at Marne-La-Vallée, 45 minutes from Central Paris by car or train, Euro Disney is most easily accessible by RER trains, from Châtelet-Les-Halles and Gare de Lyon (Direction Marne-La-Vallée and check that Marne-La-Vallée is illuminated on the platform signs, to ensure that the train goes all the way to Euro Disney). By road, the A4 leads from the south west of the *périphérique* to Exit 14 Parc Eurodisncy. There are direct buses from both Charles de Gaulle-Roissy and Orly airports.

CULTURE PLUS

MUSEUMS

Most museums charge an entrance fee; for those that are state owned expect to pay between 10 and 25 francs (half price on Sunday). Reductions are usually given for children, senior citizens and students – on production of a valid card.

If you don't like waiting in queues and you intend to visit several museums it is a good idea to purchase a *Carte Musées* from the tourist office, Métro or museum ticket office. This pass enables you to visit 65 museums or monuments in Paris or in the Ile de France region and costs 50 francs for one day, 110 francs for three days or 160 francs for five days.

The museums listed here are open every day, mornings and afternoons (opening is variable on public holidays). As a general rule, national museums are closed on Tuesday and municipal museums on Monday. Remember, most close for a long lunch from noon–12.30pm to around 2.30pm, although the major ones are often open continuously, especially during the summer months.

Centre National d'Art et de Culture Georges Pompidou, 19 Rue Beaubourg, 75004. Tel: 42.77.12.33. This is a huge arts centre at the heart of Paris, which holds regular exhibitions to celebrate the creativity of the 20th century. Also houses the National Museum of Modern Art, the Industrial Design Centre, the Public Information Library and the Institute for Acoustic and Musical Research. Open noon–10pm (weekends 10am).

Cité des Sciences et de l'Industrie la Villette, 30 Avenue Corentin Cariou, 75019. Tel: 40.05.70.00. New complex, opened in 1986, including the Géode, an auditorium where the spectator feels part of the image; the Argonaute (submarine), the Inventorium and the Planetarium. Closed Monday.

Espace Montmarte Salvador Dali, 11 Rue Poulbot, 75018. Tel: 42.64.44.80. Over 300 works on display. Open everyday from 10am–6pm and until 7pm in July and August.

Galerie Nationale du Jeu de Paume, Place de la Concorde, Jardin des Tuileries, 75001. Tel: 47.03.12.50. Recently renovated, former Impressionist museum, now showing modern works of art: sculpture, photography, cinema, etc. Closed Monday and mornings except weekends.

Institut du Monde Arabe, 1 Rue des Fossés St-Bernard, 75005. Tel: 40.51.38.38. Collection of riches of the Arab-Islamic world from the 7th to the 19th century in a remarkable building opened in 1987. The 9th-floor restaurant offers panoramic views of the Seine. Open 1–8pm, closed Monday.

Musée Antoine Bourdelle, 16 Rue Antoine Bourdelle, 75015. Tel: 45.48.67.27. Recently extended, the home and workshop of sculptor Antoine Bourdelle displays most of his works. Closed Monday.

Musée Auguste Rodin, Hôtel Biron, 77 Rue de Varenne, 75007. Tel: 47.05.01.34. Displays the works and personal collection of Rodin, including *The Gates of Hell* and the *Burghers of Calais* in the garden. Closed Monday.

Musée Balzac, 47 Rue Raynouard, 75016. Tel: 42.24.56.38. The *Cabane de Passy*, home of the writer from 1840–47. Closed Monday.

Musée d'Art Juif, 42 Rue des Saules, 75018. Tel: 42.57.84.15. Religious objects, models of synagogues and works by Pissaro, Chagall and Lipchitz. Closed Friday, Saturday and Jewish holidays.

Musée d'Art Moderne de la Ville de Paris, 11 Avenue du Président Wilson, 75016. Tel: 47.23.61.27. Features works by the Cubists and the Fauvists among others. Closed Monday.

Musée D'Orsay, 1 Rue de Bellechasse, 75007. Tel: 45.49.49.49. One of the newer museums, in the former Orsay train station, displaying works of art (including cinema and photographic arts) from the latter half of the 19th century to World War I. Closed Monday.

Musée de l'Armée, Hôtel National des Invalides, 6 Place Vauban, 75007. Tel: 45.55.37.70. Weapons, uniforms and the tomb of Napoleon I.

Musée de l'Orangerie des Tuileries, Place de la Concorde, 75001. Tel: 42.97.48.16. Home to numerous Impressionist works, including Monet's famous *Nympheas*, and 20th-century works. Closed Tuesday.

Musée de la Monnaie, 11 Quai Conti, 75006. Tel: 40.46.55.35. History of France told in its money, medals and other documents. Open 1–6pm (9pm Wednesday), closed Monday.

Musée de la Poste, 34 Boulevard Vaugirard, 75015. Tel: 42.79.23.00. History of the development of the French postal service. Closed Sunday.

Musée de la Sculpture en Plein Air, Quai St. Bernard, 75005. Tel: 43.26.91.90. This vast garden on the banks of the Seine displays recent sculptures from Gilioli, Zadkine, César etc.

Musée des Arts de la Mode, Union des Arts Décoratifs, Pavillon de Marson, 109 Rue de Rivoli, 75001. Tel: 42.60.32.14. French fashion from the 18th century to the present day: 30,000 costumes. Closed Monday and Tuesday.

Musée du Cinéma Henri Langlois, Palais de Chaillot, Aile Passy, Place de Trocadéro, 75116. Tel: 45.53.74.39. Shows the history and development of the cinema. Closed Tuesday.

Musée du Louvre, Pyramide, Cour Napoléon, 75001. Tel: 40.20.50.50. The world's largest museum, and still growing; the new Richelieu gallery is due to open this year displaying Islamic collections. The museum has five major departments; its most famous exhibits being the *Venus de Milo*, Leonardo da Vinci's *Mona Lisa* and the *Victory of Samothrace*. Closed: Tuesday. There is a separate entrance for the **Musée des Arts Decoratifs**, 107–109 Rue de Rivoli, 75001. Closed Monday and Tuesday. Tel: 42.60.32.14.

Musée Grévin, 10 Boulevard Montmartre, 75009. Tel: 47.70.85.05. Waxworks displaying 500 famous personages from French history and contemporary life. Open daily 1–7pm (opens 10am during school holidays). Also visit the **Musée Grévin Forum** at Les Halles for an evocation of the *belle époque*. Tel: 40.26.28.50.

Musée Marmottan, 2 Rue Louis Boilly, 75016. Tel: 42.24.07.02. Now houses the Impressionists, including 100 of Monet's works. Closed Monday.

Musée National du Moyen-Age Thermes de Cluny, 6 Place Paul Painlevé, 75005. Tel: 43.25.62.00. Medieval treasures, including the *Lady and the Unicorn* tapestry, saved from ruin in the 19th century and displayed on the site of the Gallo-Roman thermal baths. Closed Tuesday.

Musée National Eugène Delacroix, 6 Rue de Furstenberg, 75006. Tel: 43.54.04.87. Paintings and memorabilia in the painter's former studio. Closed Tuesday.

Musée Picasso, Hôtel du Juigné-Salé, 5 Rue de Thorigny, 75003. Tel: 42.71.25.21. Collection of over 200 paintings and other artworks. Closed Tuesday.

Musée Victor Hugo, Hôtel de Rohan Guéménée, 6 Place des Vosges, 75004. Tel: 42.72.10.16. The home of the author for 16 years; drawings, documents and memorabilia. Closed Monday.

Musée Zadkine, 100 bis Rue d'Assas, 75006. Tel: 43.26.91.90. Renovated studio where the sculptor lived and worked until his death (1967). Closed Monday.

NIGHTLIFE

The indispensable *l'Officiel des Spectacles* and *Pariscope* are the key magazines to buy with their weekly update, every Wednesday, on what is happening.

CABARETS

The Crazy Horse, 12 Avenue George V, 75008. Tel: 47.23.32.32. Two to three shows per night.

Paradis Latin, 28 Rue Cardinal-Lemoine, 75005. Tel: 43.29.07.07. Two shows Monday and Wednesday–Sunday. Built in 1889 by Gustav Eiffel, and reopened as a theatre in 1977.

Le Lido, 116 Avenue des Champs-Elysées, 75008. Tel: 40.76.56.10. Three shows daily. The slickest of all Parisian cabarets.

Moulin Rouge, Place Blanche, 75011. Tel: 46.06.00.19. Three shows a night. Tourist prices, and you can hardly get near for the tour buses.

Folies-Bergère, 32 Rue Richer, 75009. Tel: 42.46.77.11. Similar to the above.

Le Lapin Agile, 22 Rue des Saules, 75018. Tel: 46.06.85.87. Métro Lamarck-Caulaincourt. Old-fashioned mayhem in Picasso's old haunt. Get there early for a seat. You'll need to understand French.

NIGHTCLUBS & DISCOS

Régine's, 9 Rue de Ponthier, 75007. Tel: 43.59.21.13. The most famous night club in Paris, frequented by the rich and famous, and hard to get into (membership usually necessary). The disco is open 11.30pm until dawn; also there is one restaurant.

Les Bains, 7 Rue du Bourg l'Abbé, 75003. Tel: 48.87.01.80. Trendy venue in old converted public baths. Disco open midnight–5am.

Folies Pigalle, 11 Place Pigalle, 75018. Tel: 48.78.25.56. Very popular disco in an area that never sleeps.

Le Balajo, 9 Rue de Lappe, 75011. Tel: 47.00.07.87. Old ball-room, popular venue attracting chic crowd to its hot Latin and rock and roll music. Open 11pm–5am Monday, Thursday–Saturday.

Sherezade, 3 Rue de Liège, 75009. Tel: 48.74.70.76. Spectacular Middle-Eastern decor with good dance music. Open 11pm–5am Tuesday–Thursday, midnight–5am Friday and 5pm–11pm Saturday.

La Locomotive, 90 Boulevard de Clichy, 75009. Tel: 42.57.37.37. Rough, ready and mainstream. Enormous.

Le Moloko, 26 Rue Fontaine, 75009. Tel: 48.74.50.26. Chic, sharp and bedraggled – they're all here. For cocktails, a glass of wine, or a boogie.
Le Palace, 8 Rue du Faubourg Montmartre, 75009. Tel: 42.4610.87. Large multi-storeyed club. Europop and youngish crowd, but can be funky.

JAZZ CLUBS

Caveau de la Huchette, 5 Rue de la Huchette, 75006. Tel: 43.26.65.05. Young clientele for this jazz in a cellar. Open 9.30pm–2.30am Monday–Friday, 9.30pm–4am Saturday and Sunday.
New Morning, 7–9 Rue des Petites-Ecuries, 75010. Tel: 45.23.51.41. For aficionados. Concerts commence at 9.30pm.
La Cigale, 120 Boulevard de Rochechouart, 75018. Tel: 42.23.38.00. Popular club but do telephone beforehand for details of concerts.
Le Montana, 28 Rue St. Benoit, 75006. Tel: 45.48.93.08. Has performances every night.
Le Sunset, 60 Rue des Lombards, 75001. Tel: 40.26.46.60. Restaurant on the ground floor, jazz in basement around 10.30pm. Closed Sunday.

CINEMA

Cinema programmes in Paris change every Wednesday. Films marked V.O. are screened in the original version (not dubbed into French). The following cinemas frequently show films in English.
Les Forums Cinemas Orient Express, Rue de l'Orient-Express, 75001 Paris. Tel: 42.33.42.36.
Gaumont Champs-Elysées, 66 Avenue des Champs-Elysées, 75008 Paris. Tel 43.59.04.67.
Le Grand Rex, 1 Boulevard Poissonière, 75002 Paris. Tel: 42.36.83.93. A single theatre with the largest screen in Paris.
UGC Biarritz, 79 Avenue des Champs-Elysées, 75008 Paris. Tel 45.62.20.40.
La Pagode, 57bis Rue de Babylone, 75007 Paris. Tel: 47.05.12.15. The latest films in a Japanese setting. Good tea.

THEATRE & OPERA

The Comédie Française is renowned for its classical productions, but there is a good choice of theatre, concerts, ballet and opera for all tastes in the capital. Some of the major venues are listed below.
Comédie Française, 2 Rue Richelieu, 75001 Paris. Tel: 40.15.00.15.
Opéra Garnier, 8 Rue Scribe, 75009 Paris. Tel: 40.01.25.41. A misleading name as this beautiful building, with its Chagall ceiling, is now devoted to ballet.
Opéra Bastille, 2bis Place de la Bastille, 75002 Paris. Tel: 44.73.13.00. Booking tickets is a time-consuming pastime so be prepared to be patient.

Théâtre du Châtelet, 2 Rue Edouard-Colonne, 75001 Paris. Tel: 42.33.00.00. Modern opera and occasionally modern dance companies.
Théâtre de la Madeleine, 19 Rue de Surène, 75008 Paris. Tel: 42.65.07.09.
Théâtre du Palais Royal, 38 Rue Montpensier, 75001 Paris. Tel: 42.97.59.81.

SPORTS

PARTICIPANT

Parisians expend most of their energies in their lively exchange of views, be it from behind the wheel of a car or the butt of a cigarette. Nevertheless, Paris caters reasonably well for the sport enthusiast. You can find information on sporting events in *Le Figaro* each Wednesday or by phoning Allé-Sports between 10.30am–4.30pm Monday–Friday. The latter will also be able to give you information on sporting facilities within the city.

HORSE-RIDING

Manège de Neuilly, 19 bis Rue d'Orléans, 92200. Tel: 46.24.06.41.
Poney-Club de la Carthoucherie, Bois de Vincennes. Tel: 43.74.61.25.

TENNIS

Centre du Tennis du Jardin du Luxembourg. Tel: 42.34.20.00.
Centre Sportif d'Orléans, 7–15 Avenue Paul Appell, 75014. Tel: 45.40.55.88.
Courcelles, 221–229 Rue de Courcelles, 75017. Tel: 47.31.31.66.

FITNESS CENTRES

Club Quartier Latin, 19 Rue Pontoise, 75005. Tel: 43.54.82.45. Health club with squash courts and pool.
Gymnase Club, 17, Rue du Débarcadère, 75008. Tel: 45.74.14.04. Health club with step classes, weights, sauna and pool. Day pass 130 francs.

SWIMMING

Piscine Suzanne-Berlioux, 10 Place de la Rotonde, 75001. Tel: 42.36.98.44. Part of the Forum des Halles. Has a 50-metre (55-yard) pool.
Piscine Georges Vallery, 148 Avenue Gambetta, 75020. Tel: 40.31.15.20. Built for the 1924 Olympic Games.

SPECIAL INFORMATION

DOING BUSINESS

Business travel now accounts for roughly a third of French tourism revenue. This important market has led to the creation of a special Conference and Incentive Department in the French Government Tourist Office in both London and New York (*see Useful Addresses*) to deal solely with business travel enquiries. They will help organise hotels, conference centres and incentive deals for any group, any size.

Paris is a world leader for conferences, exhibitions and trade fairs and the capital's facilities are impressive; many châteaux now offer luxurious accommodation for smaller gatherings – and you can even organise a congress at Euro Disney.

For anyone wishing to put on a major business event in Paris, the first line of contact is the Bureau des Congrés de Paris, Office du Tourisme, 127 Champs-Elysées, 75008 Paris. Tel: 47.20.60.20.

There are several tour operators who specialise in conference organisation. For example:
Convergences, 120 Avenue Gambetta, 75020 Paris. Tel: 43.64.77.77, fax 40.31.01.65.
SOCFI, 14 Rue Mandar, 75002 Paris. Tel: 42.33.89.94, fax: 40.26.04.44.
Voyages Hamelin, 31 Rue Bergère, 75009 Paris. Tel: 48.01.86.00, fax: 40.22.94.12.
Wagons Lits Tourisme, 40 Rue Kléber, B.P. 244, 92307 Levallois Perret. Tel (1) 47.59.47.43.

Another good source of business information and assistance are the Chambres de Commerce et d'Industrie. Here you can obtain details about local companies, assistance with the technicalities of export and import, interpretation/translation agencies and conference centres – indeed, most chambers of commerce have conference facilities of some kind themselves.

There are French Chambers of Commerce in key cities around the world (in London tel: 071-225 5250) which exist to promote business between the two countries. At the same London address is the French Trade Exhibitions, 2nd floor, Knightsbridge House, 197 Knightsbridge, London SW7 1RB. Tel: 071-225 5566.

A calendar of trade fairs all over France is published every year and this is available in August, for the following year, from the Chambre de Commerce et d'Industrie de Paris, 16 Rue Chateaubriand, 75008 Paris.

CHILDREN

Weekly magazines like *l'Officiel des Spectacles* and *Pariscope* give details of plays, films, puppet shows and circuses. They also list baby-sitting services. In better hotels, the concierge can make arrangements for child care.

Most hotels have family rooms so children do not have to be separated from parents and a cot (*lit bébé*) can often be provided for a small supplement, although it is a good idea to check availability if booking in advance.
Babysitting Service, tel: 46.37.51.24 or 46.47.89.98.
Marionnettes du Luxembourg, tel: 43.26.46.47 or 43.29.50.97. Phone beforehand to check the time of the next performance.

GAYS

The best source of information for Gays is the national *Gai Pied* Guide (published in French, sold in the UK). If you need urgent help or information, try the Paris-based Gay Switchboard (SOS Homosexualité), tel: 46.27.49.36, where there are English-speakers; note, however, that this service is only active Wednesday and Friday from 6pm until midnight.

DISABLED

A guide, *Où Ferons Nous Etape?* (published 1990 in French only), lists accommodation throughout France suitable for the disabled, including wheelchair users, but if you have specific needs you must check with the hotel when booking. The book is available (for 40 francs by post) from the Association des Paralysés de France, Service Information, 17 Boulevard August Blanqui, 75013 Paris. Tel: 45.80.82.40. This organisation may also be able to deal direct with specific enquiries and can provide addresses of their branches throughout France.

The Comité National Français de Liaison pour la Réadaption des Handicapés (CNFLRH), is based at 38 Boulevard Raspail, 75007 Paris. Tel: 45.48.90.13. They offer a good information service for visitors to France with special needs and publish a useful free guide in French/English entitled *Touristes Quand Même* which gives information about access at airports, stations, tourist sites, restaurants, etc. as well as where to hire wheelchairs and other aids.

Specifically for young people, the Centre

d'Information et de Documentation Jeunesse, 101 Quai Branly, 75740 Paris Cedex 15, tel: 45.67.35.85, provides information on services for young less able travellers. It publishes *Vacances pour Personnes Handicapées* and annual leaflets on activity and sports holidays for young disabled people.

Taxis are obliged to take passengers with wheelchairs but if you intend to travel around a lot by taxi you can order a specially-adapted car, the day before, by telephoning 40.05.12.15. Neither the Métro nor the RATP buses are designed for wheelchair users.

STUDENTS

There are several French tour operators which organise study tours and language courses (*see Schools and Courses above* for a longer list):

Accueil des Jeunes en France, 12 Rue des Barres, 75004 Paris. Tel: 42.72.72.09. Offers French study programmes, inexpensive accommodation (or with a family), and tours for individuals or groups.

Centre des Echanges Internationaux, 104 Rue de Vaugirard, 75006 Paris. Tel: 45.49.26.25. Sporting and cultural holidays and educational tours for 15 to 30-year-olds. Non-profit making organisation.

Once in France, students will find a valid student identity card is useful in obtaining discounts on all sorts of activities, including admission to museums and galleries, cinemas, theatre etc. If you do not have your student matriculation card with you reductions may sometimes be allowed by showing your passport.

The **Centre d'Information et Documentation de Jeunesse** (CIDJ), based at 101 Quai Branly, 75740 Paris Cedex 15, tel: 45.67.35.85, is a national organisation which disseminates information pertaining to youth and student activities. The noticeboard at Quai Branly is a mine of useful information regarding accommodation and events.

USEFUL ADDRESSES

FRANCE

Air France, 119 Champs Elysées, 75384 Paris Cedex 08. Tel: 43.23.81.81. Central reservations: tel: 45.23.61.61.

Maison de la France, 8 Avenue de l'Opéra, 75001 Paris. Tel: 42.96.10.23.

Customs Information. Tel: 40.24.65.10.

Tourist Office, 127 Avenue des Champs-Elysées, 75008 Paris. Tel: 49.52.53.54, fax: 49.52.53.00. Open 9am–8pm. Smaller tourist offices are located at all railway stations except Saint-Lazare.

Automobile Club, 8 Place de la Concorde, 75008 Paris. Tel: 42.66.43.00. Also has a taped message in English listing the main events in the city on 47.20.88.98.

SNCF Information. Tel: 45.82.50.50. Reservations: tel: 45.65.60.60.

Information Service (in English) freephone: 05.20.12.02.

Traffic Information (in English – mainly the autoroutes), tel: 47.05.90.01.

UK & IRELAND

French Government Tourist Office, 178 Piccadilly, London W1V 0AL. Tel: 071-491 7622, fax: 071-493 6594.

Air France, 158 New Bond Street, London W1Y 0AY. Tel: 071-499 9511.

29–30 Dawson Street, Dublin 2. Tel: 77-8272 (reservations: tel: 77-8899).

Consulat Général de France, 21 Cromwell Road, London SW7 2DQ. Tel: 071-581 5292. Visa section is located at: 6a Cromwell Place, London SW7. Tel: 071-823 9555.

11, Randolph Crescent, Edinburgh EH3 7TT. Tel: 031-225 7954.

French Embassy, 58 Knightsbridge, London SW1X 7JT. Tel: 071-235 8080. Commercial department: 21-24 Grosvenor Place, London SW1X 7HU. Tel: 071-235 7080. Cultural department: 23 Cromwell Road, London SW7. Tel: 071-581 5292.

US & CANADA

Air France, 666 Fifth Avenue, **New York**, NY 10019. Tel: 212-315 1122 (toll-free reservations: 1-800-237 2747).

8501 Wilshire Boulevard, Beverly Hills, Los Angeles, CA 90211. Tel: 213-688 9220.

979 Ouest Boulevard de Maisonneuve, Montreal, Quebec H3A 1M4. Tel: 514-284 2825.

151 Bloor Street West, Suite 600, Toronto, Ontario M5S 1S4. Tel: 416-922 3344.

French Government Tourist Office, 610 Fifth Avenue, Suite 222, New York, NY 10020-2452. Tel: 212-757 1125, fax: 212-247 6468.

9454 Wilshire Boulevard, Beverly Hills, Los Angeles, CA 90212-2967. Tel: 213-272 2661.

645 North Michigan Avenue, Suite 630, Chicago, Illinois 60611-2836. Tel: 312-337 6301.

Cedar Maple Plaza, 2305 Cedar Springs Road, Suite 205, Dallas, Texas 75201. Tel: 214-720 4010, fax: 214-702 0250.

Business Travel Division, 610 Fifth Avenue, Suite 222, New York, NY 10020-2452. Tel: 212-757 1125, fax: 212-247 6464.

French Government Tourist Office, 1981 McGill College, Tour Esso, Suite 490, Montreal H34 2W9, Quebec. Tel: 514-288 4264, fax: 514-845 4868.

30 St. Patrick Street, Suite 700, Toronto, M5T 3A3 Ontario. Tel: 416-593 6427.

EMBASSIES & CONSULATES

Australia: 4 Rue Jean Rey, 75015 Paris. Tel: 40.59.33.00.

Canada: 35 Avenue Montaigne, 75008 Paris. Tel: 47.23.01.01.

Denmark: 77 Avenue Marceau, 75016 Paris. Tel: 44.31.21.21.

Germany: 34 Avenue d'Iéna, 75016 Paris. Tel: 42.99.78.00.

India: 15 Rue Dehodencq, 75016 Paris. Tel: 45.20.39.30.

Ireland: 4 Rue Rude, 75016 Paris. Tel: 45.00.20.87.

Japan, 7 Avenue Hoche, 75008 Paris. Tel: 47.66.02.22.

Netherlands: 7 Rue Eblé, 75007 Paris. Tel: 43.06.61.88.

New Zealand: 7 Rue Léonard de Vinci, 75016 Paris. Tel: 45.00.24.11.

Norway: 28 Rue Bayard, 75008 Paris. Tel: 47.23.72.78.

Sweden: 17 Rue Barbet-de-Jouy, 75007 Paris. Tel: 45.55.92.15.

United Kingdom: 35 Rue du Faubourg St. Honoré, 75008 Paris. Tel: 42.66.91.42. Consulate: 9 Avenue Hoche, 75008 Paris. Tel: 42.66.38.10.

United States: 2 Rue St Florentin, 75001 Paris. Tel: 42.96.14.88.

FURTHER READING

FICTION & AUTOBIOGRAPHY

Unless otherwise indicated these books are published by several houses.

A Moveable Feast, by Ernest Hemingway.

The Belly of Paris, by Emile Zola.

Notre Dame de Paris, by Victor Hugo.

Au Bon Beurre, by Jean Dutourd. Paris: Folio.

Le Père Goriot, by Honoré de Balzac.

Down and Out in Paris and London, by George Orwell.

NON-FICTION

France Today, by John Ardagh. London: Pelican.

The French, by Theodore Zeldin. London: Collins Harvill.

The Identitiy of France, by Fernand Braudel. London: Fontana Press.

A History of Modern France (3 volumes covering 1715–1962), by Alfred Cobban. London: Pelican.

France 1848–1945 (2 vols), by Theodore Zeldin. Oxford University Press.

The Food Lover's Guide to France, by Patricia Wells. London: Methuen.

Hugh Johnson's Pocket Wine Book, by Hugh Johnson. London: Mitchell Beazley.

OTHER INSIGHT GUIDES

Other *Insight Guides* and *Insight Pocket Guides* which highlight destinations in this region are: *Insight Pocket Guide* Paris, *Insight Guides* Normandy, Côte d'Azur, Burgundy, Loire Valley and France.

ART/PHOTO CREDITS

Photography by

Page 7, 14/15, 16/17, 24/25, 38/39,   **Ping Amranand**
46/47, 48/49, 52L, 53, 56, 58/59, 62,
64, 80/81, 82, 83, 85, 86/87, 94/95,
96/97, 104, 107, 112, 113, 116, 119,
122/123, 128, 131, 136, 139, 141,
142, 143, 145L, 146, 147, 150, 151,
158/159, 165, 166, 169, 177, 178, 181,
182, 183, 193, 203, 208, 211, 217,
230/231, 232/233, 204, 240

42, 43   **Archiv Für Kunst und Geschicte,**
Berlin
29, 70/71, 148/149   **Steve Van Beek**
36/37   **Bridgeman Art Library**
74, 144, 173   **Andrew Eames**
30L, 33L&R, 61, 73, 75, 77, 105,   **Annabelle Elston**
106L&R, 110, 111, 124, 125, 132,
137, 152, 171, 184, 190, 214

22, 23   **IAURIF, Paris**
20/21, 50, 52R, 54, 55, 57, 63, 78/79,   **Catherine Karnow**
92/93, 98/99, 130, 133, 140, 167, 170,
172, 176, 195, 215, 236, 238, 239,

45   **Grupo Mayher**
12/13   **Robert Harding**
26/27, 28, 31, 40   **Musées de la Ville de Paris**
30R, 32, 34, 35   **Photo Bibliotéque Nationale,**
Paris
100   **Paul Van Riel**
72   **Maria Ángeles Sánchez**
237   **Tony Stone Worldwide**
18/19, 60, 65, 66, 67, 68, 69, 76, 84,   **Bill Wassman**
109, 114, 115, 117, 118, 120/121, 126,
127, 129, 134/135, 145R, 154, 155,
157, 161, 162, 163, 168, 174/175,
179, 180, 185, 186/187, 188, 189, 191,
192, 194, 198/199, 200, 201, 202,
204, 205, 206/207, 210, 212, 213,
216, 218, 219, 220/221, 222, 224,
225, 226, 227

229   **Walt Disney Company**

Maps   **Berndtson & Berndtson**

Illustrations   **Klaus Geisler**

Visual Consultant   **V. Barl**

263

INDEX

D

E

F

Faïencerie de Gien 239
Fantasyland 227
fascism 42–43
Faubourg St Honoré 209
Festival Disney 223, 228
Fiat Tower 193
Fifth Republic 44
First Republic 39
Fitzgerald, F. Scott 167, 170
flea markets 219
flower market 126
Folies-Bergère 152
Fontaine des Innocents 83, 129
Fontaine des Quatre Saisons 182
Fontainebleu 236, 237
food 61–68
Forêt de Lyons 238
Forum des Halles 133
Fouquet, Nicolas 237
Fouquier-Tinville, Antoine 126
Franklin, Benjamin 116
Franks 29, 122
François I 33, 237
François II 33
French language 172, 173
Fronde 34
Front Populaire 42–43
Frontierland 224–225
Futurism 90

G

Gabriel, Jacques-Ange 83, 116
Galerie Adrien Maeght 172
Galerie Colbert 111
Galerie des Glaces – Versailles 235
Galerie des Variétés 113
Galerie Vivienne 111, 209, 212
Galerie Véro-Dodat 111
Galeries Lafayette 85, 114, 209, 218
galeries 85, 111, 113, 114, 209, 211–212, 218
Gare de l'Est 81
Garnier, Charles 84, 114, 177
Gaulle, Charles de 43–44, 161, 181
Gaultier, Jean-Paul 111
Gautier, Théophile 128
Geneviève, Sainte 29
Géode, La 193, 202, 203
German occupation 42–43, 168, 182, 204
Gien 239
Gill, André 155
Giraudoux, Jean 21, 53
Giscard d'Estaing, Valéry 44
Giverny 235, 238
Gothic style 82
Goujon, Jean 83
Grand Canal – Versailles 235
Grand Palais 84, 117
Grande Arche, La 75, 189, 190–191
Grande Halle – Défense 203
Grataloup, Guy-Rachel 195
Guimard, Hector 85, 157
guilds 31
Guise, Henri de 33

H

Halévy, Ludovic 173
Halles, Les 31, 122, 129, 132–133, 209
Hameau – Versailles 236
Hameau des Artistes, Le 156
Hamman 166
Haussmann, Baron 40–41,74, 84, 105, 125, 144, 177, 199, 203, 204
haute cuisine 63–64
Heloïse 31, 125
Hemingway, Ernest 76, 115, 165, 167, 169, 170, 218
Henri II 33, 139
Henri III 33, 129
Henri IV 33–34, 74, 83, 125, 129, 137, 140, 151, 166
Henry VI of England 109
Hitler, Adolf 42, 118, 180
homelessness 56, 119
hotels
  Biron 181, 182
  Carnavalet 83, 141
  Cheyenne,228
  Crillon 116
  d'Aumont 138
  de Beauvais 138
  de Cluny 161, 162
  de Lamoignan 141
  de Lanzun 128
  de Monnaies 172
  de Rohan 142
  de Sens 138
  de Sully 140
  Dieu 126
  Lambert 127
  Lutetia 181
  Matignon 181
  New York 228
Hôtel de Ville – Compiègne 237
Hôtel de Ville – Paris 85, 122, 128, 137
housing 53, 56, 119
Hugo the Great 30
Hugo, Victor 30, 40, 111, 113, 122, 140, 162, 163, 173
Huguenots 33–34, 129
Hundred Years' War 31
Hurricane Disco 228

I

Île de France 22
Île de la Cité 21, 81, 122
Île Saint-Louis 34, 127
immigrants 55–56, 65–66
"Immortals" 173
Impressionism 42, 90
Indian community 66
Indochina 43
Indochinese Temple and Tropical Garden 204
Information Centre – La Défense 192
Institut de France 172
Institut du Monde Arabe 166
Invalides, Les 34, 177, 180
Isy Brachot gallery 172

N

O

P

A
B
C
D
F
G
H
I
J
a
b
c
d
e
.
g
h
i
j
k
l